Wallace and Natural Selection

Yale Studies in the History of Science and Medicine, 8

WALLACE
and
NATURAL SELECTION

by H. Lewis McKinney

New Haven and London, Yale University Press, 1972

To my wife

Contents

Illustrations

Maps

Acknowledgments

In many ways books grow like trees in a dense forest. Under propitious circumstances, many flourish and reach maturity; others are not so fortunate. This book has attained its full growth because of generous support from the Woodrow Wilson Foundation, the National Institutes of Health (grant 4–FL–GM–14, 342) and the University of Kansas Research Fund.

My individual debts are many, but I am particularly indebted to Mr. and Mrs. A. J. R. Wallace and Mr. and Mrs. Richard R. Wallace for their generous hospitality, unlimited help, and kind permission to use and quote from their grandfather's manuscripts, which have greatly illuminated not a few perplexing problems concerning evolutionary biology.

Two of my professors and friends have perhaps made the difference in my struggle for existence. Professor Leonard G. Wilson has by wise example and kindness rescued me from fates much worse than I would otherwise have met. He has also contributed much to this work by his excellent suggestions; by allowing me, in his typically unselfish manner, a preview of his excellent work, *Sir Charles Lyell's Scientific Journals on the Species Question* (1970), my own work has been greatly enhanced. Professor Henry Guerlac, Cornell University, always a rich source of ideas, has provided many critical insights, excellent suggestions, and other vital help. His high scholarly standards and extensive knowledge serve as models of the scholarly tradition. I am deeply grateful to them both.

I am also indebted to the following organizations and individuals for their assistance: The American Museum of Natural History; The American Philosophical Society; Birmingham (England) Public Libraries; British Museum; British Museum (Natural History); University of California, Berkeley and Los Angeles; Cambridge University Library; Imperial College, London; The Linnean Society of London; The University of Liverpool; The London Library; London School of Economics; Royal Botanic Gardens, Kew; Royal College of Physicians; Royal Geographical Society of London; The Royal Society; University of Texas; Wellcome Historical Medical Library; Wilbur Applebaum, University of Illinois, Peter R. Knights, York Univ.,

Toronto, and Dr. Robert M. Stecher, Cleveland, Ohio for a transcript
of his Darwin-Bates letters. To the many others who have replied to
my queries, my thanks also.

                                                              H. L. McK.

Indian Hills
Lawrence, Kansas
1971

Introduction

Few events in intellectual history are more fascinating than the generation of fundamental ideas. The more significant the concept, the greater our fascination, particularly when simultaneous discovery is involved. The story of how the concept of natural selection was formulated has been discussed often by historians and scientists, and the focus of attention is usually on Charles Darwin, who eventually published his monumental *On the Origin of Species by Means of Natural Selection* (1859). Alfred Russel Wallace, who shared the glory of discovery with Darwin, previously has not received the same scrutiny, despite his major role in the development of evolutionary biology.

Numerous reasons for Wallace's independent moment of genius in 1858, however, have been suggested. Philip Darlington has observed that Wallace was led to his momentous discovery by the facts of zoogeography, the geographical distribution of animals. Indeed, he says, both Darwin and Wallace reached the same conclusions in the same way: "Both men first deduced the fact of evolution primarily from what they saw of animal distribution and both then drew the same explanation from the same source, from Malthus." Erik Nordenskiöld and Gerhard Wichler have arrived at essentially the same conclusion. Gerald Henderson also has observed that "an abiding interest in the geographical distribution of species and varieties was to lead Wallace over the same ground as Darwin and to the same conclusions."[1] This view is very widely held, and a recent book comprised of papers by various authorities on zoogeography

> . . . is dedicated to the memory of two great zoogeographers, Charles Darwin and Alfred Russel Wallace, whose observations and reflections on the distribution of animals provided much of the evidence that led them, just one hundred years ago, to propose to the world the epochal concept of Organic Evolution.[2]

1. Darlington, "Darwin and Zoogeography" (1959), p. 309. Nordenskiöld, *The History of Biology* (1928), pp. 486–87. Wichler, *Charles Darwin* (1961), pp. 148–49. Henderson, *Alfred Russel Wallace* (1958), p. 35. See also pp. 5–6.
2. Hubbs, *Zoogeography* (1958), p. iii. See also Ghiselin, *The Triumph of the Darwinian Method* (1969), p. 32.

Other suggestions have also been made. Loren Eiseley, while noting the influence on Wallace of Sir Charles Lyell's *Principles of Geology,* suspects nevertheless that Darwin himself provided the crucial stimulus for Wallace. In *Darwin's Century,* Eiseley suggests that although Wallace definitely worked out his views independently, he may have been influenced by certain hints either in Darwin's *Journal of Researches* or in his letters to Wallace. Eiseley concludes that "without the stimulus of Darwin, there might have been no Wallace, just as without the stimulus of Wallace, Darwin might never have got around to formal publication."[3]

Without elaborating, Arthur Lovejoy implies that Wallace discovered natural selection in 1858 because from 1847 onward "his mind was occupied with the problem of explaining the cause and modus operandi of evolution."[4] James Marchant, the editor of Wallace's letters, assumed much the same thing, but added that from 1847 until "the early part of 1855—nearly 10 years later—no reference is found either in Wallace's life or correspondence to the one absorbing idea towards which all his reflective powers were being directed;" moreover, he wrote "nothing further of importance until the second essay" three years later.[5]

Wilma George also appreciates Wallace's early interest in the species question, but she feels that "he had not apparently given it much thought" during his trip in the Amazon region; it was not, she maintains, until Wallace had left South America that the "problem of localization of groups of animals interested him for the evidence it contributed to the theory of common descent." While Wallace was in the Malay Archipelago "he could not ignore what he observed; he must find an explanation for it."[6] Later, in 1855, Wallace announced his conversion to the belief in organic evolution; and Malthus's *On Population* provided in 1858 the ultimate key.

These commonly held, representative views are based almost entirely on the familiar published accounts found in Wallace's auto-

3. Eiseley, *Darwin's Century* (1961), pp. 156–57. Cf. pp. 291–92.

4. Arthur O. Lovejoy, "The Argument for Organic Evolution before the *Origin of Species,* 1830–1858" in Glass, *Forerunners of Darwin* (1959), p. 362

5. Marchant, *Alfred Russel Wallace: Letters and Reminiscences* (1916), pp. 75, 83. Henceforth the American edition will be cited *WLR.* Abbreviations used in this work will be found on pp. xviii-xix.

6. George, *Biologist Philosopher* (1964), pp. 19, 24–25, 58.

biography[7] and in Marchant's life of Wallace. Recently, works have appeared which utilize limited amounts of unpublished manuscript materials. Wilma George, for example, has used some unpublished documents, but following her policy of studying Wallace's published writings "with the emphasis on his scientific contribution," she has made only limited use of these resources.[8] In general, the unpublished sources have not received sufficient attention.

Wallace's unpublished notebooks and journals, however, contain much information fundamental to any full understanding of the development of his thoughts on evolution. Two notebooks and two journals, now at the Linnean Society of London, are of particular interest.[9] Although the earliest notebook, begun immediately after his arrival in the Malay Archipelago, is largely devoted to lists and descriptions of animal species, there are a number of entries in the first part of this manuscript which indicate Wallace's interest in the species question. I shall refer to this as the Wallace 1854 Notebook. The first 182 pages of another notebook (having entries up to 1859) apparently continue Wallace's early notes on the species question.[10] Because of his extensive notes on these pages, I have designated this notebook the Wallace Species Notebook.[11] Wallace's unpublished journals, upon which he based his work *The Malay Archipelago*, also contain other information necessary for this study, and I shall refer many times

7. Wallace, *My Life: A Record of Events and Opinions* (1905). Hereafter cited as *My Life*. The English and American editions are paginated slightly differently. There was a second edition in one volume in 1908.

8. George, *Biologist Philosopher*, p. x. See also pp. 40–41, 48, 53, 57–58. Although Williams-Ellis, *Darwin's Moon* (1966), has also used unpublished MSS, she is careless when quoting. See esp. pp. 40–41, 71, 83–84. My recent investigations of Wallace and his work do refer to unpublished materials (McKinney, "Alfred Russel Wallace and the Discovery of Natural Selection," (1966), pp. 333–57; also my doctoral dissertation, same title, Cornell University, 1967). Similar materials have been cited by Beddall, "Wallace, Darwin, and the Theory of Natural Selection" (1968), pp. 261–323. Some errors are corrected in McKinney, "Wallace's Earliest Observations on Evolution: 28 December 1845" (1969), pp. 370–73.

9. For a preliminary list, see Bibliography, Wallace MS materials.

10. The back half is paginated from the back of the middle section and is devoted primarily to lists of species. On pp. 68–69 are notes for an address which may have been made after his return to England in 1862.

11. Although the earliest dated entry is of 12 March 1855, there is reason to believe that a large number of important undated entries were made before February 1855. See chapter 3.

to the ones written during 1856, 1857, and 1858.[12] Obvious errors
of grammar, spelling, etc. have been silently corrected.

The various sources of information about Wallace's life and
thoughts—his notebooks, journals, published and unpublished letters,
autobiography, interviews, book annotations, and other materials—
tell us that as early as 1845 Wallace was converted to the idea that
species originated through natural, evolutionary processes. Although
his trip to the Amazon basin (1848–52) confirmed his predilection,
Wallace lost most of his evidence when his ship sank upon his return
to England. Consequently, his published works of 1852 and 1853
contain only fleeting glimpses of his heretical ideas on species. We
do know, however, that he discussed his ideas with Henry Walter
Bates no later than 1850.

In 1855 Wallace first publicly announced his belief in evolution,
and from February 1855 until February 1858 he assiduously collected
evidence to discover how evolution occurs. The path to discovery,
therefore, was direct, and Wallace himself has informed us that the
final key to the mystery was provided by the work of Malthus, *An
Essay on the Principle of Population*. Curiously enough, the question
of *why* this was the case seems not to have been asked before. Both
published and unpublished sources, independently, furnish a definite
answer to this important question.

Since Wallace did publish some of his views on evolution at least
three years before discovering natural selection, we might anticipate
some public or at least private response to this work; indeed, Lyell's
important journals on the species question[13] vividly demonstrate

12. I shall refer to these as: Journal, 1856–57 (running from 13 June 1856
to 9 March 1857); and Journal, 1857–58 (from 13 March 1857 to 9 March
1958). The Linnean Society of London also has Wallace's journal of his visit to
America in 1886–87, American Journal, 1886–87, and two other journals,
also compiled in the Malay Archipelago, which I have designated: Journal,
1858–59 (from 25 March 1858 to about 29 October 1859) and Journal,
1859–61 (from 29 October 1859 to just after 4 May 1861). These four
journals from the Malay Archipelago are not paginated, except for the beginning of Journal, 1856–57. Apparently, at first he had decided to paginate, but
upon finding that he had so many additions to make, he began to number
entries. Reference made to these journals will be to entries only.

13. Wilson, *Sir Charles Lyell's Scientific Journals on the Species Question*
(1970). Henceforth cited as *Lyell Journals*. I shall refer to the original paging
in the journals.

that Wallace's early pronouncement on evolution in 1855—"On the Law which Has Regulated the Introduction of New Species"—had a profound effect on both Sir Charles Lyell and Charles Darwin.[14] In fact, this important paper provided the direct stimulus causing Darwin to begin on 14 May 1856 what he designated his Species Sketch, which in expanded form became *On the Origin of Species by Means of Natural Selection* (1859). Wallace's contributions to the early history of evolutionary biology, therefore, were far greater than has been previously realized; that is the theme of this book.

14. This article was first published in September in the *AMNH, 16,* 2 (1855), 184–96, and has been reprinted in a number of places; Wallace, *Contributions to the Theory of Natural Selection* (1870), pp. 1–25 [minor changes are evident]; Pantin, "Alfred Russel Wallace: His Pre-Darwinian Essay of 1855" (1959), pp. 139–53. Facsimile reprint. Also in McKinney, ed., *Lamarck to Darwin* (1971), pp. 69–82. I shall refer to Wallace's article as the 1855 Paper. The original pagination will always be used.

Abbreviations

AMNH	*The Annals and Magazine of Natural History.*
DJR (1839)	Charles Darwin, *Journal of Researches into the Geology and Natural History of the Various Countries Visited by H.M.S. Beagle.* New York and London, 1952. Facsimile Reprint of the First Edition of 1839.
DJR (1845)	———, *Journal of Researches into the Natural History and Geology of the Countries Visited During the Voyage of H.M.S. "Beagle" Round the World.* London, 1845. Second Edition.
1855 Paper	A. R. Wallace, "On the Law which Has Regulated the Introduction of New Species," *The Annals and Magazine of Natural History, 16,* 2 (1855), 184–96.
HJB	Sir William Jackson Hooker, ed., *Hooker's Journal of Botany and Kew Garden Miscellany.*
LLD	Francis Darwin, ed., *The Life and Letters of Charles Darwin.* 2 vols., New York, 1959.
LLL	Mrs. [Katherine] Lyell, *Life, Letters, and Journals of Sir Charles Lyell, Bart.* 2 vols., London, 1881.
Lyell Journals	Leonard Wilson, ed., *Sir Charles Lyell's Scientific Journals on the Species Question.* New Haven and London, 1970.
MA	A. R. Wallace, *The Malay Archipelago: The Land of the Orang-Utan and the Bird of Paradise. A Narrative of Travel with Studies of Man and Nature.* London, 1883. 7th ed.
MLD	Francis Darwin and A. C. Seward, eds., *More Letters of Charles Darwin.* 2 vols., New York, 1903.

My Life	A. R. Wallace, *My Life: A Record of Events and Opinions.* 2 vols., London, 1905. Paginated slightly differently than the American edition of the same year.
NS	A. R. Wallace, *Contributions to the Theory of Natural Selection.* London, 1870.
Palm Trees of the Amazon	A. R. Wallace, *Palm Trees of the Amazon and their Uses.* London, 1853.
Principles (1830, 1832, 1833)	Sir Charles Lyell, *Principles of Geology.* 3 vols., London, 1830–33. 1st ed.
Principles (1835)	———. 4 vols. 4th ed.
Principles (1837)	———. 4 vols. 5th ed.
Principles (1857)	———. 9th ed. First Published 1853. Reprinted 1857.
Principles (1872)	———. 2 vols. 11th ed.
Travels on the Amazon	A. R. Wallace, *A Narrative of Travels on the Amazon and Rio Negro.* London, 1853. A second edition was published in 1889 et seq.
Vestiges (1844)	Robert Chambers, *Vestiges of the Natural History of Creation.* London, 1844. 1st ed.
Vestiges (1845)	———. 3rd ed.
Vestiges (1853)	———. 10th ed.
WLR	James Marchant, ed., *Alfred Russel Wallace: Letters and Reminiscences.* New York and London, 1916. The illustrated English edition is in 2 volumes.

1 Development of a Naturalist
1823–1848

Most of what we know about Alfred Russel Wallace's early life from 1823 until 1848 is based on his autobiographical writings, particularly *My Life: A Record of Events and Opinions,* and a few interviews; the family prayer book, now in the possession of the Wallace grandsons, provides the dates of his birth and baptism. The original sources for these years, which Wallace himself drew upon in 1905, disappeared until recently when many invaluable letters and other material were located in an old trunk. Nevertheless, we still must rely heavily on Wallace's own accounts, which are sometimes inaccurate. Annotated books from Wallace's early library frequently fill gaps.

Alfred Russel Wallace, the seventh child of Thomas Vere Wallace and Mary Anne Greenell, was born on 8 January 1823 in Usk, Monmouthshire. Five years later, his family moved to Hertford, where in 1830 he began his only formal education in the one-room Hertford Grammar School, which was, as he later described it, "a bad one."[1] This brief contact with formal education apparently did not profoundly influence the course of his life. After six years of studying Latin he was unable to translate properly a page of Vergil's *Aeneid,* although he did learn enough to "understand the specific descriptions of birds and insects in that tongue" and to appreciate Latin etymological derivation of English words.

Two or three years of French were somewhat more efficacious, enabling him to read simple French books, and, no doubt, preparing him to converse reasonably well in that language while in the Malay Archipelago. Geography as taught from Pinnock's *School Geography* was as uninteresting as "learning the multiplication table both in the painfulness of the process and the permanence of the results." That he should later excel in the geographical study of animal distribution, however, should be no more surprising than the fact that Charles Darwin became an excellent geologist in spite of Professor Jameson's dull lectures at Edinburgh. Students, of course, often rise above their

1. *My Life,* vol. I, chapters I–III. Poulton, "Alfred Russel Wallace, 1823–1913" (1924), p. xxxii.

uninspired teachers. His mathematical studies were limited to a little Euclid and algebra, while as for history, "whatever little knowledge of history I have acquired has been derived more from Shakespeare's plays and good historical novels than from anything I learned in school." Fortunately, Wallace read voraciously at home, where he had access to a wide variety of classics and travel books.[2]

At Christmas 1836, at the age of thirteen,[3] Wallace left school, and the following summer was apprenticed to his brother William, a surveyor with whom he worked for the most part until mid-December 1843. During his solitary rambles while surveying the English moors and mountains, Wallace "first began to feel the influence of nature and to wish to know more about the various flowers, shrubs, and trees I daily met, but of which for the most part I did not even know the English names." He was then scarcely aware that such a discipline as systematic biology existed. His initial interests arose from a chance remark overheard in 1836:

> A lady, who was governess in a Quaker family we knew at Hertford, was talking to some friends in the street when I and my father met them, and stayed a few moments to greet them. I then heard the lady say, "We found quite a rarity the other day—the Monotropa; it had not been found here before." This I pondered over, and wondered what the Monotropa was. All my father could tell me was that it was a rare plant; and I thought how nice it must be to know the names of rare plants when you found them. However, I did not even know there were books that described every British plant.[4]

Unfortunately, his brother's apathy toward botany temporarily arrested Wallace's interests.

It was not until 1841 that he decided to satisfy his curiosity by purchasing a cheap paperback on botany published by the Society for the Diffusion of Useful Knowledge. In such a humble manner began his study of nature. This practical handbook was his constant companion for a year before he stumbled upon a notice of John Lindley's *Elements of Botany,* which claimed to aid students wishing "to add to their incipient knowledge of the forms of plants an ac-

2. *My Life,* vol. I, pp. 51–55, 74–76.
3. Ibid., p. 79. Cf. p. 1. Many authors state that he was fourteen.
4. Ibid., pp. 106, 110–11, 229.

quaintance with their structure and economy."[5] Yet Wallace was disappointed to discover that Lindley's work, which he acquired in July 1842, contained little information really useful to him. As he later remarked, he especially deplored the conspicuous absence of any indication of the geographical distribution of the species described. Nevertheless, he borrowed J. C. Loudon's *Encyclopedia of Plants* from a friend and entered copious notes in the margins and on interleaved pages of his Lindley's *Elements*.[6] On the page facing the title page, Wallace copied two long passages from Charles Darwin's *Voyage of the Beagle*. Here we may observe in sharp focus Wallace's growing love of botany:

"I am strongly induced to believe that as in music, the person who understands every note will if he also possesses a proper taste more thoroughly enjoy the whole so he who examines each part of a fine view may also thoroughly comprehend the full and combined effect. Hence a traveller should be a *Botanist,* for in all views plants form the chief embellishment. Group masses of naked rock even in the wildest forms and they may for a time afford a sublime spectacle but they will soon grow monotonous. Paint them with bright and varied colours and they will become fantastic; clothe them with vegetation, and they must form at least a decent if not a most beautiful picture."[7]

Soon mere identification of species gave way to a desire to collect, and during his spare moments Wallace began to form a herbarium. His brother William thought botanical pursuits a foolish waste of time, and Wallace himself "only looked upon it as an intensely interesting occupation for time that would be otherwise wasted." Nevertheless, the sensations of delight then experienced closely resembled those which later excited and commanded his attention:

5. Ibid., pp. 192–93. Lindley, *Elements of Botany* (1847), p. vi. Wallace's personal copy of the fourth edition is at the Linnean Society of London.

6. Loudon's book contained descriptions and figures of nearly 10,000 English species, using the Natural and Linnaean classifications. Loudon, *An Encyclopedia of Plants* (1836), pp. iii, xix–xx, 1–2, 1051–86.

7. Quoted by Wallace with a few alterations and added emphasis, from Darwin, *Journal of Researches into the Geology and Natural History of the Various Countries Visited by H. M. S. Beagle.* Facsimile Reprint of the First Edition of 1839 (1952), p. 604. I shall also cite the second edition of 1845. Henceforth cited as *DJR*.

Even when we were busy I had Sundays perfectly free, and used them to take long walks over the mountains with my collecting box, which I brought home full of treasures. I first named the species as nearly as I could do so, and then laid them out to be pressed and dried. At such times I experienced the joy which every discovery of a new form of life gives to the lover of nature, almost equal to those raptures which I afterwards felt at every capture of new butterflies on the Amazon, or at the constant stream of new species of birds, beetles, and butterflies in Borneo, the Moluccas, and the Aru Islands.

Still, Wallace was far from being even a proficient amateur although he had experienced a profound aesthetic response to nature, and he continued: "I knew the wild rose, bramble, hawthorn, buttercup, poppy, daisy, and fox glove, and a few others equally common and popular, but this was all. I knew nothing whatever as to genera and species, nor of the large numbers of distinct forms related to each other and grouped into natural orders."[8]

Even by the time he left for the Amazon in 1848, he still could name only a "moderate proportion" of the species in his collection. For Wallace the Amazon expedition was to serve as his first real training ground in science just as had the *Beagle* voyage for Darwin. Nevertheless, the years between 1837 and 1844 were important for his growing awareness of natural science and thus constituted a scarcely perceptible turning point of his life.

His experiences at Leicester confirmed and strengthened this new emphasis in his life. About December 1843, his brother William's surveying business began to decline, and early in 1844 Wallace had to look for a new job. Surprisingly enough, in view of his limited educational background, he secured a position as a Master at the Collegiate School at Leicester where he taught English, arithmetic, surveying, and beginning drawing.[9] He spent his leisure hours at the local library indulging his ever growing interest in natural science; there he read Alexander von Humboldt's *Personal Narrative of Travels in South America*—a fascinating book whose lofty descriptions of tropical verdure, especially of Teneriffe, had already lured Charles Darwin to the tropics—and the Reverend T. R. Malthus's *Essay on the Principle of Population,* a book which, although of great

8. *My Life,* vol. I, pp. 193–96.
9. Ibid., pp. 229–30.

significance early in Wallace's life, was soundly rejected later: "The theory propounded by Malthus is the greatest of all delusions."[10]

Probably in 1842, he had also read Darwin's *Voyage of the Beagle* and by 1846 he had reread it. This of course would have acquainted him with the views of Charles Lyell, and by April 1846 Wallace had read Lyell's *Principles* at least once.[11] He read Robert Chambers's heretical *Vestiges of the Natural History of Creation* (1844 et seq.) in the fall of 1845 after he had left Leicester.[12] While all these books profoundly influenced his life, Humboldt's *Personal Narrative* and Darwin's *Voyage of the Beagle* lured him to the tropics. In fact, Darwin's allusion to "the vivid descriptions in the Personal Narrative of Humboldt, which far exceed in merit anything I have read on the subject," may have caused him to read Humboldt's work in the first place.[13] Certainly, a passage Wallace took from Darwin suggests that he was dreaming of the exotic tropics quite early:

"When one wishes to find language to express ones ideas, epithet after epithet is found too weak to convey to those who have not visited the intertropical regions the sensation of delight which the mind experiences. I have said the plants in a hothouse fail to communicate a just idea of the vegetation, yet I must recur to it. The land is one great, wild, untidy, luxuriant hothouse which nature made for her menagerie. . . . In my last walk I stopped again and again to gaze on these beauties, and endeavoured to fix for ever on my mind, an impression which I know sooner or later must fail. The form of the orange tree, the cocoa nut, the palm, the mango, the tree fern, the banana, will remain clear and separate; but the thousand beauties that unite these into one perfect scene, [—the gorgeous beauty of the delicate flowers, the luxuriant verdure [?] of the crowded

10. Rockell, "The Last of the Great Victorians," (1912), p. 662. *My Life,* vol. I, p. 232. Cf. Wallace, *Social Environment and Moral Progress* (1913), chap. 16, especially p. 161.

11. *My Life,* vol. I, pp. 133, 162, 256. Wallace wrote the date "July 1842" on the title page of his copy of Lindley's *Elements* facing the excerpts from Darwin's work.

12. Wallace first mentions Chambers's *Vestiges* in a letter written to H. W. Bates on 9 November 1845. See note 25 below.

13. Darwin (1839), p. 604. These words follow on the same page as the quotation copied by Wallace (note 7 above), and we may safely assume that he read them. Wallace also refers to Humboldt and Bonpland on p. 125 of his copy of Lindley's *Elements*.

vegetation and all the attendant beauties of a tropical forest—]
must fade away, leaving behind like some tale heard in childhood a picture full of indistinct but most beautiful figures."[14]

On 30 September 1842 Wallace purchased a copy of William
Swainson's *A Treatise on the Geography and Classification of Animals* (1835), which he annotated very heavily. Even at this early date
his interest in zoogeography was great, and his mind was essentially
unprejudiced by religious preconceptions. Swainson had attempted
to harmonize scripture, geology, and zoology by citing Dr. J. C.
Prichard, who argued that some animals in Australia and South
America could have been created after the Noachian flood. Wallace
objected strenuously: "a most absurd and unphilosophical hypothesis!!
—by it how do you account for remains of different species of
Kangaroo and other animals peculiar to Australias in deep encased [?]
and in solid rock. To what ridiculous theories," he continued, "will
men of science be led by attempting to reconcile science to scripture!"[15]

We can see in these notations his ability even during the 1840s to
focus his mind on relevant issues. He questioned Swainson's observation "that the primary causes which have led to different regions of
the earth being peopled by different races of animals, and by laws
by which their dispersion is regulated, must be forever hid from
human research." And he specifically denied that "the various tribes
of organized beings were originally placed by the Creator in certain
regions, for *which they are by their nature peculiarly adapted.*"[16]
Although he knew not the specific answers, he believed firmly that
natural laws, not natural theology, promised solutions. By 1845, he
was prepared to accept an answer by Robert Chambers that evolution
occurred through ordinary generation.

Of equal importance to Wallace during this formative period of
his life was the lasting friendship established at Leicester with Henry
Walter Bates, an enthusiastic entomologist who greatly expanded

14. Wallace took these words with slight change from *DJR* (1839), p. 591.
The words within the brackets are Wallace's own which suggests that he was
somewhat carried away by Darwin's prose.

15. Wallace's copy of Swainson (1835), p. 5. He thought that Prichard's
reference to the flood being limited to the habitable world, and not universal
was "rather better, but still a useless attempt to work a coincidence where
there was never meant to be an agreement."

16. Ibid., p. 9. Italics by Wallace. He wrote "No" in the margin.

Wallace's scientific horizons by introducing him to the wonders of collecting butterflies and beetles. Bates was the son of a local hosiery manufacturer; in 1838 his formal education terminated and he was apprenticed in the family trade. He opened and swept out a warehouse in the morning but spent all his spare moments diligently pursuing insects in nearby Charnwood Forest. Before Wallace's arrival in Leicester, Bates was already known to entomologists for a short paper on coleopterous insects. Thus Wallace could only benefit from such a friendship, as is evident from his early impressions of Bates:

> I found that his specialty was beetle collecting, though he also had a good set of British butterflies. Of the former I had scarcely heard, but as I already knew the fascinations of plant life I was quite prepared to take an interest in any other department of nature. He asked me to see his collection, and I was amazed to find the great number and variety of beetles, their many strange forms and often beautiful markings or colouring, and was even more surprised when I found that almost all I saw had been collected around Leicester, and that there were still many more to be discovered.[17]

A rank amateur, Wallace had no idea that beetles were either so numerous or varied—one thousand different kinds within ten miles, so Bates told him!—and his curiosity was whetted. Since he could not find many new plants around Leicester, Wallace obtained a collecting bottle, pins, and a box, bought a copy of James Francis Stephens's *A Manual of British Coleoptera, or Beetles* and began collecting assiduously.

After his brother William's death in February 1845,[18] Wallace

17. H. W. Bates (1825–92) was educated at Creaton's boarding school at Billesden, a large village about nine miles from Leicester. See Edward Clood, "Memoir" [of H. W. Bates] prefaced to Bates, *The Naturalist on the River Amazons* (1892), pp. xxii–lxxxix, and McKinney, "Henry Walter Bates" (1970), 500–04. I shall also cite the two-volume first edition of Bates's work (1863). *My Life*, vol. I, p. 237.

18. This date is incorrectly given in *My Life*, vol. I, pp. 14, 239, as February 1846, and most biographers cite this date. A letter to W. G. Wallace, Alfred Russel Wallace's son, from E. B. Poulton, dated 28 August 1923, points out this error and also refers to *My Life*, vol. I, p. 230 which says that Wallace was in Leicester one year, i.e. from 1844–45. W. G. Wallace has corrected this error in his personal copy of the rare one-volume second edition of *My Life* (1908), p. 129. This book and the letter cited above are in the possession of the Wallace grandsons. Cf. Poulton (1924), p. viii.

returned briefly to surveying; but he continued to correspond with his friend Bates, to collect plants and insects enthusiastically, and to read widely. Moreover, he was certain after his year at Leicester that he had no desire to teach, and he soon discovered that surveying had its unpleasant side—bill collecting. Besides, he was becoming more and more enraptured by the study of nature.

This consuming interest led Wallace to suggest to Bates, when they were exchanging specimens in the summer or autumn of 1847, that they should journey to the tropics to collect specimens.[19] The flowing prose of William H. Edwards's book, *A Voyage Up the River Amazon*, which described the Amazon basin as the garden of the world, turned their attention to Pará (now Bélem) and the Amazon:

> Promising indeed to lovers of the marvelous is that land, where the highest of Earth's mountains [the Andes so they thought] seek her brightest skies, as though their tall peaks sought a nearer acquaintance with the most glorious of stars; where the mightiest of rivers roll majestically through primeval forests of boundless extent, concealing, yet bringing forth the most beautiful and varied forms of animal and vegetable existence; where Peruvian gold has tempted, Amazonian women have repulsed, the unprincipled adventurer; and where Jesuit missionaries, and luckless traders, have fallen victims to cannibal Indians, and epicurean anacondas.[20]

The eminent botanist Sir William J. Hooker had observed that "no one can read the published narrative of a visit to the *Amazon River*

19. Bates (1892), p. vii, said that Wallace suggested the trip in the autumn of 1847. Although Wallace stated in *My Life*, vol. I, p. 254, that they met in the summer and decided (implying jointly) on a trip to the tropics, he appears to have said on other occasions that he suggested the trip, and such a suggestion is consistent with his character. Dawson, "A Visit to Dr. Alfred Russel Wallace" (1903), p. 176.

20. Edwards, *A Voyage up the River Amazon* (1847), p. 11. This lofty style pervades the entire book. Edwards (1822–1909), an American lawyer and entomologist, was the son of William Edwards, founder of the hide and leather industry of the United States, and the great grandson of Jonathan Edwards, the great divine. His trip in 1846 to the Amazon resulted in *Voyage up the River Amazon*. Later he published *The Butterflies of North America*, "one of the finest contributions to the biology of insects that has come from the United States." L. O. Howard, "William H. Edwards," *Dict. Amer. Biog.* vol. VI, pp. 46–47.

by Mr. Edwards . . . without feeling a conviction that there is a glorious field for the botanist, and very much too an unexplored one."[21] They were encouraged by conversations with Edward Doubleday of the British Museum, who showed them some exquisite new species of butterflies collected near Pará. Moreover, the author of *A Voyage Up the River Amazon,* an American who happened to be in England on business, intensified their interest, and Edwards even wrote letters of recommendation for Wallace and Bates.[22] The decision was quickly made.

The specific purpose of their trip was, according to Bates, "to make for ourselves a collection of objects, dispose of the duplicates in London to pay expenses, and gather *facts,* as Mr. Wallace expressed it in one of his letters, *towards solving the problem of the origin of species,* a subject on which we had conversed and corresponded much together."[23] And Wallace already had definite prejudices regarding this question, for Robert Chambers's anonymously published *Vestiges of the Natural History of Creation* (1844) had convinced him that development occurred by means of the ordinary process of reproduction (Fig. 1).

I well remember the excitement caused by the publication of the *Vestiges* and the eagerness and delight with which I read it. Although I saw that it really offered no explanation of the process of change of species, yet the view that change was effected, not through any unimaginable process, but through the known laws of reproduction commended itself to me as perfectly satisfactory, and as affording the first step towards a more complete and explanatory theory.[24]

In a letter of 28 December 1845 to Bates, Wallace had observed about that controversial book:

21. *Hooker's Journal of Botany and Kew Garden Miscellany* 1 (1849), 20. Henceforth cited *HJB.*

22. *My Life,* vol. I, p. 265. Later in 1886–87, while giving the Lowell Lectures in the United States, Wallace again met Mr. Edwards, this time at his home in Coalburgh, West Virginia. Ibid., vol. II, pp. 136, 139, 140.

23. Bates (1892), p. vii. Italics are mine.

24. Wallace, *The Wonderful Century* (1898), pp. 137–38. Three editions of Chambers' *Vestiges of the Natural History of Creation* will be cited in this work. The first edition will be cited *Vestiges* (1844), the third edition *Vestiges* (1845), and the tenth *Vestiges* (1853).

Fig. 1. Robert Chambers, *Vestiges* (1884)

I have a rather more favorable opinion of the "Vestiges" than you appear to have. I do not consider it as a hasty generalization, but rather as an ingenious hypothesis strongly supported by some striking facts and analogies but which remains to be proved by more facts and the additional light which future researches may throw upon the subject. It at all events furnishes a subject for every observer of nature to turn his attention to; every fact he observes must make either for or against it, *and it thus furnishes both an incitement to the collection of facts and an object to which to apply them when collected.* I would observe that many eminent writers give great support to the theory of the progressive development of species in animals and plants.[25]

And collect facts is precisely what Wallace did from that time on, as he remarked in 1855:

It is about ten years since the idea of such a law [regarding the evolution of species] suggested itself to the writer of this essay and he has since taken every opportunity of testing it by all the newly ascertained facts with which he has become acquainted, or has been able to observe himself. These have all served to convince him of the correctness of his hypothesis.[26]

Although he carefully omitted any specific reference to that heretical book, it is clear from a later remark that Wallace was referring to the developmental hypothesis of the *Vestiges:*

Ever since I had read the *Vestiges of Creation* before going to the Amazon, I continued at frequent intervals to ponder on the great secret of the actual steps by which each new species had been produced, with all its special adaptations to the conditions of its existence. . . . I myself believed that [each species] was a direct modification of the preexisting species through the ordinary process of generation as had been argued in the *Vestiges of Creation.*[27]

25. See McKinney (1969) for the dating of this letter as well as the published and original texts. I shall always cite the original text when referring to this important letter. Italics are mine. p. 372.

26. 1855 Paper, p. 185.

27. Wallace, "My Relations with Darwin in Reference to the Theory of Natural Selection" (1903), p. 78.

In fact, the influence of the *Vestiges,* to which I shall have occasion to return many times, can scarcely be overemphasized. Wallace set out for the Amazon jungles specifically to gather facts "towards solving the problem of the origin of species" with a definite point of view, and because he was dissatisfied with his efforts in England:

> I begin to feel rather dissatisfied with a mere local collection; little is to be learnt by it. I sh[oul]d like to take some one family to study thoroughly, principally with a view to the theory of the origin of species. By that means I am strongly of [the] opinion that some definite results might be arrived at. Can you assist me in choosing one that it will be [*sic*] not be difficult to obtain the greater number of the known species.[28]

Before closing the letter, he observed that his "favorite subject" was "the variations, arrangement, distribution, etc. of species."

Although the trip to the Amazon was a matter of high adventure as well as an escape from uninspiring environments, it was perhaps above all else an audacious field trip testing the heretical developmental hypothesis of Robert Chambers's *Vestiges of the Natural History of Creation.*

28. *My Life,* vol. I, pp. 256–57. Last sentence from the original letter.

2 Animal and Plant Distribution in the Amazon Basin

Wallace and Bates departed from Liverpool on 26 April 1848, arriving at Pará thirty-one days later on 28 May (*Fig. 2*). They were eager to begin exploring and quickly set to work in the nearby jungles collecting more than four hundred different insects in the first two weeks. The itinerary for their first two years included the environs of Pará, the Tocantins River, and the Amazon as far as Barra (now Manaus) where the Amazon and Rio Negro converge. Although they had already been exploring much of the time independently, at this point the two naturalists separated permanently, Wallace taking the largely unknown regions of the Rio Negro and Bates departing for the upper Amazon.[1]

In light of Wallace's predilection for the idea that species originate through evolution, we might expect to find in his subsequent publications based on his Amazon expedition either forthright statements or at least strong hints of these ideas. Unfortunately, on 6 August 1852, when Wallace was returning to England, his ship burst into flames and sank, taking with it his entire magnificent private collection of specimens gathered after leaving Pará, the three most interesting years of his journal, his entire collection of live animals, and numerous notes and sketches. He saved only his sextant, notes and sketches on palm trees, his Rio Negro diary, some notes for a map of the Rio Negro and Uaupés rivers (see Map 1), and 203 sketches of Amazonian fish. Despite these extensive losses, Wallace did publish some very interesting observations regarding the geographical distribution of organisms; this evidence confirmed his belief that species evolve.[2]

1. Poulton (1924), pp. x–xii. *WLR*, pp. 21–24. Bates stayed a total of eleven years and returned to England in 1859 with a very large collection of insects including more than 8,000 new species. For a full description of their travels see the classic work of Bates, Wallace's *Travels*, or Woodcock, *Henry Walter Bates* (1969).

2. *Wallace, A Narrative of Travels on the Amazon and Rio Negro* (1853), pp. iv, 393, 400–01. A list of his live specimens is found on pp. 382–83. Hereafter referred to as *Travels on the Amazon*. A second edition, with very few changes, appeared in 1889. There were various title pages for this edition.

Fig. 2. A. R. Wallace, age 24 (1848) (from a daguerreotype)

Dover Publications has reprinted this edition with an introduction by H. Lewis McKinney. References to the second edition will be to the Dover reprint. *My Life,* vol. I, pp. 303–06, 313–14. His specimens, unfortunately, had not been shipped home earlier, and he lost the opportunity to have one of the very finest European collections of American species. His notes on the geography of the Rio Negro and Uaupés Rivers resulted in Wallace, "On the Rio Negro" (1853), pp. 212–17. His map of the Uaupés River was the most accurate one available until the present century. *My Life,* vol. I, pp. 316–21. His collection

Since Wallace had sent only one brief paper, "On the Umbrella Bird," to England before his return, virtually our entire knowledge of how his ideas developed is based on two books and a number of papers written after his return. When we recall that his collections were at the bottom of the sea, we must expect certain limitations; nevertheless, portions of this work definitely prefigure Wallace's 1855 Paper.

Although Wallace was principally concerned "with the varied and interesting animal productions of the country, [he] yet found time to examine and admire the wonders of vegetable life which everywhere abounded"[3] (Fig. 3). He was most certainly not an accomplished botanist, but he did not neglect the geographical distribution of plants. Most of his botanical observations, however, were mere generalizations in narrative form like the following:

> The forests of the Amazon are distinguished from those of most other countries by the great variety of species composing them. Instead of extensive tracts covered with pines, or oaks, or beeches, we scarcely ever see two individuals of the same species together, except in certain cases, principally among the palms.[4]

To the Brazilian palms, Wallace devoted a small volume which, as a result of his valuable information on their uses, native names, and geographical distribution, has become a fundamental work. He

---

of some 203 sketches of Amazonian fish was donated to the British Museum (Natural History). Ibid., pp. 285–87 (with plates). See also Wallace, "On some Fishes Allied to Gymnotus," (1853), pp. 75–76.

3. Wallace, *Palm Trees of the Amazon and their Uses* (1853), p. iii. Hereafter cited as *Palm Trees of the Amazon*. Reprinted with an introduction by H. Lewis McKinney (1971).

4. *Travels on the Amazon*, pp. 435–36. His *Travels* contains innumerable references of this nature. See especially pp. 10–12, 23–25, 32–36, 154. Compare Wallace's descriptions with those of an accomplished botanist Richard Spruce, who was also in the Amazon region at this time. Letter from Spruce to Sir W. J. Hooker in *HJB, I* (1849), 345. Some especially scurrilous remarks on Wallace's casual treatment of botany are found in an anonymous review in *The Gardener's Chronicle*. "It is clear that the author's knowledge of natural history is superficial, and that of botany, in particular, excessively narrow; and hence his narrative often loses its value, as well as much of its interest, from the absence of precision in the facts recorded." Anonymous, *The Gardener's Chronicle and Agricultural Gazette* (1853), p. 839.

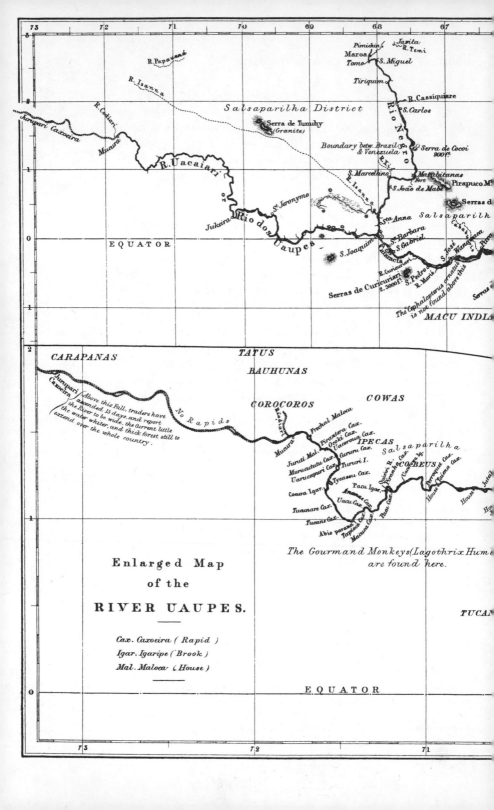

Enlarged Map
of the
RIVER UAUPES.

Cax. Caxoeira (Rapid)
Igar. Igaripe (Brook)
Mal. Maloca (House)

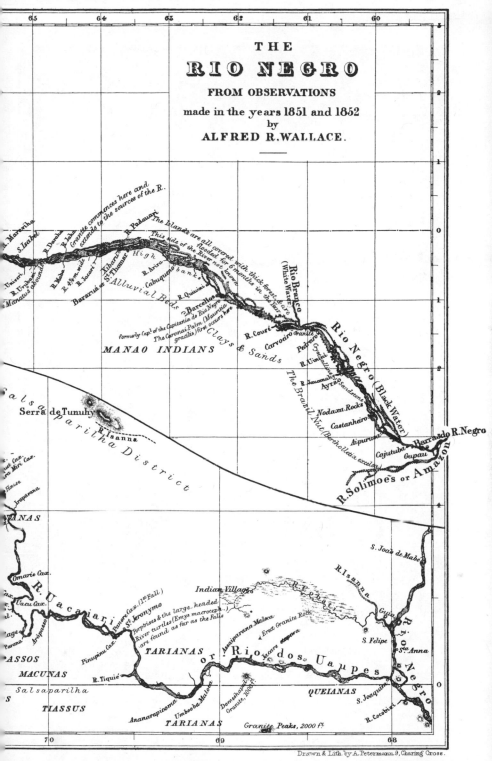

Map 1. The Rio Negro and Uaupés Rivers

Fig. 3. Drawing of a jungle tree by Wallace (courtesy of the Linnean Society of London)

added at least eleven new species to the scientific literature.[5] One species, which he called *Acrocomia lasiospatha* (Martius), was later found to be a new species and was appropriately renamed *Acrocomia wallaceana*. In general, his geographical observations were precise, and for some species such as the *Leopoldinia major* and the *Mauritia gracilis,* Wallace is considered the authority for their distribution. A striking example of his exact geographical determination of a species concerns the *Leopoldinia piassaba* which he was able to restrict to an area of three hundred square miles.[6]

Scholarly reaction to Wallace's contribution to palm tree literature varied. One reviewer recommended it in glowing terms "as a highly valuable companion to the great work on Palms by Martius," a highly complimentary observation since K. F. P. von Martius had published the outstanding monograph on all the palms known up to 1850, and was, in fact, the world's leading expert on palm trees.[7] On the other hand, Sir William Jackson Hooker—the leading English expert on palms, Director of the Royal Botanical Gardens at Kew, and father of Joseph Dalton Hooker—found little value in Wallace's book. "This work," he wrote, "is certainly more suited to the drawing room table than to the library of the botanist."[8] Ironically, Hooker was quite pleased by Seemann's *Popular History of the Palms and Their Allies,* although its author, Berthold Seemann, an eminent Prussian

5. Wallace thought that he had probably discovered fourteen new species (see *Palm Trees of the Amazon*). Of these, eleven still remain. One, which Wallace could not name for lack of fruit or flower, was later named by R. Spruce as the new species, *Bactris bidentula,* according to J. Barbosa Rodrigues (Dahlgren, *Index of American Palms* (1936), p. 71). Dahlgren gives copious references. Another species of *Bactris* which he could not identify is unknown. Still another, *Astrocaryum humile,* has been reclassified as a *Bactris humilis,* a new species. (See Dahlgren, pp. 28, 58.) The 11 new species are: *Leopoldinia major, L. piassabe, Euterpe catinga, Mauritia carana, M. gracilis, M. pumila, Geonoma rectifolia, Bactris elatior, B. macrocarpa, B. tenuis, B. integrifolia.*

6. Dahlgren (1936), pp. 13, 119, 207. *Palm Trees of the Amazon,* pp. 19–20.

7. Anonymous, *"Review of the Palm Trees of the Amazon* by A. R. Wallace" (1854), p. 56. Martius, *Historia Naturalis Palmarum* (1823–50). The illustrations are magnificent.

8. [Sir W. J. Hooker], "Review of *Palm Trees of the Amazon,"* (1854), p. 62. This statement summarizes the tone of the entire review.

botanist, had plagiarized many passages from Wallace's work![9] Perhaps the fact that Seemann was an expert botanist whereas Wallace was obviously a tyro had some bearing on the matter, but an even stronger reason for Hooker's approbation may well have been that his son Joseph had helped prepare Seemann's book. Possibly an additional reason for Hooker's condemnation of Wallace's book was that Wallace, the amateur, had dared in *Palm Trees of the Amazon* to refute Sir W. J. Hooker, the expert.[10] If any bitterness between the two ever resulted, it completely disappeared, for when Wallace was in the Malay Archipelago, Hooker published Wallace's botanical letters.

Modern authorities have also refuted Sir W. J. Hooker's harsh words: "Of . . . publications dealing exclusively with New World palms, Wallace, *Palm Trees of the Amazon,* is a small volume which occupies a notable place." Professor Liberty Hyde Bailey has described it as pleasant, interesting, and notable.[11]

Although Wallace's botanical interests are evident in the *Palm Trees of the Amazon,* he was primarily concerned with the distribution of animals. This was indeed one of his major interests: "There is," he wrote, "no part of natural history more interesting than the study of the geographical distribution of animals."[12] And it may be instructive to recall some important observations on this subject made by Sir Charles Lyell in his *Principles of Geology,* a book which profoundly influenced Wallace's thinking (as it did Darwin's) and which he probably took with him to South America in 1848.[13] Lyell opened his chapter on "Laws which Regulate the Geographical Distribution of Species":

9. Compare Wallace, *Palm Trees of the Amazon,* pp. 47–50, 43–45 with Seemann, *Popular History of Palms and Their Allies* (1856), pp. 252–53, 331–33. [Hooker], "Review of *Popular History of Palms and Their Allies,* by Berthold Seemann" (1856), p. 92.

10. Seemann (1856), p. viii. Hooker, "Piacaba: Fiber and Fruit of the *Coquilla Nut, Attelea Funifera,* Mart.," *HJB, 1* (1849), 121–23. Refuted in *Palm Trees of the Amazon,* pp. 20–21.

11. Dahlgren (1936), p. 287. Bailey, *Gentes Herbarum* (1933–49), vol. III, p. 41; vol. IV, p. 449; vol. VIII, p. 41.

12. *Travels on the Amazon,* p. 469.

13. Osborn, "Alfred Russel Wallace" (1913), pp. 523–37, especially 523, note 1, and 524. Cf. Osborn, *Impressions of Great Naturalists* (1928), between pp. 66–67, photograph of a letter from Wallace to Osborn, dated 16 June 1912.

Next to determining the question whether species have real existence, the consideration of the laws which regulate their geographical distribution is a subject of primary importance to the geologist. It is only by studying these laws with attention, by observing the positions which groups of species occupy at present, and inquiring how these may be varied in the course of time by migrations, by changes in physical geography, and other causes, that we can hope to learn whether the duration of species be limited, or in what manner the state of the animate world is affected by the endless vicissitudes of the inanimate.[14]

The words of Robert Chambers in the *Vestiges* on geographical distribution also no doubt had their impact; he had reached four general conclusions on this subject: (1) Numerous distinct foci of organic creation exist on earth. (2) As far as classes and orders are concerned, the production of organisms is closely related to the local conditions of climate, etc. Diversity, which apparently is not the result of physical or geographical reasons, occurs in the lower gradations. (3) The logical inference is that this diversity is effected by "minute and inappreciable causes" which give the organic development law a specific direction in these lower subdivisions. (4) Development has occurred at different rates on the various continents, with the greatest amount having occurred in the eastern continent, the next in the western, and the least in Australia. Geological and geographical antiquity of the regions may cause this inequality.[15]

When observing the areas occupied by certain species of Amazon monkeys, Wallace discovered that three broad rivers—the Amazon, Rio Negro, and Madeira—marked out four large divisions of the Amazon region which he designated as the provinces of Guiana, Equador, Peru, and Brazil. He thought that these boundaries were precise and that certain species were not found on both sides of them. Thus a gray and white tamarin (*Jaccus bicolor*) is always found north of the Amazon and east of the Rio Negro in the Guiana province. An

14. I have used many different editions of Lyell's book during this investigation and will cite Lyell's work the following way: [first edition in 3 vols.] *Principles* (1830), (1832), (1833); [fourth edition in 4 vols., the edition used by Wallace when he was in the Malay Archipelago] *Principles* (1835); [ninth in 1 vol.] *Principles* (1857); [eleventh in 2 vols.] *Principles* (1872). Reference is to *Principles* (1835), bk. III, chap. V, p. 22.

15. *Vestiges* (1845), pp. 190–91.

Amazonian woolly-monkey is found in the Peru district, never east of the Rio Negro. In the neighborhood of Pará a yellow-handed howler (*Mycetes Beelzebub {sic}*) and a Negro tamarin (*Jaccus tamarin*) are always found south of the Amazon. Wallace also observed the rare and markedly delimited Uakari monkeys; each variety, accordingy to Hill, "is further restricted within the general range to comparatively small areas adjacent to the banks of the larger rivers, which formed barriers to their spread and to the intermingling of the different races. This was appreciated by both Wallace (1852, 1853) and Bates (1863), and has been stressed especially by Forbes (1880)."[16]

Wallace's observations were, of course, limited by his itinerary and the length of time he spent in the various areas; nevertheless, his generalizations regarding the pronounced effects of river barriers on the distribution of monkeys were perceptive and have been confirmed by the later works of W. C. Osman Hill and others. Sanderson has observed, for example, that

> it is of particular interest to note that [the] distribution of these [three distinct types of *Cebus* monkey in the coastal area of Surinam] is limited by the four large rivers—the Courantijne and the Coppename, the Suriname and the Marowijne—which cut the area from south to north. . . .
> It is hard to suggest what changes in the environment sufficient to affect the animals occur between the blocks of forest encompassed by parts of rivers in Suriname. The soil, vegetation and climate appear to be identical, but the varieties of *Cebus* face

16. Wallace, "On the Monkeys of the Amazon," (1852), pp. 107–10. *Jaccus bicolor* = *Marikina bicolor* of Hill, *Primates, Comparative Anatomy and Taxonomy* (1957), vol. III, p. 248. Hill's map (pp. 250–51) completely corroborates Wallace's observation by vividly displaying the delimiting geographical effect of river barriers on monkey distribution. *Lagothrix Humboldtii* = *Lagothrix cana cana* of Hill, vol. V, pp. 243–44; Hill's map, located between pages 244 and 245, again demonstrates the pronounced effect that river barriers have on the geographical distribution of monkeys. *Mycetes Beelzebub {sic}* = *Alouatta belzebul belzebul* according to Hill, vol. V, pp. 131–32; *Jaccus tamarin* = *Tamarin Tamarin tamarin*, Hill, vol. III, pp. 204, 207. For a graphic presentation of the distribution of *A. belzebul belzebul* and *T. tamarin tamarin* see the maps in vol. V, between pp. 136–37, and vol. III, p. 203. On the Uakari monkeys, Hill, vol. IV, p. 243; see especially the map between pp. 238 and 239.

each other across rivers less than a quarter of a mile and sometimes not even a hundred yards across.[17]

As for the *capuchin* monkeys, Sanderson states that "their distribution appears to be determined by rivers which even when small form effective barriers between recognizable races or species."[18]

Birds obviously are less geographically delimited than are monkeys. Yet, as Wallace pointed out, three species of the genus *Psophia*, the Trumpeters, are remarkably separated by rivers. The Green-winged Trumpeter (*Psophia viridis*) lives only on the south bank of the Amazon and east of the Madeira River as far as the forests of Pará. North of the Amazon the Green-winged Trumpeter gives way to the Common Trumpeter (*Psophia crepitans*), and west of the Madeira and south of the Amazon occurs another closely allied form, the White-winged Trumpeter (*Psophia leucoptera*). Some of the Jacamars (*Galbulae*) are likewise restricted in range by rivers, as are many other species.[19] Bates was also impressed by this phenomenon, and the fact is now common knowledge among ornithologists.[20]

Although insects generally have greater means of dispersal than do mammals and birds, there are examples which demonstrate that large rivers limit their distribution also. Two species of butterflies offer a striking example. Thus Wallace says that *Callithea sapphira* is always found south of the Amazon, while just across the river to the north is found the closely allied *Callithea leprieuri*.[21]

17. Sanderson, "A Brief Review of the Mammals of Suriname" (1949–50), p. 767.

18. Sanderson, *Living Mammals of the World* [1955], p. 75.

19. *Travels on the Amazon*, pp. 472–75. Wallace, *The Geographical Distribution of Animals* (1876), vol. II, p. 358. Peters, *Check List of Birds of the World* (1934), vol. II, p. 156. These birds do not fly well. Other members of the genus are likewise limited by rivers. For a list of species separated by the Amazon from closely allied species see Sclater and Salvin, "List of Birds collected by Mr. Wallace on the Lower Amazons and Rio Negro" (1867), p. 594. *Galbula viridis* = *G. galbula* (Peters, *Check List of Birds*, vol. VI, p. 6). It apparently is not restricted by the Amazon.

20. Bates (1863), vol. I, p. 343. George J. Wallace, *An Introduction to Ornithology* (1955), p. 250.

21. *Travels on the Amazon*, p. 474. Bates corroborates Wallace's conclusion but also states "The upper Amazons fauna, nevertheless, contains a very large proportion of Guiana Species." Bates (1863), vol. I, p. 343. Wallace also observed that fish were restricted in their distribution. *Travels on the Amazon*, p. 325.

It is a simple matter for a person familiar with the theory of common descent to explain these phenomena: species isolation (either
physiographic or biotic) has been followed by variation and divergence
from the original stock. Eventually, of course, significant genetic differences can accumulate. Closely allied species, therefore, are found
proximate to each other—for example, on opposite sides of barriers—
because they were once part of the same parent population which has
been divided into daughter populations and evolved over a period of
time. In both his Species Notebook (46–49) and in his 1855 Paper,
(189–190) Wallace recognized that the evidence afforded by these
phenomena supported the concept of evolution, and we also find a very
suggestive question in his notebook begun in 1854 immediately after
Wallace arrived in the Malay Archipelago: "?how many of the land
birds are found in the countries on both sides of the Ganges."[22] On
the fifth page following this remark is another illuminating comment:
"Geoffroy St. Hilaire believes [in the] mutability of species. [Wm.]
Whewell, Hist{ory of the} Ind{uctive} Sc{iences} Vol. 3, p. 630."
Since the date "Sunday, July 1854" is on the opposite page, these
notes were made shortly after his arrival in the Archipelago on about
6 March 1854 and before he had carried out any significant or extensive exploration.

Considering his point of view—he was from 1845 onward an evolutionist seeking evidence to support his views—it is apparent that
Wallace recognized the significance of his remarks made in 1852 and
1853 concerning the geographical distribution of birds, insects, fish,
and palms, all of which he mentions in his 1855 Paper (189).

The evidence adduced there and on the following page led Lyell
to observe:

it was clear that the evidence which most powerfully influenced
his mind was that derived from his own experience of the geo-

22. Not paginated. This is a comment on article No. 77, presented in May
1854. Capt. Robert C. Tytler, "Observations on the Fauna of Barrackpoore,"
AMNH, 13, 2(1854), 365–76. Wallace would have received this issue from
about three to six months after it was published, that is sometime between
August and October 1854, and he definitely would have read the issue since
his two books, Palm Trees of the Amazon and Travels on the Amazon were
reviewed there in glowing terms. Ibid., pp. 56–58. In Wallace's Species Notebook," p. 8, he also observed "Insects [are] different on two sides of [the] Col
de Tende in [the] Alps [North of Nice]."

graphical distribution of species, and especially of birds and insects.[23]

Moreover, Wallace had probably discussed the general theoretical portion—as well as some of the evidence—of his 1855 Paper with Henry Walter Bates no later than 1850; this is strongly suggested by a letter Bates wrote Wallace on 19 November 1856.[24]

Furthermore, Wallace's observations stand out boldly in contrast to the paucity of exact information concerning species distribution before 1852. Wallace himself complained:

> In the various works on natural history and in our museums, we have generally but the vaguest statements of locality. S. America, Brazil, Guiana, Peru, are among the most common; and if we have "River Amazon" or "Quito" attached to a specimen, we may think ourselves fortunate to get anything so definite: though both are on the boundary of two distinct zoological districts, and we have nothing to tell us whether the one came from the north or south of the Amazon, or the other from the east or the west of the Andes. Owing to this uncertainty of locality, and the additional confusion created by mistaking allied species from distant countries, there is scarcely an animal whose exact geographical limits we can mark out on the map.[25]

This conspicuous lack of precision regarding South American fauna occurs, for example, in Georges Cuvier's *The Animal Kingdom.* "Brazil" is the most common area designated, but Cuvier also cites the general location "South America;" the banks of rivers are not infrequently given, but only *rarely* is the right or left bank indicated.[26] Even Wallace himself did not realize the precise delimiting effect of river barriers (as well as barriers of other kinds) until some time after his arrival in South America;[27] in fact, the vast majority of naturalists

---

23. *Principles* (1872), vol. II, p. 277.
24. See chapter 3, p. 29.
25. "On the Monkeys of the Amazon," p. 109.
26. Cuvier, *The Animal Kingdom* (1827–39), vol. V, pp. 24–43, especially p. 42. He is specific on pp. 36–38. For a more vague account of geographical distribution see Gray, *Catalogue of Monkeys, Lemurs, and Fruit-Eating Bats in the Collection of the British Museum* (1870), pp. 42–52; South America is a frequent location given.
27. *My Life,* vol. I p. 377.

generally did not understand the specific importance of the evidence until after Darwin's *On The Origin of Species* was published in 1859. As late as 1867 Sclater and Salvin could state: "It is in fact only within the last few years that the importance of giving exact localities to objects of natural history has met with the appreciation it deserves."[28]

That Wallace did not publicly commit himself in 1852 or 1853 to the doctrine of evolution when discussing the geographical distribution of species should not at all surprise us, for he had suffered extensive losses while returning to England, and would not have openly espoused a scientific heresy with so little concrete evidence. Wallace was, however, mentally prepared to understand what he saw; he discussed the issues with Bates; he used the evidence in his notebooks, and brought it to bear very powerfully on the question of evolution in his 1855 Paper. Furthermore, he continued throughout his life to support evolution most effectively with the facts adduced from the geographical distribution of organisms, reaching a high point in 1876 with the publication of his monumental *The Geographical Distribution of Animals*.

28. Sclater and Salvin (1867), p. 566.

3 On the Organic Law of Change
1854–February 1855

Despite his valuable experiences in the Amazon region, Wallace had very little to show for his four years in the jungles other than his new reputation as a diligent and zealous collector (Fig. 4). Even his two books, *Palm Trees of the Amazon* and *Travels on the Amazon,* were not particularly well received at first—indeed, Darwin complained that the *Travels* lacked enough facts. But above all, the species problem had not been solved, so Wallace decided to set out once more to gather facts. This time, however, he ruled out South America, for his friend Bates, the botanist Richard Spruce, and a good ornithologist were already working there.[1] He decided instead to explore a new territory and finally selected the Malay Archipelago after examining the insect and bird collections of the British Museum and the collections in the Linnean Society as well as the Royal Botanic Gardens at Kew—and perhaps because of a suggestion made by the *Vestiges.*[2] Such a trip would of course be very expensive, so Wallace turned for aid on about 30 June 1853 to the Royal Geographical Society whose president, Sir Roderick Murchison, he had met. He proposed to explore thoroughly the natural history of the Malay Archipelago, understandably adding that he would also endeavor to "pay much attention to Geography." Wallace also referred to his well-known work in South America and explained that the loss of his valuable collections, books, and instruments had compelled him to request free passage to the Archipelago on a government ship. He had secured a promise of assistance from a former medalist of the Royal Geographical Society, Sir James Brooke, who was also the Rajah of Sarawak, Borneo, a fact which no doubt invigorated an already strong proposal.[3]

1. *My Life,* vol. I, pp. 302, 326.
2. See chapter 4.
3. See Appendix I for the full text of Wallace's request. Sir James Brooke (1803–68) was born at Banaras, India and educated in England. After running away from school, he received military training. Having received a sizable inheritance from his father's estate in 1835, Brooke purchased a 142 ton schooner which he eventually sailed to Borneo in December 1838. He made a very favorable impression on the government of Sarawak, and during his second visit of 1840, Brooke actively helped suppress a native rebellion. He was richly rewarded with full control of the government; the Sultan bestowed

Fig. 4. A. R. Wallace, age 30 (1853) (courtesy of A. J. R. Wallace and R. R. Wallace)

formal recognition in 1842. By effecting various reforms, Brooke restored
order and also attempted to eliminate the Malay and Dayak pirates. His vigor-
ous action provoked anger in England, and the British House of Commons
charged him with cruel and illegal conduct. As Lord Palmerston observed,
however, Brooke "retired from the investigation with untarnished character
and unblemished honour." His visit to England in 1847 was a rousing success,
and he was officially appointed British Commissioner and Consul General of
Sarawak. In the following year, he was knighted. A Chinese immigrant insur-

With the promise of assistance from Sir Roderick, Wallace was anxious to depart, and when prospects for obtaining passage to the Archipelago appeared dim, he offered to go to "Eastern Africa" if the Society thought it best.[4] Finally, however, after an abortive departure on a ship recalled at the last moment to the Crimea because of the war there, he boarded the steamer *Euxine* to begin a trip which lasted from 1854 until 1862, covering some fourteen thousand miles. His collections were enormous, amounting to some 125,660 specimens of natural history gathered from Sumatra, Java, Borneo, Timor, the Moluccas, New Guinea, Aru, and many lesser islands of the Malay Archipelago[5] (see Map 2 for the route of Wallace's travels in the Archipelago).

Soon after arriving in the Archipelago, Wallace "decided to keep a complete set of certain groups [of animals] from every island or distinct locality" which he visited. The purpose: to work out the "geographical distribution of animals of the Archipelago, and throw some light on various other problems"—the origin of species.[6] In commenting on H. W. Bates's reaction to his 1855 Paper, Wallace revealed that he was giving the species problem considerable thought:

> To persons who have not thought much on the subject I fear my paper on the succession of species will not appear so clear as it does to you. *That paper is, of course, only the announcement of the theory, not its development. I have prepared the plan and written portions of an extensive work embracing the subject in all its bearings and endeavoring to prove what in the paper I have only indicated.*[7]

---

rection in 1857 cost him his house, valuable library, and almost his life; in 1863 he turned over his duties to his nephew Charles Johnson Brooke and returned to England. Shortly thereafter the British government formally recognized his territory as an independent state. *Dict. Nat. Biog.*, vol. II, pp. 1336–38.

4. Wallace to Dr. Norton Shaw, Secretary of the Royal Geographical Society of London, 27 August [1853], unpublished letter, Royal Geographical Society of London.

5. For the length of his stay on the various islands and the success of his insect collecting see Wallace, "Notes on the Localities Given in *Longicornia Malayana*, with an Estimate of the Comparative Value of the Collections made at Each of Them," (1869), pp. 691–96.

6. *My Life,* vol. I, p. 385. He regretted that he had not been more careful in his collecting while in the Amazon. Ibid., pp. 377–78.

7. Letter dated 4 January 1858. *WLR,* p. 54. Italics are mine.

This illuminating letter suggests at least two important points: (1) Before he wrote his important 1855 Paper in February of that year, Wallace had already written the plan and portions of a book on the species problem. (2) His statement, "That paper is, *of course,* only the announcement of the theory, not its development," indicates, as does the sentence which precedes it, that he and Bates had discussed Wallace's ideas on evolution no later than their last meeting in the Amazon basin, namely, before 26 March 1850 when Bates and Wallace separated at Barra (Manaus). Wallace's revealing comment is a direct response to Bates' statement: "The theory I quite assent to, and, *you know,* was conceived by me also, but I profess that I could not have propounded it with so much force and completeness."[8] Curiously, Wallace also wrote Charles Darwin in 1857 (Fig. 5) that he was thinking deeply about the species problem, and had written a detailed plan to prove evolution occurs:

> It was [most interesting to learn from your very acceptable letter] of May last, that my views on the order of succession of species were in accordance with your own; for I had begun to be a little disappointed that my paper had neither excited discussion nor even elicited opposition. The mere statement and illustration of the theory in that paper is of course but preliminary to an attempt at a detailed proof of it, the plan of which I have arranged, & in fact written, but which of course requires much [work in European] libraries and collections, a labor which I look [forward to when I return.][9]

These two letters clearly demonstrate Wallace's early work on a book discussing evolution as a valid scientific theory.

We have already seen two suggestive remarks in the 1854 Notebook which indicate the direction of Wallace's thoughts very shortly

8. Letter dated 19 November 1856. Ibid., p. 53. Italics are mine in both cases. Bates left Barra for Ega, the first town of any importance on the Solimões, on 26 March 1850. Wallace left soon afterwards for the Rio Negro. Bates, *The Naturalist on the River Amazons* (1892), p. 177.

9. Letter fragment, Wallace to Darwin, 27 September 1857, Cambridge University Library. Later in this work I shall refer to the reverse side of the fragment. Words in brackets have been reconstructed by me from the parts of words remaining, combined with familiarity with his style and other letters written during this period.

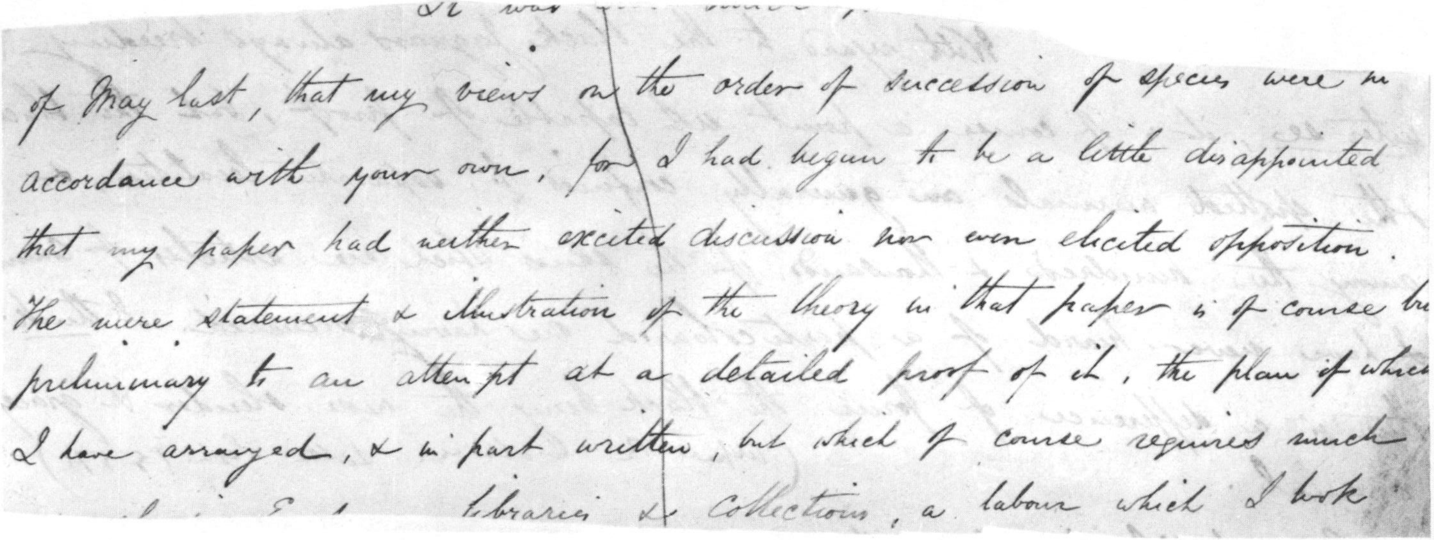

Fig. 5. Fragment of a letter from A. R. Wallace to Charles Darwin, 27 September 1857 (courtesy of The University Library, Cambridge)

after his arrival in the Orient; another full page of notes will be discussed later in specific connection with Wallace's 1855 Paper. We also find in the 1854 Notebook additional notes from books which he apparently read at the Singapore Library:

> *Annals of Nat. Hist.* Vol. 18 Edentata [are] allied by internal structure to birds and *reptiles*—but more nearly to reptiles. Birds are allied to reptiles? Mammalia and birds have both branched out of reptiles, not from *the other*.[10]

Additional notes on some fossil human bones, ethnology—with the first of some curious references to use of bows and arrows, a subject also discussed in his Species Notebook—and a note clipped from the 1854 Horticultural Society publication on an "experiment of sowing the miserable grass *Aegilops ovata* year after year until it became wheat," are the extent of Wallace's sparse note-taking concerning evolution. This notebook obviously is not the important one referred to in his letters to Bates and Darwin, although the first pages of the book do contain some interesting remarks as we have seen.[11]

The notes for Wallace's book, however, are contained in the notebook which I have designated the Wallace, Species Notebook. His letters to Bates and Darwin inform us that portions of his book, tentatively entitled *On the Organic Law of Change,* antedate the 1855 Paper which was "only the announcement of the theory." It would appear, then, that the undated plan and concluding remarks for his book[12] precede his 1855 Paper. The plan of his book on evolution remarkably illuminates his frame of mind:

> We must at the outset endeavour to ascertain if the present condition of the organic world is now undergoing any changes, of what nature and to what amount, and we must in the first place assume that the regular course of nature from early Geological Epochs to the present time has produced the present state of things and still continues to act in still further changing it. While

10. Wallace, 1854 Notebook, [p. 3] not paginated. Italics are Wallace's. The article referred to is Edward Fry, "On the Relation of the *Edentata* to the Reptiles, especially of the Armadillos to the Tortoises," *AMNH, 18* (1846), 278–80.

11. The example of the grass is entered again in Species Notebook, p. 44.

12. That is from page 35 possibly as far as 53, and perhaps even from page 31.

the in-organic world has been strictly shown to be the result of a series of changes from the earliest periods produced by causes still acting, it would be most unphilosophical to conclude without the strongest evidence that the organic world so intimately connected with it had been subject to other laws which have now ceased to act, and that the extinctions and productions of species and genera had at some late period suddenly ceased. The change is so perfectly gradual from the latest Geological to the modern epoch that we cannot help believing the present condition of the earth and its inhabitants to be the natural result of its immediately preceding state modified by causes which have always been and still continue in action.[13]

As T. H. Huxley remarked: "Consistent uniformitarianism postulates evolution as much in the organic as in the inorganic world," and Wallace was clearly applying Charles Lyell's uniformitarian geological principles to the organic world. But Lyell thought that he was being consistent by stating that if the average state of the inorganic world has remained constant, then so also has the state of the organic world. Ergo, evolution of new forms cannot occur.[14] The fact remains, however, that Wallace's book on the species question was developing *primarily* by using many of Lyell's own arguments concerning geology to disprove Lyell's rejection of the idea that species evolve, a point Wallace felt was contradictory to the former. And it is not surprising that Wallace should have found Lyell to be a gold mine of evidence, for as Loren Eiseley has pointed out, all the essential ingredients for natural selection—the struggle for existence, the ecological balance of species, the extinction of species in the geological record (as well as some very interesting remarks on the geographical distribution of

13. Species Notebook, pp. 35–36. Wallace does not supply the preliminary words "On the" to the title of his book, but an exceedingly large number of his scholarly articles begin with these words. Two famous examples are "On the Law which has Regulated the Introduction of New Species" (1855) and "On the Tendency of Varieties to depart Indefinitely from the original Type" (1858). I think it highly likely that his book would have begun in the same way.

14. For an excellent discussion of uniformitarianism see Hooykass, *Natural Law and Divine Miracle* (1959); the second printing was entitled *The Principle of Uniformity* (1963). See also M. J. S. Rudwick, "A Critique of Uniformitarian Geology: A Letter from W. D. Conybeare to Charles Lyell, 1841," *Proc. Amer. Philos. Soc., III,* 5 (1967), 272–87.

organisms)—are found in the *Principles of Geology*.[15] Furthermore, an excellent discussion of the evolutionary ideas espoused by Lamarck also appears in volume two of the first edition (1832), and Wallace was quite familiar with these passages:

> Many of Lamarck's views are untenable and it is easy to controvert them but not so the simple question of a species being produced in time from a closely allied distinct species which, however, may of course continue to exist as long or longer than its offshoot.[16]

Thus Wallace on the one hand agreed wholeheartedly with Lyell's cogent arguments establishing that geological changes which have shaped the world as it now is have occurred slowly over millions of years; but on the other hand, he refused to believe that the same changes did not also occur in the biological world and accumulate over eons of time: evolution *did* occur and Lyell could not convince Wallace otherwise in spite of the eloquent arguments marshaled against the Lamarckian hypothesis.

Wallace argued with Lyell's *Principles* at great length, but only some of the most important issues will be considered here: namely, Lyell's contention that species vary only within limits; that different species in different localities having similar conditions are the products of special creation; and that there is a constant balance of species. There is no reason, Wallace stated, to believe Lyell's statement

> that varieties of some species may differ more than other species do from each other—without shaking our confidence in the reality of species. . . . Is it not a mere prepossession or prejudice like that in favor of the stability of the earth which he [Lyell] has so ably argued against? In fact *what positive evidence have we that species only vary within certain limits?*[17]

15. Eiseley, *Darwin's Century*, pp. 102–03.

16. Species Notebook, p. 44. Wallace later noted a sarcastic observation by Darwin: "Lamarck would have been delighted with the fact [of a blind burrowing animal, the Tucutucu, *Ctenomys Brasiliensis*], had he known it when speculating (probably with more truth than usual with him) on the gradually acquired blindness of the *aspalax*. . . ." Ibid., p. 60. *DJR* (1845), p. 52. Also it will be recalled that immediately after conceiving natural selection, Wallace thought over the deficiencies of Lamarck. *My Life*, vol. I, p. 362.

17. Species Notebook, p. 39. Italics are mine. See Lyell, *Principles* (1835), bk. III, chap. 2.

Wallace then argued that if all varieties of dog except one were to die and that one, the spaniel for example, were spread over the entire earth and subjected to all types of climates, food, etc., over long geological ages, might not new, quite distinct varieties arise? And if the same experiment were continued, the same result would ensue: more new varieties would arise. These varieties would be produced at birth and would breed true. Now conceivably other species might also vary to the same extent, and granted unlimited variation over eons of time, there is reason to suppose that the variety of forms seen in the organic world could be accounted for by natural laws.

Wallace was especially irritated that Lyell categorically rejected this obvious and suggestive evidence:

> In a few lines Lyell passes over the varieties of the Dog and says there is no transmutation. Is not the change of one original animal to two such different animals as the Greyhound and the bulldog a transmutation? Is there more essential difference between the ass, the quagga and the zebra than between these two varieties of dogs?[18]

Wallace's concluding remarks regarding the dog—a favorite example for evolutionists—are incisive:

> Lyell says "it has been shown that a short period of time is inefficient to bring about all the changes possible in a species." But this is altogether begging the question. We can only produce a certain change in a limited time, but it no means follows that other change cannot & has not been brought about requiring long periods. Does Mr. Lyell think that from any one race of dogs the greyhound, bulldog, & spaniel can be produced in a short space of time?[19]

The idea of very slow, continuous change operating over exceedingly long periods of time was central to Wallace's argument, and he had decided to close his proposed book with a lengthy botanical ex-

---

18. Ibid., p. 437 ff. and Lamarck, *Zoological Philosophy* (1914), pp. 110–11. For a new translation see McKinney, ed., *Lamarck to Darwin* (1971), pp. 9–17. Wallace's argument is remarkably close to Lamarck's. Compare Darwin, *On the Origin of Species* (1967), a Facsimile Reprint of the First Edition of 1859, pp. 163–67. Unless otherwise noted, all references to the *Origin* will be to this edition. Species Notebook, p. 41.

19. Species Notebook, p. 43.

ample, which discloses an implicit awareness of the struggle for existence:

> ?Introduce this and disprove all Lyell's arguments first at the *commencement of my last chapter.* Lyell argues that one species could not change into another by a change of external circumstances because, while the change was taking place, *other species already accustomed to those circumstances would displace them.* But this must always be on the supposition of a rapid, not a gradual change. He says if the Temperature of Etna were lowered, the pine would descend & displace the oak & the chestnut; and these latter [trees] would descend and displace the olive & the vine before either of these species could be modified by external circumstances so as to support these changes." This is highly improbable.

Wallace then argued that if the temperature fell only one degree every thousand years, at the end of ten thousand years the oaks and chestnuts would have had sufficient time to adapt to the temperature change. During his long period, however, the several species would undergo gradual modification. As a result new and better adapted species must arise. Thus, granted Lyell's lengthy geological periods for organic change, new species eventually would appear as modifications of older, more poorly adapted ones.[20]

The concept of special creations especially annoyed Wallace, for he considered it to be a clumsy, artificial, and unnecessary contrivance to save the phenomena and preserve established ideas on species. Instead of illuminating the problem, however, these "special creations" only conjured up additional mysteries by inventing processes contrary to the known order of nature. Hence, they were merely unnecessary— and somewhat absurd—hypotheses adduced to explain why there were so many *different* species over the world in *similar* climates. As for the Galapagos Islands and St. Helena, Wallace asked why their flora and fauna are similar to, but not the same as, those of the nearest mainland.

> If they are special creations, why should they resemble those of the nearest land? Does not that fact point to an origin from that

20. Ibid., pp. 51–52. First italics are Wallace's, the second are mine. (See also Lyell, *Principles* (1835), bk. III, chap. X, pp. 161–62.)

land? Again, in these islands are found species peculiar to each island, and not one of them containing all the species found on the others as would be the case had one been peopled with new creations and the others left to become peopled by varied currents etc. from it. Here we must suppose special creations in each island of peculiar species though the islands are all exactly similar in structure, soil, and climate & some of them within sight of each other.[21]

Indeed, the concept of special creations posed many difficulties, for if it were accepted as true, then it would be logical to assume that all islands distant from the mainland (or other land) would have peculiar flora and fauna. But recently formed volcanic or coral islands have only stragglers from the nearest land and no unusual species. Again, it is illogical to suppose that these islands would be populated for centuries in a natural manner before special creations were introduced. "According to Mr. Lyell's own arguments they would hardly be able to *hold their own against the previous occupants* of the soil and there would have to be a special *extermination* to make room for the new and peculiar species."[22]

The counter argument might have been that the special creations were added immediately after the formation of the new island; nevertheless there would ensue a struggle between new arrivals and new creations for ecological niches; and according to Wallace, the new arrivals would have the advantage. This process would be contrary to the present order of nature, "for none of the islands which we have any reason to believe have been formed since a very late geological era, are inhabited by such peculiar species." On the other hand, islands of considerable antiquity *do* have inhabitants found nowhere else.[23]

Wallace's conclusion echoed Lyell's arguments for geological uniformity:

A long succession of generations appears therefore to have been requisite to produce those peculiar productions found no where else but allied to those on the nearest land. The change like every other change in nature was no doubt gradual and the supposition that other species were successively produced closely allied to

21. Ibid., pp. 46–47.
22. Ibid., pp. 47–48. Italics are mine.
23. Wallace notes in the margin: "This must be proved." Ibid., p. 48.

those existing, and that while this was going on the original or some of the first formed species died out, exactly accords with the facts as we find them and the process of peopling new islands at the present day.[24]

In his paper of 1855, Wallace also discussed—carefully avoiding specific, dangerous conclusions about evolution—the peculiar phenomena of the flora and fauna of the Galapagos and St. Helena Islands. These observations greatly impressed Lyell.[25]

Concerning the so-called balance of species, Wallace strongly doubted that the phrase had meaning.

Lyell talks of the "balance of species being preserved by plants, insects, & mammalia & birds all *adapted* to the purpose." The phrase is utterly without meaning. Some species are very rare, others very abundant. Where is the balance? Some species exclude all others in particular tracts. Where is the balance? When the locust devastates vast regions and causes the death of animals and man, what is the meaning of saying the balance is preserved. [Are] the Sugar Ants in the West Indies [as well as] the locusts which Mr. Lyell says have destroyed 800,000 men an instance of the balance of species? To human apprehension there is *no balance but a struggle in which one often exterminates another.* When animals or plants become extinct, where is the balance?[26]

The struggle for existence, here explicitly described, had for some time occupied a central place in Wallace's thinking; indeed, he had first used this specific phrase in *A Narrative of Travels on the Amazon and Rio Negro* (1853) while discussing the question of whether slavery is good or justifiable:

Can it be right to keep a number of our fellow-creatures in a state of adult infancy—of unthinking childhood? It is the responsibility and self-dependence of manhood that calls forth the highest powers and energies of our race. It is the *struggle for existence,* the *"battle of life,"* which exercises the moral faculties and calls

24. Ibid., pp. 46–49. Other entries regarding St. Helena are found on the following pages: pp. [Third page of writing but not paginated], and 151.
25. See chapter 7.
26. Species Notebook, pp. 49–50. Italics mine. See *Principles* (1835), bk. III, chap. VIII, p. 116.

forth the latent spark of genius. The hope of gain, the love of power, the desire of fame and approbation, excite to noble deeds, and call into action all those faculties which are the distinctive attributes of man. [27]

Although Wallace definitely was aware of the struggle for existence before opening his Species Notebook, he was nevertheless deeply impressed by the specific, vivid descriptions of the struggle found in Lyell's *Principles of Geology*. [28]

Nevertheless, at times in his Species Notebook Wallace's youthful impatience overcame him and his criticism sometimes became quite caustic:

> The varieties of the *Primrose* adduced by Lyell are *complete proof of the transmutation of species*. It only shows the impossibility of convincing a person against his will. Where an instance of the transmutation is produced, he turns round and says— "You see, they are not species; they are only varieties."[29]

These relatively brief but representative excerpts point forward very definitely to Wallace's 1855 Paper; they also show that Wallace recognized the importance of his observations on the geographical distribution of species. In one place he rejected Lyell's idea that species vary solely because of temperature, climate, etc. and observed that "in the most equable climates of the tropics, numberless varieties exist linking together the most closely allied species.[30]

In a number of places the continuing profound influence of the *Vestiges* is apparent; often Wallace used similar language. We have already seen that he considered the primrose to be a direct proof of evolution. Furthermore, Hugo De Vries later in the century performed

27. *Travels on the Amazon*, p. 121. Italics are mine. The date in brackets at the top of the page is June 1849. Although his book was published in 1853, and the observation could have been made then, it is not improbable that Wallace's observation on the struggle for existence actually was made in 1849.

28. See chapter 5 for a discussion of this point. There are many references in the *Principles* to the struggle for existence. Dr. Robert Young, Cambridge University, has counted without effort at least sixteen references in vol. II (1833, 2nd ed.) alone.

29. Species Notebook, p. 42. Italics are mine. See *Principles* (1835), bk. III, chap. II, pp. 446–48.

30. Ibid., p. 41.

experiments with the *Oenothera lamarckiana,* the Evening Primrose, which eventually led him to rediscover the work of Mendel. Chambers in the *Vestiges* said of the primrose: "It has been shown that the primrose, cowslip, oxslip, and polyanthus, are varieties of one species, produced by peculiar conditions."[31] Even Huxley, who was shocked by the unscientific methodology of *Vestiges,* was struck by this evidence. Lyell quoted him on 24 April 1856 as saying in connection with the species question: "The oxslip, says Huxley, is not known on the continent. It is a British permanent variety or race of the Primrose."[32]

A favorite example of Wallace, Lamarck, and Darwin was that of the dog.[33] This animal had intrigued Chambers also:

> Thus, the various families of dogs, although so different in external form and even in physical character, are all held as of one species, because under certain changed conditions, the peculiarities of form and instinct will all disappear, and a tendency will be shown to go back to a common and apparently original type.[34]

Again, both Wallace and Chambers agreed that the number of vertebrae common to different mammals argues for a common ancestry;[35] both believed that over long periods of time species gradually change into other species:

> Who is to say where this power of conditions has its limit? Or, admitting that it has a limit short of species-transition in the present state of the physical world, who is to say that it had not a little more power in the geological ages, and did then move the animated families on from one specific type to another? It will be said no one pretends to deny the possibility of such power; we only require proof. See proof, then, in the facts of geology, for species did in those ages follow each other in an order at once of

31. *Vestiges* (1845), p. 167.
32. *Lyell Journals,* I, pp. 145–46. Cf. *Life, Letters, and Journals of Sir Charles Lyell, Bart.* Edited by Mrs. Katherine Lyell (1881), Vol. II, p. 212. Henceforth cited *LLL.*
33. See note 18 above. Also *On the Origin of Species,* Ch. 1.
34. *Vestiges* (1845), p. 167.
35. Ibid., pp. 146–47; Species Notebook, pp. 32–33.

development and of time. This, indeed, is not a demonstration; but take it for what it is—ground of a strong probability.[36]

In the Species Notebook, Wallace, like Chambers, clearly recognized the important implications of the paleontological record. Their observations on this subject again show remarkable similarities. As in the case of the dog, Wallace's point of departure for his arguments was Lyell's *Principles of Geology:*

"Some of the more ancient Saurians approximated more nearly in their organization to the types of living Mammalia than do any of the existing reptiles." Lyell Vol. I, p. 231.[37] which? just what I want. Lyell says the Didelphys [Didelphidae—opossum] of the Oolite is fatal to the theory of progressive development.[38] Not so if low[ly] organized mammalia branched out of *low* reptiles or fishes. All that is required for the progression is that *some* reptiles should appear before Mammalia & birds or even that they should appear together. In the same manner reptiles should not appear *before fishes,* but it matters not how soon after them. As a general rule let Naturalists determine that one class of animals is higher organized than another, & all that the development theory requires is that *some* specimens of the lower organized group should appear earlier than *any* of the group of higher organization.[39]

Wallace's views apparently originated from Chambers's statements "on the succession of animal forms in the course of time." Chambers had said:

Our earth, as we have seen, bore crinoidea before it bore the higher echinodermata. It presented crustacea before it bore fishes, and when fishes came, the first forms were those ganoidal and placoidal types which correspond with the early foetal condition of higher orders. Afterwards there were reptiles, then

36. *Vestiges* (1845), p. 169. Compare, for example, Wallace's views on the dog quoted above.

37. Wallace slightly changed the wording. *Principles* (1835), bk. I, chap. IX, p. 231.

38. Ibid., p. 234. This is not referred to in the eleventh edition and was, therefore, probably a taxonomical mistake. Not an exact quotation.

39. Species Notebook, p. 37. Italics by Wallace.

mammifers, and finally, as we know came man. The tendency of all these illustrations is to make us look to *development* as the principle which has been immediately concerned in the peopling of this globe, a process extending over a vast space of time, but which nevertheless connected in character with the briefer process by which an individual being is evoked from a simple germ.[40]

Wallace examined this progression point by point.

Now vertebrated animals are usually allowed to be the highest form of animal life. They appear Geologically after the mollusca & Radiata. Fishes are universally declared the lowest of the vertebrata. They appear first. Reptiles are universally considered as higher than fishes but lower than Birds & Mammalia. They are found next in succession. The Marsupiata [Marsupialia] are generally allowed to be one of the lowest forms of the Mammalia, & it is one of them which appears first while the highest form, the Quadrumana, appears considerably later. Thus not one fact contradicts the progression.[41]

According to Wallace, there are supposed contradictions only because scientists felt that the highest forms of one group should appear in the paleontological record before the lowest forms of the succeeding group appear. The answer, said Wallace, is that "each group goes on progressing after other groups have branched from it. They then go on in parallel or diverging series & may obtain their max[im]a together."[42] Wallace also discussed the interesting problems of the fossil record in his 1855 Paper, mentioning many of these same facts: "Mollusca and Radiata existed before Vertebrata, and the progression from Fishes to Reptiles and Mammalia, and also from the lower mammals to the higher, is indisputable."[43] The gradual changes occur in a branching series analogous to a branching tree, a concept also used by Charles Darwin. The interesting point is that Wallace's thoughts on the fossil record appear to be a direct outgrowth of the arguments adduced in Chambers's *Vestiges*.[44]

40. *Vestiges* (1845), p. 53. Italics by Chambers.
41. Species Notebook, pp. 37–38. Cuvier's "Radiata" has been broken into the Echinodermata and Coelenterata.
42. Ibid., pp. 38–39.
43. 1855 Paper, pp. 190–91.
44. Chambers' extensive influence will also be discussed in the next chapter in connection with Wallace's law.

Obviously, by February 1855 Wallace had pinpointed the necessary problems to explore, and he had clearly recognized the intense struggle for existence, the ecological balance of species, and the important fact that gradual change occurring over a long period may ultimately result in the origin of distinctly new species. But the final solution to the species problem continued to elude him:

> We are like children looking at a complicated machine of the reasons of whose construction they are ignorant, and like them we constantly impute as causes what is really effect in our vain attempts to explain what we will not confess that we cannot understand.[45]

It was comparable to the "fragments of a dissected map—a picture or a mosaic—[an] approximation of [the] fragments shew that all gaps have been filled up."[46] He understood a large part of that mosaic: slow, natural forces are at work in the organic world; as a result of the struggle for existence, some species die out, others survive; and given enough time for gradual changes to occur new species would eventually appear. The one crucial missing ingredient was the survival of the fittest; nevertheless, he was prepared by February 1855 to make his first public pronouncement on the species question.

45. Species Notebook, p. 33.
46. Ibid., p. 53.

4 "On the Law Which Has Regulated the Introduction of New Species" February 1855

The publication of the "polarity theory" in 1854 by the English naturalist Edward Forbes caused Wallace to present some of his views on the species question before having discovered the key to the mystery. Forbes had argued that "the scale of the first appearance of groups of beings of any degree is *most clearly not one of organic progression.*[1] ... Nevertheless in the relative arrangements, so to speak, of generic types in time, there is an indication of the working of a general law of another kind, and one which seems to me to depend on *the manifestation of the relation of Polarity.*"[2] According to him more genera were produced during the early parts of the Paleozoic period and during the later part of the Neozoic (i.e. Mesozoic + Cenozoic) than during other comparable geological time spans. These periods of intense production formed the extremes of the "great circle of the system of nature;" they were a "Divine scheme of organized nature." In short, according to Forbes, "polarity" was "an attribute or *regulating law* of the *divinely originating* scheme of creation." He concluded by saying:

> If it be true, as I believe it to be, then the truth that it contains is most important; if it prove in the end to be a misrepresentation, it will at least have served the good purpose of stimulating inquiry in a fresh direction.[3]

1. Italics are mine.
2. Italics by Forbes, "On the Manifestation of Polarity in the Distribution of Organized Beings in Time," (1851–54), pp. 429–30. This paper was read on Friday, 28 April 1854, and was reprinted in a number of places; for example: *The Edinburgh New Philosophical Journal,* 57 (1854), 332–37. An abbreviated form of the "polarity hypothesis" by Forbes first appeared in the conclusion of his presidential address presented on 17 February 1854. Edward Forbes, "Address Delivered at the Anniversary Meeting of the Geological Society of London on the 17th February 1854," *Quart. J. Geolog. Soc. Lond.,* 10 (1854), lxxvii–lxxxi. I shall cite the presentation at the Royal Institution.
3. Ibid., pp. 430–33. Italics are mine.

Of the stimulating effect of Forbes's paper there can be no doubt, for Wallace remarked: "It was the promulgation of Forbes's theory which led me to write and publish, for I was annoyed to see such an ideal absurdity put forth when such a simple hypothesis will explain *all the facts.*"[4] A particularly absurd notion, in Wallace's opinion, was that of a "Divine" scheme of creation, for this implied that one could find evidence of design in nature. In his Species Notebook he discussed *"Proofs of Design."* According to the *Cyclopedia of Natural History* (Vol. 2, p. 55), the three scars on a cocoa nut were designed by the wisdom of God. For example, one is *soft,* rather than hard and impenetrable, in order to allow an "embryo" to emerge. Wallace commented:

> Is not this absurd? To impute to the supreme Being a degree of intelligence only equal to that of the stupidest human beings. What should we think, if as a proof of the supreme wisdom of some philosopher, it was pointed out that in building a house, he had made a door to it, or in contriving a box [he] had furnished it with a lid!—Yet this is the kind and degree of design imputed to the Deity as a proof of his infinite wisdom. Could the lowest savage have a more degrading idea of his God?

On the following two pages he again attacked ideas in which natural phenomena are explained in terms of the design of God. In challenging such an explanation of the number of vertebrae in animals, he said:

> Here are several gratuitous statements and inferences. The writer seems to have been behind the scenes at the creation & to have been well acquainted with the motives of the Creator. A humbler mortal may suppose that the same power which enabled the elephant & giraffe, the whale and the camel to perform all their functions with 7 neck bones could also have formed birds to perform theirs with the same number, with still further modifications of form & structure. The writer, however, places a limit to the power of the creator in this direction. He says this could not have been done, "it was necessary to give them more."[5]

4. *WLR,* p. 54. Italics by Wallace.
5. Species Notebook, pp. 31–33.

Thus Forbes's attempt to elucidate previously unexplained natural phenomena by resorting to a mysterious creator was clearly unforgivable. That Forbes *assumed* "to a great extent the completeness of our knowledge of the whole series of organic beings which have existed on the earth" was another fatal error; in Wallace's opinion, this was another fundamental reason for rejecting the hypothesis.[6] These, then, were the immediate stimuli which moved Wallace to publish.

The course of Wallace's thoughts on the species question has been examined in the previous chapter; in addition Wallace specifically wrote that "during the evenings and wet days I had nothing to do but to look over my books and ponder on the problem which was rarely absent from my thoughts," namely, how do species originate? He then went on to describe his extensive preparation for a discussion of the subject:

Having always been interested in the geographical distribution of animals and plants, having studied Swainson and Humboldt, and having now myself a vivid impression of the fundamental differences between the Eastern and Western tropics; and having also read through such books as Bonaparte's "Conspectus," already referred to, and several catalogues of insects and reptiles in the British Museum (which I almost knew by heart), giving a mass of facts as to the distribution of animals over the whole world, it occurred to me that these facts had never been properly utilized as indications of the way in which species had come into existence. The great work of Lyell had furnished me with the main features of the succession of species in time, and by combining the two I thought that some valuable conclusions might be reached.[7]

6. 1855 Paper, p. 195.
7. *My Life,* vol. 1, pp. 354–55. Swainson, *A Treatise on the Geography and Classification of Animals* (1835). As mentioned in chapter 1, Wallace owned a copy of this book. Swainson, *The Natural History and Classification of Fishes, Amphibians, and Reptiles* (1838–39), and the "Zoogeography" of Swainson in Murray, *An Encyclopedia of Geography* (1834). Humboldt and Bonpland, *Personal Narrative of Travels to the Equinoctial Regions of the New Continent, During the Years 1799–1804* (1818–29) Bonaparte, *Conspectus Generum Avium* (1832).

Wallace's 1854 Notebook contains observations on another work which also exerted a profound influence on his thought: namely, François Jules Pictet's *Traité de paléontologie, ou Histoire naturelle des animaux fossiles considérés dans leurs rapports zoologiques et géologiques.*[8] Although Wallace appears never to have mentioned Pictet's name again, he took extensive notes on Pictet's large work on paleontology, and his 1855 Paper bears remarkable similarities to Pictet's ideas, as Wallace's notes of 1854 demonstrate:

From Pictet's Paleontology Laws of Geological development
1. Species [have a] limited Geolog[ical] duration.
2. Contemporaneous spec[ies] generally appear[e]d or disap[peare]d together.
3. [The] older [the] fauna, [the] gtr. [greater the] differences from recent [fauna].
4. Recent faunas [are] more diversified than anc[ien]t [ones].
5. [The] most perfect animals [are] recent.
6. [The] order of appearance [is] like [the] order of development.
7. From [the] birth to [the] death of a species, genus, or family, [there is] no interruption.
8. Faunas shew temp[erature] has varied?

8. F. J. Pictet (1809–1872) was born in Geneva into one of the oldest and most distinguished families there. His father was a politician as well as a scientist and friend of A. P. de Candolle, with whom the young Pictet ultimately studied. In 1829 he received a bachelor of science degree at the Academy in Geneva. The following year, he studied at the Jardin des Plantes in Paris for six months and came into contact with Cuvier, Étienne Geoffroy Sainte Hilaire, Flourens, Latreille, and particularly Victor Audouin, who became one of his closest friends. Before going to Paris, Pictet had worked at the Museum of Natural History in Geneva arranging and classifying the collections. Upon returning to Geneva, he began work in entomology and subsequently made a name for himself in that subject, especially with his work published during 1841–45. In the early 1840s his attention shifted more and more to paleontology, and since there were no good textbooks available in French, he published a four volume *Traité de paléontologie* (Geneva, 1844–46). A second, revised edition was published later (Paris, 1853–57). This monumental work listed all known kinds of animal fossils and discussed then current ideas on species. Pictet also wrote many other monographs on Swiss paleontology. See *Archives des Sciences Physiques et Naturelles, 43* (1872), 342–413, which contains an extensive list of his works. See also *Quart. J. Geolog. Soc. Lond., 29* (1873), xlv–li, esp. xli–xlii.

9. Ancient species [were] more widely distributed.
10. Fossil animals [were made on the] same plan as living [ones].

[Comments]
1. Undisputed.
2. ?generally unimportant.
3. True, with specific exceptions.
4. Doubtful, but [this] does not affect [the] develop[men]t theory.
5. *True* when a whole series can be traced; often apparently false.
6. Important.
7. Very important, undisputed.
[8. omitted]
9. ?Because [there was] more sea & therefore more equal temp[erature].
10. Undisputed. Important.[9]

A careful comparison of Wallace's geological propositions of his 1855 Paper, found in Appendix II, with notes from Pictet's *Paléontologie* reveals that Wallace had incorporated certain points from Pictet, although, of course, not all these points were original with him. For example:

(WALLACE)

7. In each period, however, there are peculiar groups, found nowhere else, and extending through one or several formations.

(PICTET)

1. Species [have a] limited Geolog[ical] duration.

(WALLACE)

8. Species of one genus, or genera of one family occurring in the same geological time are more closely allied than those separated in time.

(PICTET)

3. [The] older [the] fauna, [the] gtr. [greater the] differences from recent [fauna].

9. 1854 Notebook, [p. 15], not paginated. An entry on the facing page is dated "May/54."

(WALLACE)

9. . . . in geology the life of a species or genus has not been interrupted.

(PICTET)

7. From [the] birth to [the] death of a species, genus, or family, [there is] no interruption.[10]

In a discussion of the geological propositions, we find further similarity:

(WALLACE)

Much discussion has of late years taken place on the question, whether, the succession of life upon the globe has been from a lower to a higher degree of organization. The admitted facts seem to show that there has been a general but not a detailed progression. Mollusca and Radiata existed before Vertebrata, and the progression from Fishes to Reptiles, and also from the lower to the higher, is indisputable.[11]

(PICTET)

5. [The] most perfect animals [are] recent.

Despite Pictet's obvious influence,[12] it would be quite misleading to underrate the profound influence of Lyell's *Principles,* for the entire work of Wallace is grounded upon the uniformitarian principles including large time periods as advocated by Lyell. As we have seen, the plan of Wallace's proposed book *On the Organic Law of Change* was that the uniformitarian principles in geology were to be applied rigorously to biology, and in Wallace's 1855 Paper, Lyell was specifically quoted in connection with extinction: "The extinction of species, however, offers little difficulty, and the *modus operandi* has been well illustrated by Sir C. Lyell in his admirable 'Principles.'"[13] Although

10. Forbes had said the same thing, (1851–54), p. 429. See also de Beer, *Darwin Notebooks,* vol. 2, no. 5, (1960) p. 171, note 4; Darwin, *Origin of Species,* pp. 315 and 343; and Darwin's "Essay of 1844," in de Beer, *Darwin and Wallace, Evolution by Natural Selection* (1958), p. 185.

11. 1855 Paper, pp. 190–91.

12. The general influence of Pictet deserves careful examination, for Darwin also cites his work a number of times. See, for example, *Origin of Species,* pp. 302, 305, 313–16, 335, 338. Curiously, neither Lyell in his *Principles* (1872) nor Geike in *The Founders of Geology* (1905) mentions Pictet and his work.

13. 1855 Paper, p. 190.

Wallace would fight to the death with Lyell about evolution, he fully accepted his geological principles, at least at that time. In fact, one might say that to some extent he accepted those principles *more* fully than Lyell himself, who refused to accept evolution until the 1860s.

We have also noticed that Wallace's previous work on the geographical distribution of species pointed forward specifically to his 1855 law which I shall discuss later. Indeed some of the most cogent evidence is adduced from the data: "Closely allied species are often found in the same or closely adjoining districts," as Wallace had himself observed earlier in the cases of the toucans, hummingbirds, fish, monkeys, butterflies, etc. Although these examples were by no means unique,

> hitherto no attempt has been made to explain these singular phaenomena, or to show how they have arisen. Why are the genera of Palms and of Orchids in almost every case confined to one hemisphere? Why are the closely allied species of brown-backed Trogons all found in the East, and the green-backed in the West? Why are the Macaws and the Cockatoos similarly restricted? Insects furnish a countless number of analogous examples;—the Goliathi of Africa, the Ornithopterae of the Indian Islands, the Heliconidae of South America, the Danaidae of the East, and in all, the most closely allied species found in geographical proximity. The question forces itself upon every thinking mind—why are these things so? They could not be as they are had not law regulated their creation and dispersion.[14]

The influence of Chambers' *Vestiges* is perceptible in Wallace's paper in a number of places not yet mentioned. An obvious one is that of rudimentary organs, a subject sharply focused on by Lamarck and Chambers:

> The rudimentary organs, as those not fully developed for use are called, appear most conspicuously in animals which form links between various classes. . . .
> The limbs of all the vertebrate animals are, in like manner, on one plan, however various they may appear. In the hind-leg of a horse, for example, the angle called the hock is the same part which in us forms the heel: and the horse and other quadrupeds,

14. Ibid., pp. 189–90.

with certain exceptions, walk, in reality, upon what answers to
the toes of a human being. In this and many other quadrupeds the
fore part of the extremities is shrunk up in a hoof, as the tail of
the human being is shrunk up in the bony mass at the bottom of
the back. The bat, on the other hand, has these parts largely
developed. The membrane, commonly called its wing, is framed
chiefly upon bones answering precisely to those of the human
hand; its extinct congener, the Ptero-dactyle, had the same membrane extended upon the fore-finger only, which in that animal
was prolonged to an extraordinary extent. In the paddles of the
whale and other animals of its order, we see the same bones as
in the more highly developed extremities of the land mammifers;
and even the serpent tribes, which present no external appearance
of such extremities, possess them in reality, but in an underdevel-
oped or rudimental state.[15]

Wallace used the same incorrect definition of rudimentary organs,
accepting them as incipient rather than as vestigial features, and he
referred to "the minute limbs hidden beneath the skin in many of the
snake-like lizards, the anal hooks of the boa constrictor, the complete
series of jointed fingerbones in the paddle of the Manatus and whale."
He also adduced Chambers's botanical examples of rudimentary floral
envelopes, stamens, and carpels.[16]

Moreover, it is not mere coincidence that Chambers closed his chapter on the "Mental Constitution of Animals" in precisely the same
way as Wallace closed his paper on organic change:

It is most interesting to observe into how small a field the whole
of the mysteries of nature thus ultimately resolve themselves.
The inorganic has been thought to have one comprehensive law,
GRAVITATION. The organic, the other great department of mun-
dane things, rests in like manner, on one law and that is DEVEL-
OPMENT.[17]

Wallace ended his 1855 Paper in this manner:

Granted this law and many of the most important facts in
Nature could not have been otherwise, but are as necessary deduc-

15. *Vestiges* (1845), pp. 146–47.
16. 1855 Paper, p. 195. Compare with *Vestiges* (1845), p. 148.
17. *Vestiges* (1845), p. 251. Italics by Chambers.

tions from it, as are the elliptic orbits of the planets from the law of gravitation.[18]

Furthermore, it is obvious that Wallace's law itself is strongly reminiscent of the conclusion of the heretical *Vestiges* which said:

> The idea then, which I form of the progress of organic life upon the globe—and the hypothesis is applicable to all other similar theatres of vital being—is, *that the simplest and most primitive type, under a law to which that of like-production is subordinate, gave birth to the type next above it, so that this produced the next higher, and so on to the very highest*, the stages of advance being in all cases very small—namely, from one species only to another; so that the phenomenon has always been of a simple and modest character.[19]

Of course Lamarck had said essentially the same thing: "every individual possessing life always resembles very closely those from which it sprang."[20] Although ostensibly arriving by a somewhat different path Wallace stated in a similar vein: *"Every species has come into existence coincident in both space and time with a pre-existing closely allied species."* All three of these statements explain "the natural system of arrangement of organic beings, their geographical distribution, their geological sequence, the phenomena of representative and substituted groups in all their modifications, and the most singular peculiarities of anatomical structure"[21] as Wallace claimed for his law; but Wallace's law was rigorously mechanistic—no intervening supernatural being was necessary at any time—and his evidence, devoid of the repugnant errors of the *Vestiges,* was marshaled in a most overpowering manner.[22] In fact, Sir Charles Lyell later wrote to Wallace:

18. 1855 Paper, p. 196.

19. *Vestiges* (1844), p. 222. *Vestiges* (1845), p. 170 is almost identical. Italics by Chambers.

20. Lamarck (1809), p. 35. Lamarck's theory of evolution is discussed in its various stages in Packard, *Lamarck: The Founder of Evolution* (1901), chapters 16 and 17.

21. 1855 Paper, pp. 186, 196. Italics by Wallace.

22. Both Lamarck and Chambers felt that there was a supreme author of nature and her laws, nevertheless, Chambers felt that he had gone "beyond the French philosopher to a very important point, the original Divine con-

I have been reading over again your paper published in 1855 in the *Annals* on "The Law which has regulated the Introduction of New Species", passages of which I intend to quote, not in reference to your priority of publication, but simply because *there are some points laid down more clearly than I can find in the work of Darwin itself, in regard to the bearing of the geological and zoological evidence on geographical distribution and the origin of species.*[23]

Although Wallace had borrowed facts from Lyell, Chambers, Lamarck, Pictet, and others, he had woven all these facts together with his own personal discoveries into a unique, cogent argument—described by Huxley as a "powerful essay." Its outstanding virtue was that scientifically acceptable data were utilized to support "some kind of evolution." With the death of Forbes few others were fully qualified to discuss Wallace's novel synthesis of facts, and the public silence of the scientific world was conspicuous. Private reactions, however, were quite another matter as we shall see. Nevertheless, Wallace had presented his case for evolution, and he lacked only a mechanism for the change—all this fully three years before discovering natural selection. The next important question to examine is: In what way did Wallace's case for evolution develop during that interim period?

---

ception of all the forms of being which these natural laws were only instruments in working out and realizing." *Vestiges* (1845), p. 177. See Lamarck, *Zool. Philos.* (1914), pp. 36, 41, 180, 342. Both appear to have been deists. Wallace was an agnostic at that time.

23. *WLR*, pp. 279–80. Letter dated 4 April 1867. Italics are mine.

5 On the Organic Law of Change

February 1855–February 1858

For Wallace, the period from February 1855 until February 1858—that is, between the writing of his two important papers on the species question—is generally thought of as an essentially unimportant lull in his thoughts about evolution. Indeed, Marchant has remarked that "Wallace wrote nothing further of importance [after his 1855 Paper] until the second essay which more fully disclosed his view of the origin of species."[1] Recently, Wilma George, Gerald Henderson, and Barbara Beddall have alluded to some interesting remarks made by Wallace during this period,[2] but for the most part very little evidence has been adduced to disprove the belief that this period was one of silent meditation on Wallace's part, followed abruptly and unexpectedly by his recollection of Malthus and the formulation of the principle of natural selection.

During this period, however, Wallace was carefully gathering evidence in support of the evolutionary hypothesis, just as he had been before he published his 1855 Paper. In his Species Notebook we can see the kind of evidence, the direction of his thoughts, and the manner in which he was marshaling this evidence. His papers written during this period together with a letter to H. W. Bates supply additional information.

Considering the remarkably similar conclusions arrived at by Wallace and Charles Darwin, it is not surprising that much of the evidence they gathered came from precisely the same sources. Indeed, if Wallace had finally published *On the Organic Law of Change,* it would have resembled *On the Origin of Species* in many ways; the resemblance arises, of course, from their mutual reliance upon Lyell's great *Principles of Geology.* Both naturalists owed a far greater debt to this work than to any other, including that of Malthus. Although Wallace strongly disagreed with Lyell's views on species, he nevertheless was profoundly influenced by Lyell's cogent arguments regarding geological change and candidly admitted his debt:

1. *WLR,* p. 83.
2. George (1964), pp. 58–59. Henderson (1958), p. 45. Beddall (1968), pp. 280–89.

Along with Malthus I had read, and been even more impressed by, Sir Charles Lyell's immortal 'Principles of Geology' which taught me that the inorganic world—the whole surface of the earth, its seas and lands, its mountains and valleys, its rivers and lakes, and every detail of its climatic conditions, were and always had been in a continual state of slow modification.[3]

As we know, Darwin carefully studied the first edition of Lyell's *Principles* during the voyage of H.M.S. *Beagle* (1831–36).[4] It seems evident that the extensive annotations he later made in his copy of Lyell's fifth edition—published in March 1837—are significant especially when we recall the statement in his Journal that he had opened his first notebook on the transmutation of species in July 1837, because in March of that year he "had been greatly struck" by the character of South American fossils and by the interesting species of the Galapagos Islands. As he added later, "these facts (especially latter) origin of all my views."[5] It must have been obvious to Darwin as he read Lyell's recapitulation of his discussion of the reality of species that his observations on the Galapagos species and the South American fossils contradicted Lyell's conclusions. Indeed, Darwin's extensive annotations on Lyell's recapitulation demonstrate (1) that he was aware of the significance of Lyell's statements—they had to be disproved if transmutation was to be established, and (2) that he had read Lyell's work at about the same time that he had begun his full-scale assault on the species question from the evolutionary point of view. Loren Eiseley, on the other hand, has argued that Darwin opened his first notebook in 1837 because in January 1837 Edward Blyth had published a significant paper commenting on natural selection.[6] I think

3. Linnean Society of London (1908), p. 118.

4. Volume one of Darwin's copy of the *Principles* (first edition) is "reasonably fully annotated." Although the second volume has only a single annotation (the word "Galapagos") and some of the index pages remain uncut, "Charles studied the volume with care for he makes many references to it in his correspondence. . . . " S. Smith, "The Origin of the 'Origin,' " (1959), pp. 2–3.

5. Quoted by Smith, ibid., p. 3. See de Beer, ed., "Darwin's Journal," vol. 2, no. 1, (1959) p. 7.

6. Eiseley, "Charles Darwin, Edward Blyth, and the Theory of Natural Selection," (1959), pp. 94–158. Eiseley reiterates his thesis in a later article, "Darwin, Coleridge, and the Theory of Unconscious Creation," (1965), pp. 588–602, esp. 597. I shall have occasion to return to his observations in my conclusions.

that it is more important that Lyell's fifth edition of the *Principles* was published in March 1837, *the same month,* Darwin tells us, that he was "greatly struck" by the implications of the South American fossils and Galapagos species.

Furthermore, as Darwin himself observed, no one could read Lyell's great work without seeing geology through his eyes; nor did his influence stop with geology: "the future historian will recognize [Lyell's *Principles*] as having produced a revolution in natural science."[7] Even the most cursory examination of Darwin's *Origin* and his Notebooks on Transmutation of Species will disclose Lyell's profound influence. Obviously, Lyell's arguments formed the essential fabric of Darwin's own arguments.

Of Wallace's debt to Lyell there also can be no doubt. We have already seen that Wallace's proposed book on evolution, like Darwin's, was grounded on Lyell's uniformitarian principles but applied to the organic world;[8] that, on the other hand, he took issue with Lyell's views on species, and had planned to close his book with an extended refutation of these views; and further that uniformitarian principles permeate his 1855 Paper. Specific reference is made to Lyell's ideas on extinction. Moreover, it appears that at about the time he thought of natural selection, Wallace was again disputing Lyell's contention that the change of species is accomplished in very short periods of time and that indefinite divergence ultimately would be deleterious to individuals:

> In Lyell's recapitulation of facts as to [the] reality of species, he says: "Lastly. The entire variation from the original type which any given kind of *change* can produce may usually be effected in a brief period of time, after which no further deviation can be obtained by continuing to alter the circumstances *though ever so gradually;* indefinite divergence either in the way of improvement or deterioration being prevented & the least possible excess *beyond the defined limits* being fatal to the existence of the individual."[9]

7. Darwin, *On the Origin of Species,* p. 282.
8. Wallace used Lyell's fourth edition when he was in the Malay Archipelago. Species Notebook, p. 4 from the front but not paginated as are later pages.
9. In his own copy of the *Principles,* Darwin underlined the words "improvement or deterioration" and added in the margin "if this were *true* adios

Here rests the whole question[10] & Lyell *assumes* it in his favour.
He assumes that only *change{s}* of *circumstances* produce variety.
How then do varieties constantly occur in the same place & under
the same circumstances as the original species? How can he prove
that variation may not go on at a rate commensurate with Geo-
logical changes? How can man's hasty experiments settle this?
His "though ever so gradually" is a gratuitous assumption.
What are "the defined limits,"—he assumes that they exist.[11]

Wallace's famous paper, "On the Tendency of Varieties to Depart
Indefinitely from the Original Type,"[12] apparently was a direct refutation of Lyell's contentión, quoted above, that "the entire variation
from the original type" is effected quickly and within prescribed
limits. When these ill-defined boundaries were exceeded, extinction
followed. Wallace had already fought this battle with Lyell, using
the example of the dog,[13] and both of his earlier accounts strikingly
anticipated his paper of 1858. As he remarked in his notebook, "Here
rests the whole question," and we find in Wallace's conclusion of that
famous paper the very same language that had been used by Lyell:

> We believe we have now shown that there is a tendency in
> nature to the continued progression of certain classes of *varieties*
> *further and further from the original type*—a progression to
> which there appears no reason to assign any *definite limits* [and
> which] by minute steps, in various directions, but always checked
> and balanced by the necessary conditions, subject to which alone
> existence can be preserved, may, it is believed, be followed out
> so as to agree with all the phaenomena presented by organized

theory." S. Smith (1959), p. 4. Lyell's observations are found in *Principles*
(1835), bk. III, chap. IV, p. 21, point number 4. The complete recapitulation
from this edition is reprinted in McKinney (1971), pp. 41–42.

10. Italics are mine.

11. Except as noted, the italics are Wallace's. Species Notebook, pp. 149–50.

12. Wallace's paper was first read on 1 July 1858, and published in the
Journal of the Proceedings of the Linnean Society of London, Zoology, III,
(1859), pp. 53–62 and has been reprinted in many places. I shall refer to the
reprint in Wallace's *Contributions to the Theory of Natural Selection* (1870),
chap. II, pp. 26–44. Henceforth this volume will be cited *NS*. The first footnote and all the captions in the text are later additions by Wallace. Also reprinted in McKinney (1971).

13. See above chapter 3, p. 35.

beings, their *extinction and succession in past ages,* and all the extraordinary modifications of form, instinct and habits, which they exhibit.[14]

The striking similarities between Wallace's notes on point number four of Lyell's recapitulation respecting species change and the argument of Wallace's paper of 1858 on natural selection—especially the conclusion quoted above—seem to show that Wallace had this specific reference in mind as he wrote his paper, and was in fact directing his argument against that very passage. Evidently, when Wallace took notes for his paper of 1858, he examined his notebooks and utilized the evidence contained therein. Some examples of this procedure will be adduced in the following pages.

Furthermore, it is entirely possible that Wallace followed in his conclusion the sequence of his examination of his notebook or at least his estimation of the importance of his own notes. In his work *Darwinism,* Wallace says that "in order to show how little effect these writers [on transmutation, i.e. Lamarck and Chambers] had upon the public mind, I will quote a few passages from the writings of Sir Charles Lyell, as representing the opinions of the most advanced thinkers of the period immediately preceding that of Darwin's work" (1889, p. 4). What Wallace did not state was that these quotations were taken directly from the versions in his own Species Notebook and thus only indirectly from the *Principles of Geology.* Both the content and the sequence are extremely interesting:

> When recapitulating the facts and arguments in favour of the invariability and permanence of species, he [Lyell] says: "The entire variation from the original type which any given kind of change can produce may usually be effected in a brief period of time, after which no further deviation can be obtained by continuing to alter the circumstances, though ever so gradually, indefinite divergence either in the way of improvement or deterioration being prevented, and the least possible excess beyond the defined limits being fatal to the existence of the individual."[15] In another place he maintains that "varieties of some species may differ more than other species do from each other without shaking

---

14. *NS,* pp. 43–44. All italics, except for the first word, are mine.
15. A direct quotation from Species Notebook, pp. 149–50.

our confidence in the reality of species."[16] He further adduces
certain facts in geology as being, in his opinion, "fatal to the
theory of progressive development,"[17] and he explains the fact
that there are so often distinct species in countries of similar
climate and vegetation by "special creations" in each country.[18]

These quotations may possibly indicate, roughly, the manner in which
Wallace examined his notebook immediately before writing his
famous paper of 1858. Whatever the precise sequence, there can be
no doubt of the direct influence of Lyell's work in general and more
specifically point number four of the recapitulation. It is possible
that even the phrase "the struggle for existence" came from Lyell's
discussion of the sugar ants and locusts, quoted above,[19] in which
fierce struggle led to the extermination of certain species. Indeed,
Wallace quoted this very example in his paper of 1858 and observed
that the least numerous and more feeble varieties would suffer first:

> Now, let some alteration of physical conditions occur in the dis-
> trict—a long period of drought, *a destruction of vegetation by
> locusts,* the irruption of some new carnivorous animal seeking
> "pastures new"—any change in fact tending to render existence
> more difficult to the species in question, and tasking its utmost
> powers to avoid complete *extermination;* it is evident that of all
> the individuals composing the species, those forming the least
> numerous and most feebly organized variety would suffer first,
> and, were the pressure severe, must soon become *extinct.*[20]

Eventually, then, only the superior varieties would remain. There
seems to be little doubt, especially since Lyell's evidence was used
extensively, that Wallace's conclusion that species evolve by means
of natural selection owed much to the evidence found in the *Principles.*

16. A direct quotation from Species Notebook, p. 39. See above chapter 3,
p. 34.

17. A direct quotation from Species Notebook, p. 37. As I pointed out in
chapter 3, p. 41, note 38, this is a quotation only in part.

18. A reference to Species Notebook, p. 45 (et seq.), Wallace, *Darwinism*
(1889), pp. 4–5. Wallace goes on (p. 5) to quote again directly from notes he
had taken earlier from Louis Agassiz's *Lake Superior:* Species Notebook,
pp. 140–41.

19. Chapter 3, p. 38. However, Wallace himself had already used the term
as we have seen. See chapter 3, pp. 38–39.

20. *NS,* pp. 35–36. Italics are mine.

Wallace's ideas on variation were not limited to Lyell's pronouncements, weighty though they were, for he drew information from a variety of sources, not the least of which was his own extensive experience—by 1858 he had spent about eight years in the tropics as a professional collector. Furthermore, in about July 1856 Wallace had read and taken extensive notes on an important article of 1835 by Edward Blyth, an English naturalist, who had made some very interesting observations about varieties, and who heartily recommended the "sound and excellent remarks on varieties . . . found in the second volume of Lyell's *Principles of Geology*." Thus, Wallace had read an article in essential agreement with Lyell's view but with more explicit reference to "the struggle for existence" and the survival of "the best organized," "the strongest," "the best able to maintain his ground and defend himself from every enemy."[21] Wallace took the following notes on Blyth's penetrating article:

Mr. Blyth (Loudon's *Mag. of Nat. Hist.* Vol. 8, p. 40)
Classes varieties into
1. Simple varieties or variations. In which parents produce an offspring slightly different from themselves in stature, colour, or form, & which when kept apart & propagated constitute *Breeds*.
2. Acquired variations. (?Are *these ever propagated*) Yes. which are the changes gradually produced in animals by food, climate, or other external circumstances. Such are the differences between the same animals inhabiting the mountains & the plains, a hot or a cold climate; & enjoying scanty or abundant nourishment.
3. Breeds Are simple varieties, propagated or increased by isolation either natural or artificial.

21. Blyth, "An Attempt to Classify the 'Varieties' of Animals, . . . , " (1835), pp. 46, 48. This article (as well as Blyth's 1836 and 1837 sequels) is conveniently reprinted in Eiseley's article, "Charles Darwin, Edward Blyth, and the Theory of Natural Selection" (1959), pp. 115–22. A typographical error on p. 115 gives the volume number as 3 instead of 8. I have used the original article and my page references are to the original. For a detailed discussion of Blyth and his work see McKinney, "Edward Blyth" (1970). Blyth's article is also reprinted in McKinney (1971), pp. 43–56.

4. True varieties
   Are those prominent cases of simple varieties which have
   become propagated & kept distinct from the original stock—
   as the otter sheep of N. America, the black Jaquar, the crook
   tailed cat of [the] Indian Archipelago.[22]

The immediate importance of this document is that it provides
definite evidence that at least one of the discoverers of natural selection—Alfred Russel Wallace—read and understood (a safe assumption since he had already appreciated the significance of the same
problems as they had been presented in Lyell's *Principles*) Blyth's
arguments more than two years before hitting upon the principle of
natural selection. And these arguments contain clear-cut anticipations
of ideas more fully expounded by Wallace and Darwin at a later date.
For example, in Blyth's discussion of breeds, we find an *almost*
Darwinian discussion of the struggle for existence:

the original and typical form of an animal is in great measure
kept up by the same identical means by which a true *breed* is
produced. The original form of a species is *unquestionably* better
adapted to its *natural* habits than any modification of that form;
and, as the sexual passions excite to rivalry and conflict, and the
stronger must always prevail over the weaker, the latter, in a
state of nature, is allowed but few opportunities of continuing
its race. In a large herd of cattle, the strongest bull drives from
him all the younger and weaker individuals of his own sex, and
remains sole master of the herd; so that all the young which are
produced must have had their origin from one which possessed
the maximum of power and physical strength; and which, consequently in the struggle for existence, was the best able to
maintain his ground, and defend himself from every enemy. In
like manner, among animals which procure their food by means
of their ability, strength, or delicacy of sense, the one best organised must always obtain the greatest quantity; and must, therefore, become physically the strongest, and be thus enabled, by
routing its opponents, to transmit its superior qualities to a greater number of offspring.[23]

22. Blyth (1835), pp. 40–49. The article continues to p. 53. Species
Notebook, p. 62. Italics by Wallace.
23. Blyth (1835), p. 46. Italics are Blyth's.

The familiar ring of these words immediately recalls the words both of Wallace (in his paper "On the Tendency of Varieties to Depart Indefinitely from the Original Type") and of Darwin (in his essays of 1842 and 1844 and in the *Origin*). Hindsight leads us to expect Blyth to draw what is to us the logical conclusion, namely, that assuming his arguments were true, then new, better adapted species eventually would arise to replace the inferior ones. And Blyth was willing to concede in regard to domestic species that the same law "can be easily converted by man into a means of raising different varieties," which, as he had already pointed out, "may be very unlike the original type." Furthermore, although permanent variations would rarely be perpetuated in a state of nature, he conceded:

> But it does not hence follow that among wild birds there are *no* permanently white or pied varieties; or in other words, no true partial or semi-albinoes. A blackbird with a white head has now inhabited a garden in this neighborhood for three successive years; and if the cupidity of collectors did not mark out every white or pied bird for destruction, I doubt not that I should have been able to have furnished some other similar instances of permanent variation.

Later, he went on to say that "when two animals are matched together, each remarkable for a certain given peculiarity, no matter how trivial, there is a dedicated tendency in nature for that peculiarity to *increase*," and he pointed out that in human races if nontypical variations were propagated, they "would become the origin of a new race."[24]

In spite of these astute observations, however, Blyth did not understand that he had observed the mechanism for the propagation of new species. For him natural selection was essentially a conservative force; his law was "intended by Providence to keep up the typical qualities of a species;" in a state of nature simple variations "are generally lost in the course of two or three generations," by a blending inheritance.[25]

To Wallace, however, the hypothetical swamping effect of blending inheritance was a possibility to be ignored. Since he was firmly con-

24. Ibid., pp. 43–49. Italics are Blyth's.
25. Ibid., pp. 46, 41, 46–49.

vinced that evolution occurred, there could be no such effect, nor did he believe that "by a wise provision [of the creator] the typical characters of a species are, in a state of nature, preserved,"[26] for the geological record clearly demonstrated that species do become extinct. For Wallace, there simply never was a "species barrier," to use Eiseley's interesting term; consequently, Wallace pushed on to ground where Blyth feared to tread: in all four categories of variation new forms *can,* and therefore, *must* arise—simple varieties *can* become breeds, and true varieties such as the otter (ancons) sheep *do* arise. And a most important point is that these new forms propagate their own peculiar kind. Even acquired variations (phenotypic characters) are propagated. Only a few pages before his notes on Blyth appear in his notebook, Wallace had recorded the following observation:

> New forms, miscalled species, are always starting up in every Botanic Garden. In the garden of Berlin, Link states that *Tizyphora dasyantha* after many years changed to another form which might be called *T. intermedia.*
> Lindley, Intro[duction to] Bot[any][27]

It is important to notice that Wallace attached no especial significance to Blyth's graphic description of the struggle for survival. The reason for this is simple; the concept was not new to Wallace—he had already found it plainly stated in Lyell's *Principles,* as I have mentioned above. And he also understood that extinction was a necessary consequence of the struggle; that those surviving species are better adapted to their environment; and that variations—simple, acquired, and true (permanent)—which persist can, and according to his theory, *must,* be propagated.

Yet Wallace did not perceive that natural selection, the survival of the fittest organisms, is another important consequence of the struggle for existence. He approached this concept, yet failed to seize upon it. There are at least two possible reasons for this: although aware of the difficulty animals have in procuring food, Wallace did not yet realize the vital relationship between a limited food supply and the struggle for existence. And apparently he was so close to this complex problem that he needed a new perspective. It was Malthus, not Blyth, who provided these important keys.

26. Ibid., p. 48.
27. Species Notebook, p. 59.

Wallace's obsession with animal variation in a state of nature was further reflected in an article written during these years on the natural arrangement of birds. This article furnishes an excellent example of Wallace's approach to the taxonomic problems he encountered each day as a collector. Obviously, he was opposed to mere superficial cases of analogy, such as beak structure, which had been used previously to classify birds, when natural affinities provided a more logical arrangement, particularly to the evolutionist. (Lamarck is an outstanding example.) Wallace believed that our complete ignorance of extinct forms prevented us from determining either the true direction or the extent of the affinities of the various families of birds. Rarely is a family or genus exactly intermediate between two others; consequently, Wallace represented the relationships as an irregularly branched tree. This, then, was a direct application of his evolutionary "complicated branching line of affinity" which he had described in his 1855 Paper (p. 187). He suggested that the passerine birds be regrouped into a natural arrangement as indicated by affinities; that is, one should compress the groupings into Fissirostres and Scansores, so that the insensible gradations connect the species, making it much easier to conceive their connections by intermediate links: "an *arrangement* may be possible, but a *classification may not be so.*"[28]

Because of his preconceptions, Wallace was very definitely on the right track, and these suggestions of arrangement by affinity, rather than by analogy, although not entirely novel—as is evident from Alfred Newton's historical introduction to his famous *A Dictionary of Birds*—are unmistakable adumbrations of the approach to ornithological taxonomy after 1 July 1858. As Newton observed, possibly no other branch of zoology accepted the principles of evolution sooner, and the stimulus which that concept imparted was profound. The geographical distribution of birds and their affinities were seen in a new perspective: "classification assumed a wholly different aspect."[29]

Wallace's paper of 1856 with its emphasis on natural affinity served as another public notice of his ideas on species, and turning once more to his Species Notebook we find a candid discussion of the problems of affinity:

28. Wallace, "Attempts at a Natural Arrangement of Birds" (1856), pp. 193–216, ref. 214. Also p. 195. Italics are Wallace's.
29. Newton (1896), pp. 1–78, 79.

Is not the Cetacean group rather a modification of mammalia to an aquatic life than a link connecting them with fishes? In essentials they exhibit nearly all the mammalian & scarcely any piscine characters. The skeleton is mammalian, the highly developed forearm has its parts more perfect than many terrestrial quadrupeds. In the essential characters of generation & nourishment of the young they show no tendency to depart from the mammalian type. The skin, the layer of dermal fat, the respiration are all truly mammalian. In the seals we have the first steps of the ferae, in the cetacea we see it carried much farther from the pachyderm type. The very fact of their being aquatic forms of *two orders* shews that they are both aberrant developments of their respective orders, not the foundation of the whole class which both of them cannot be.

Although the distinctions between affinity and analogy were by that time recognized—hummingbirds were no longer considered as transitions between birds and insects—"the *principles* of distinction are often lost sight of." Consequently, superficial resemblances, such as beak structure and color, were still advocated as transitional characters. He concluded:

When two groups are broadly distinguished by certain characters which are universal in each of them & are not found in any other group, we must in order to establish a transition from one to the other shew that a decided diminution of these peculiarities takes place, that the essential characters of each group have begun to vanish. As long as these most important characters remain undiminished, no alterations of external form or habits can be held to shew any signs of a transition.[30]

Since the most perfect forms embody the essential characters of the group, transitions between groups never occur by means of these typical forms but rather by the least perfectly developed ones. Bats are therefore not transitional, because they are highly developed mammals. Hummingbirds cannot possibly be transition stages "by which the birds are connected with other parts of the animal kingdom," because they are also very highly developed species of their respective orders. Likewise Insecta are not the connecting links be-

30. Species Notebook, pp. 76–78. Italics by Wallace.

tween Vertebrata and Annulosa (Annelida). In the more rudimentary organisms are to be found the transitional forms; he continued by emphasizing the importance of the universal and relatively stable characters:

> We may make another observation on the kind of characters which are the most important as showing affinities between extensive groups. It is not generally those on which the habits, motions & food of the various species depend that are of the greatest value for the purposes of classification but often on characters which seem to have little influence & to be of little importance but which yet by their universality, & by the very gradual manner in which they shew any signs of change, are strikingly characteristic of natural groups.

In birds, for example, the wings, legs and feet, and bills may vary widely, but "feathers occur with scarcely any variation throughout the whole class & the horney covering of the bill, & the hard scale like skin of the feet change not with all the variations of size, habitat & habits." Structures such as stomach, leg, and wings may vary according to changes of external form, habits, and food, and thus furnish no information additional to that available from observation. "But we have in the sternum modifications of form which do not depend immediately on external characters." There are other characters—arrangements of plumage, form of nostrils, nature of the skin—all of which "furnish excellent & very constant characters for the determination of larger groups."

From the particular treatment of birds, Wallace wished to consider more general cases:

> Now let us apply the principles here enunciated to the elucidation of some of those doubtful affinities about which Naturalists are still disagreed, namely those of the Cetacea to the fishes, the Ostriches to the Mammalia, the Penguins to the Reptiles, and the Caprimulgidae [Caprimulgiformes] to the Owls.[31]

Wallace's discussion of the species question was continued in an article published in *The Zoologist,* in which he emphasized that the concepts of "permanent" and "geographical" varieties tend to confuse

31. Ibid., pp. 78–83.

even more the issue of precisely what is meant by the term species,

> for if permanent characters do not constitute one when those
> characters are minute, then a species differs from a variety in de-
> gree only, not in nature, and no two persons will agree as to the
> amount of difference necessary to constitute the one, or the
> amount of resemblance which must exist to form the other. The
> line that separates them will become so fine that it will be exceed-
> ingly difficult to prove its existence.

This question was of major importance to the belief in the stability of
species, for unless some absolute, essential difference could be discovered, that very "fact is one of the strongest arguments against the
independent creation of species, for why should a special act of creation be required to call into existence an organism differing only in
degree from another which has been produced by existing laws?"

If special creation is not to be denied, there is but one alternative
definition:

> You must consider every group of individuals representing per-
> manent characters, however slight, to constitute a species; while
> those which are subject to such variation as to make us believe
> they have descended from a parent species, or that we know have
> so descended, are to be classed as varieties.

Of course, Wallace's alternative definition of species and varieties,
upon close examination, was equally difficult to pin down because of
the problems involved in deciding precisely what constitutes permanence; and, more important, his definition, if accepted, would openly
invite a multiplication of specific names. Obviously, Wallace had focused attention on a perplexing zoological dilemma: to be logically
consistent, biologists either had to reject special creation openly and
agree that species differ from varieties in degree only, or they had to
call *any* group with "permanent characters, however slight," a species.
This meant that "permanent varieties" would have to be classed as
species, which is the meaning of his conclusion: "The two doctrines
of 'permanent varieties' and of 'specially created unvarying species,'
are inconsistent with each other."[32]

---

32. Wallace, "Note on the Theory of Permanent and Geographical
Varieties" (1858), pp. 5887–88.

The precise significance of this article, written in 1857, becomes clear when Wallace's later publications are examined.[33] In his famous paper of 1858 on natural selection, Wallace returned specifically to the question of "permanent or true varieties"—Blyth's fourth category of varieties—and observed that there is generally no means of determining "which is the *variety* and which the original *species, . . .* except in those rare cases in which the one race has been known to produce an offspring unlike itself and resembling the other." Of course, this would be "quite incompatible with the 'permanent invariability of species,' though Lyell and others would have countered by saying that species vary only within strict limits." Wallace then observed that the general principle of the survival of the fittest causes certain varieties to depart more and more from the original type, the end result being that at some point varieties *become* species.[34] This point of view, of course, sounds very much like the first definition in his article "Note on the Theory of Permanent and Geographical Varieties;"[35] but he did not state *when* a variety becomes a species if the original species does not become extinct immediately after the formation of the new variety.

This subject is more fully elaborated in his article, read 17 March 1864, on the Papilionidae butterflies of the Malay Archipelago.[36] Here we find the most complete statement of Wallace's views on species and varieties. As a working definition, he cited Prichard's state-

33. That the meaning of his article is not completely clear may be inferred from the fact that Wilma George has cited the second definition as Wallace's own (1964, pp. 58–59) while Henderson has cited the first definition as Wallace's (1958, pp. 45, 47). Wallace specifically states at the beginning of his article (p. 5887), that he does *not* commit himself to *either* definition: "I venture to offer the following observations, which, without advocating either side of the question, are intended to point out a difficulty or rather a dilemma, its advocates do not appear to have perceived." See also Beddall (1968), pp. 288–89.

34. *NS,* pp. 27, 36. Italics are Wallace's.

35. See above p. 67.

36. Wallace, "On the Phenomena of Variation and Geographical Distribution as Illustrated by the *Papilionidae* of the Malayan Region" (1865), pp. 1–71 (and plates I–VIII). An abridged version is reprinted in *NS,* pp. 130–200 under the title "The Malayan Papilionidae or Swallow-tailed Butterflies, as Illustrative of the Theory of Natural Selection." I have cited the more accessible version in *NS,* but *all* quotations which I have cited from this article have been compared with the original article.

ment "that '*separate origin and distinctness of race, evinced by a constant transmission of some characteristic peculiarity of organization,*' constitutes a species." Ignoring the question of "origin," he focused attention on the differences or peculiarities which are permanent.

> The rule, therefore, I have endeavored to adopt is, that when the difference between two forms inhabiting separate areas seems quite constant, when it can be defined in words, and when it is not confined to a single peculiarity only, I have considered such forms to be species. When, however, the individuals of each locality vary among themselves, so as to cause the distinction between the two forms to become inconsiderable and indefinite, or where the differences, though constant, are confined to one particular only, such as size, tint, or a single point of difference in marking or in outline, I class one of the forms as a variety of the other.[37]

But the problem of species definition is actually even more complex, and following a lengthy discussion of five different categories of variation—simple variability, polymorphism, local forms, co-existing varieties, races or subspecies—Wallace made some revealing remarks:

> Species are merely those strongly marked races or local forms which when in contact do not intermix, and when inhabiting distinct areas are generally believed to have had a separate origin, and to be incapable of producing a fertile hybrid offspring. But as the case of hybridity cannot be applied in one case in ten thousand, and even if it could be applied would prove nothing, since it is founded on an assumption of the very question to be decided—and as the test of separate origin is in every case inapplicable—and as, further, the test of intermixture is useless, except in those rare cases where the most closely allied species are found inhabiting the same area, it will be evident that *we have no means whatever of distinguishing so-called "true-species" from the several modes of variation here pointed out, and into which they so often pass by an insensible gradation.*[38]

37. *NS*, p. 142. The italics are Wallace's. See Prichard, *Researches into the Physical History of Mankind* (1841–47), vol. I, p. 105. See also pp. 106–09.
38. *NS*, pp. 144–46, 161. Italics are mine.

The point of his statement is not that the term "species" is essentially useless and ready for the philosopher's wastebasket, but that the number of specific designations should not be so limited, and that forms generally known or suspected to have arisen from parent species —formerly called "permanent varieties," etc.—should also be labeled "species." Adducing evidence from a large number of eminent sources, Wallace showed that species are "most intricately combined in a tangled web of affinities, leading by such gradual steps from the slightest and least stable variations to fixed races and well-marked species," making it "very often impossible to draw those sharp dividing-lines which it is supposed that a careful study and full materials will always enable us to do."[39]

The importance of individual opinion thus becomes paramount: "there is no possible test but individual opinion to determine which of them [races and subspecies] shall be considered as species and which varieties. . . . I can find no other test that is more certain than individual opinion."[40] But differences in species designation could be minimized, he thought, by calling "species" *all* forms with some marked degree of permanence.

Thus it would appear that Wallace was advocating here the second definition in his "Note on the Theory of Permanent and Geographical Varieties." Even though the line separating varieties from species becomes very thin and subjective while the process of species formation is occurring—so much so that it may be difficult sometimes to prove its existence (definition one)[41]—a certain degree of permanence may come into being; despite the inherent difficulties encountered by the subjective nature of taxonomy, the attempt to determine species should be continued because the concept is exceedingly useful.[42]

Not surprisingly, Wallace's views on species and varieties—as presented in his "Note on the Theory of Permanent and Geographical Varieties," "On the Tendency of Varieties to Depart Indefinitely from the Original Type," and later in his article on the Papilionidae—are remarkably similar to Darwin's views as expressed in his great work.[43] A more important point to notice, however, is that Wallace's idea of

39. *NS*, p. 165.
40. *NS*, p. 160.
41. See above p. 67.
42. See Wallace, *The World of Life* (1910), pp. 11–12.
43. Darwin, *On the Origin of Species*, pp. 51–52.

species had a very early origin. As early as 1845, before he had any extensive familiarity with the subject, Wallace stated that "a permanent peculiarity not produced in any way by external causes is a distinction of species and not of mere variety."[44]

Unquestionably, then, Wallace's "Note on the Theory of Permanent and Geographical Varieties" is another distinct marker along his path to discovery. Returning to his notebook, we find yet another entry, made late in 1857, on continuous variation in nature:

> On Continents the individuals of one kind of plant disperse themselves very far, and by the difference of stations of nourishment & of soil produce *varieties,* which at such a distance not being crossed by other *varieties* & thus brought back to the primitive type, become at length permanent & distinct *species.* Then if by chance in other directions they meet with another *variety* equally changed in its march, the two have become very distinct *species* & are no longer susceptible of intermixture.[45]

In a letter to Henry Walter Bates, dated 4 January 1858, Wallace reiterated his belief in the natural, as opposed to special, creation of species:

> [Darwin] is now preparing for publication his great work on species and varieties, for which he has been collecting information twenty years. He may save me the trouble of writing the second part of my hypothesis by proving *there is no difference in nature between the origin of species and varieties,* or he may give me trouble by arriving at another conclusion, but in all events his facts will be given for me to work upon.[46]

We need discuss at this point but one other published paper, written before Wallace's 1858 paper on natural selection, and bearing directly on the species problem. In this paper, which discusses the

44. McKinney (1969), p. 372. For a discussion of the history of the species question, see Mayr, *The Species Problem* (1957). The first article "Species Concepts and Definitions," pp. 1–22, by Mayr, contains a useful bibliography, but he has quoted (p. 18) Wallace's definition of a species without reference to the extensive qualifications which I cited on pp. 69–70 above. For modern definitions of species, varieties, etc., and a bibliography of these subjects, see Mayr, *Animal Species and Evolution* (1963), p. 99.

45. Species Notebook, p. 90. Italics are Wallace's.

46. *WLR,* p. 54. Italics are mine.

natural history of the Aru Islands, Wallace presented a cogent argument, distinctly evolutionary in tone, that his 1855 law—"Every species has come into existence coincident in space and time with a preexisting closely allied species"—satisfactorily explained the anomalies of the geographical distribution of organisms on the Aru Islands.

His collections from those islands contained "many Australian genera and some species" as well as a remarkable number of species from New Guinea. "Such an identity occurs, I believe, in no other countries separated by so wide an interval of sea, for the average distance of the coast of Aru from that of New Guinea is at least 150 miles, and the points of nearest approach upwards of 100." Only islands recently separated from the nearest mainland such as Great Britain and Sicily, appeared to have fauna similar to that of the closest mainland. He concludes: "We must, therefore, suppose Aru to have once formed a part of New Guinea, in order to account for its peculiar fauna, and this view is supported by the physical geography of the islands;" namely, the shallow sea between New Guinea southward to Australia and the peculiar winding channels on Aru which appeared to have been at one time river channels fed by the mountains of New Guinea although they are now filled with salt water.

The question of why this fauna is not found in the western part of the Archipelago or, for that matter, why the same species are not found in similar climates over the world, would have been answered in only one way by most orthodox naturalists of his time. As Wallace put it:

> as the ancient species became extinct, new ones were created in each country or district, *adapted to the physical conditions of that district.*[47] Sir Charles Lyell, who has written more fully, and with more ability on this subject than most naturalists, adopts this view. He illustrates it by speculating on the vast physical changes that might be effected in North Africa by the upheaval of a chain of mountains in the Sahara. "Then," he says, "the animals and plants of Northern Africa would disappear, and the region would gradually become fitted for the reception of a population of species *perfectly dissimilar in their forms, habits, and organization.*"

What Wallace had noticed, however, was that despite exact resemblances of climate and physical features, the productions of New

47. Italics are mine.

Guinea differed "totally" from "those of the Western Islands of the
Archipelago, say Borneo." Moreover, while the physical conditions of
Australia and New Guinea were quite distinct, "the faunas of the two,
though mostly distinct in species, are strikingly similar in character."
Clearly, Lyell's speculations cannot explain why "kangaroos are especially *adapted* to the dry plains and open woods of Australia," but
were also introduced into the dense dark forests of New Guinea.
Furthermore, "we can hardly imagine that the great variety of monkeys, of squirrels, of Insectivora, and of Felidae, were created in
Borneo because the *country was adapted to them,* and not one single
species given to another country exactly similar, and at no great distance."[48] Viewed in the light of the old convictions, it was perhaps
not quite so peculiar that woodpeckers would be absent from Australia,
but their absence from the forests of New Guinea, Borneo, and
Malacca would have been a great mystery. Wallace continued:

> We cannot help concluding, therefore, that *some other law has
> regulated the distribution of existing species*[49] than the physical
> conditions of the countries in which they are found, or we should
> not see countries the most opposite in character with similar
> productions, while others almost exactly alike as respects climate
> and general aspect, yet differ totally in their forms of organic
> life.

The law to which he alluded is, of course, his own law that the
species have been created in spatial and temporal reference to previously existing closely allied species. In the past New Guinea and
Australia had enjoyed a common connection and perhaps were more
similar in climate and physical features. Later, separation occurred
with a possible modification of climate and subsequent extinction of
species less well adapted. Other similar species, however, had appeared—*evolved,* though he refrained from using such a word—in
their places in the two countries.

This process would evidently produce the present condition of
the two faunas, in which there are many allied species—few
identical. The great well-marked groups absent from the one
would necessarily be so from the other also, for however much

48. Italics are mine.
49. Italics are mine.

they might be *adapted* to the country, the law of close affinity would not allow of their appearance, except by a long succession of steps occupying an immense geological interval.

Moreover, the degree of similarity or distinctness reveals the length of time they had been separated. Since the fauna of Aru is very similar to that of Australia, the physical separation must have occurred recently. A longer undisturbed separation, say for one division of the Tertiary, would have brought about more significant changes. The longer the time, the greater the differences, with some species becoming extinct, and unreplaced in one country, while modified forms might be introduced in the other. The faunas then would display generic as well as specific differences, such as found between those of the West Indies and Mexico. If still another geological period elapsed with ensuing geological and organic changes, the relationship of Aru and Australia would resemble that existing between Madagascar and Africa where "there are many extensive groups of species forming peculiar genera, or even families, but still with a general resemblance to African forms." He concluded, in effect, that uniformitarian principles in geology can be successfully applied in biology:

> In this manner, it is believed, we may account for the facts of the present distribution of animals, without supposing any changes but what we know have been constantly going on. It is quite unnecessary to suppose that new species have ever been created "perfectly dissimilar in forms, habits, and organization" from those which have preceded them; neither do "centres of creation," which have been advocated by some, appear either necessary or accordant with facts, unless we suppose a "centre" in in every island and in every district which possesses a peculiar species.[50]

This conclusion, of course, reaffirmed the plan for his proposed book on species and also his early observations concerning the flora and fauna found on ancient islands, such as the Galapagos, whose flora and fauna resemble, yet are substantially different from, those of the mainland.[51]

50. Wallace, "On the Natural History of the Aru Islands" (1857), pp. 473–85, ref. 478. Except as noted, the italics are Wallace's.
51. Chapter 3, pp. 32–33 and 36–38.

On the eve of his discovery, there was but one essential missing ingredient—the importance of the food supply, a matter never specifically discussed in his Species Notebook. Although this subject had been alluded to in Blyth's article of 1835, Wallace does not appear to have attached any especial significance to it,[52] but notes in his journal for 1857 reveal that he had been profoundly impressed by the exceedingly wretched state of existence and physical debility of the natives of Aru. According to Wallace, this state of affairs existed because of their unbelievably precarious food supply.[53] He was therefore aware of this problem in reference to the human races of the Archipelago, and we shall see in chapter six that his ethnological interests caused him to recall Malthus in whose book he saw the laws of population and food supply writ large.

We have already noticed the importance for Wallace of Lyell's *Principles of Geology:* he directed his arguments against Lyell's definition of species while using Lyell's evidence as well as his own. Nevertheless, he also examined his notes on Blyth's paper of 1835 and in his famous paper of 1858 probably quoted from these notes in one or two places. For example, when Wallace wrote about "the belief in what are called 'permanent or true varieties,'—races of animals which continuously propagate their like, but which differ so slightly (although constantly) from some other race, that the one is considered to be a variety of the other," it is apparent that he was quoting Blyth.[54] This may also be the case when he refers to the following statement "that varieties produced in a state of domesticity are more or less unstable, and often have a tendency, if left to themselves, to return to the normal form of the parent species."[55]

That Wallace actually did reexamine his notebook carefully while writing his famous paper can be firmly established. The interesting fact that Wallace alluded to Lyell's description of the destruction of vegetation by locusts and the consequent struggle for existence has

52. Blyth, (1835), p. 53. " . . . food being so abundant, they [falcons] would soon multiply to the extirpation of their prey; which, of course, would be very speedily followed by that of preyer."

53. Journal, 1857–58, section 71.

54. NS, p. 27. Blyth (1835), pp. 46–47; Species Notebook, p. 62. See above p. 61.

55. NS, p. 26. Blyth (1835), p. 46. But he also discusses domestication in these terms while discussing Lyell. See above chapter 3, p. 35.

already been mentioned.[56] It is possible that Wallace could have seized upon Blyth's use of that term, although I think it highly improbable because of his reference to the locusts. But there is even stronger evidence that Wallace was carefully going over his notes shortly before or during the writing of his paper.

On page 54 in his Species Notebook, just eight pages before his notes on Blyth, we find the following notes:

> Owen says (Geolog. Soc. May 16, 1855) most of the extinct reptiles exemplify the law of the prevalence of a more generalized structure as compared with the more specialized structure of existing species. The Labyrinthidonts combined Sauroid with Batrachian characters. Rhynchosaurus, Sauroid with Chelonian characters. The Icthyosaurus had modifications borrowed from the class of fishes & the Pterodactyl & thus borrowed from the class of Birds & Bats. The Dicynodons had resemblances to Lizards, Crocodiles & Tryonix.[57]

A careful comparison of Wallace's notes with Owen's original paper has led me to conclude that his notes were made from a secondary source, possibly even a letter from someone in England whom he considered reliable: he uncharacteristically excluded any quotation mark; the order of notes differs from that of the article; his notes include a number of references to items not discussed or alluded to in Owen's article (e.g. the reference to pterodactyls). Nevertheless, in his paper of 1858, Wallace apparently quoted Owen *directly* when discussing species modifications via natural selection:

> It also furnishes us with a reason for that "more specialized structure" which Professor Owen states to be a characteristic of recent compared with extinct forms, and which would evidently be the result of the progressive modification of any organ applied to a special purpose in the animal economy.[58]

The words "more specialized structure" are those Wallace used on page 54 of his Species Notebook as quoted above, and are not from Owen's article. They show, however, that Wallace was in fact quoting

56. See above p. 38.
57. Owen, "Description of the Skull of a Large Species of *Dicynodon* (*D. tigriceps,* Ow.)" (1845–56), pp. 233–240. Read 16 May 1855.
58. *NS,* p. 43.

from his notebook when he wrote his paper. Apparently, Wallace recalled the work of Malthus; the idea of natural selection flashed upon him; he examined his notebooks and took notes before writing his final version.

If Wallace had quoted from his notebook even more extensively, Darwin would have received an even greater shock than he did when he wrote Lyell in June 1858: "if Wallace had my Ms. sketch written out in 1842, he could not have made a better short abstract. *Even his terms now stand as heads of my chapters.*"[59] Ironically, a number of notes taken by Wallace in his Species Notebook discussed ideas which were remarkably similar to ones espoused by Darwin, and a number of passages were taken directly from Darwin's own *Journal of Researches.*

> The Tucutucu (*Ctenomys Brasiliensis*) a burrowing animal is often found blind. This blindness though common cannot be a very serious evil, yet it appears strange that any animal should possess an organ frequently subject to be injured.[60]

After observing that Lamarck would have been delighted with such examples as the tucutucu, the Aspalax, and the Proteus,[61] Wallace returned to his observations regarding the tucutucu:

> in the Tucutucu which I believe never comes to the surface of the ground the eye is rather larger but often rendered blind & useless. No doubt Lamarck would have said that the tucutucu is now passing into the state of Proteus & Aspalax.[62]

Wallace, no doubt, would have been delighted if he had known while writing these notes in July 1856 that Darwin was going to adduce this evidence in the *Origin.* He concluded these particular notes in a very Darwinian manner:

---

59. *LLD,* Vol. I, p. 473. The primary reason being that they found the same things in Lyell. Italics are mine.

60. *DJR* (1839), pp. 58–60. See Darwin's *On the Origin of Species,* p. 137. Species Notebook, p. 60. His 1855 Paper used evidence regarding the Galapagos Islands which probably came from Darwin's *Journal.* 1855 Paper, p. 188.

61. Cf. Darwin, *On the Origin of Species,* p. 139.

62. Species Notebook, p. 60. Taken with minor changes from *DJR* (1845), p. 52.

The eyes of the nocturnal or darkness living animals are either very large & sensitive or small & imperfect. In the first case we may well believe the nocturnal habit to be the result of the organisation, the full light of day being painful to the large & highly organised visual organs as in Owls, goatsuckers, cats, etc.

In the second case the smallness or imperfection of the visual organs seems to be the result of the habits which other circumstances have bestowed upon the animal, the eyes becoming imperfect for want of use as in all other organs; as in the *Proteus,* Aspalax, & the blind insects found in caverns. The small eyes of the bat, so different from other creatures of voluntary nocturnal habits, may be accounted for by supposing them to be too weak to be used in full day. AW.[63]

Darwin had also observed in his first notebook on transmutation that von Buch in his work on the flora of the Canary Islands believed species to have arisen from varieties: "von Buch distinctly states that permanent varieties become species, p. 147–150,—not being crossed with others."[64] Wallace had noticed precisely the same phenomenon, for he wrote:

Flora of Canaries   von Buch
He then shows that plants on the exposed peak of Teneriffe when they can meet and cross do not form varieties or species while others such as *Pyrethrum* or *Cineraria* living in sheltered vallies & low grounds often have closely allied species confined to one valley or one island.[65]

Wallace had also planned to discuss in his book on evolution the instinct of bees as exemplified in the construction of honeycombs, a point which Darwin also discussed at length in the *Origin.*[66] I shall return in my conclusion to the similarities as well as the significant differences between these two naturalists.

63. Species Notebook, p. 61.
64. de Beer, ed., *Darwin Notebooks*, vol. 2, no. 2 (1960), p. 61. Both Darwin and Wallace read the French translation. Leopold von Buch, *Déscription physique des Iles Canaries* (1836).
65. Species Notebook, p. 90. Von Buch (1836), pp. 148–49, the same pages to which Darwin referred.
66. Ibid., pp. 173–77. Darwin, *On the Origin of Species*, pp. 224–35.

In this chapter we have observed Wallace continuing to apply the principles which he had long before accepted in the plan for his book *On the Organic Law of Change*. His understanding of the species question had become more sophisticated, but scarcely anything radically new had been added to it. His test of the concept of evolution at Aru had been highly satisfactory, and his observations of the wretched existence of its natives may have been crucial. But in general, the period from 1855 to 1858 may be described as rich in application, but poor in innovation. The facts all strongly supported his preconceptions, but the moment of illumination was slow in coming. Nevertheless, given Wallace's frame of mind, the evidence he was gathering, and his general intellectual background, his paper "On the Tendency of Varieties to Depart Indefinitely from the Original Type" was perhaps an inevitable result of an intense search.

6   Malthus, *On Population*

As we have seen, Wallace quickly accepted the theory of evolution as a viable hypothesis when most reputable scientists rejected it. He also recognized in the work of Sir Charles Lyell (and others) the crucial pieces of evidence which were to be adduced in support of natural selection. All this, however, occurred several years before February 1858 when Wallace wrote "On the Tendency of Varieties to Depart Indefinitely from the Original Type." Moreover, in spite of the fact that Lyell, Chambers, Pictet, Owen, and others laid necessary foundation stones for his theory, it was to T. R. Malthus's *An Essay on the Principle of Population* that Wallace constantly referred when describing the final brilliant flash of inspiration which solved the enigmatic species problem for him. Thus, although the immediate stimulus is known, an important question remains to be answered: "Why Malthus?" Why was it that Wallace, in the distant Malay Archipelago, happened to recall from the depths of his memory a book concerning problems of human population? The answer to this question greatly illuminates the direction of Wallace's thoughts before February 1858.

Wallace left rather full autobiographical accounts which describe his moment of discovery, and provide two important clues which help to answer the question posed above.[1] In the first place, Wallace,

---

1. The four best known accounts are: Wallace, *Natural Selection and Tropical Nature* (1891), p. 20; Wallace, *The Wonderful Century* (1898), pp. 138–39; Wallace, *My Life*, vol. I, pp. 360–63 [Also in the rare one-volume revised edition of 1908]; Linnean Society of London, *The Darwin-Wallace Celebration Held on Thursday, 1st July, 1908, by the Linnean Society of London* (1908), p. 111. Other accounts are: Wallace, "My Relations With Darwin in Reference to the Theory of Natural Selection," (1903), pp. 78–79. [Wallace, "Origin of the Darwinism Theory," pp. 339–44, ref. pp. 342–43 in Daniel Edwin Wheeler, ed., *Wonders of Science and Invention* (1909). Vol. 8 of Hamilton Wright Mabie, ed., *Young Folks' Treasury*. Taken verbatim from Wallace's *Wonderful Century*.] Two letters also describe his discovery: Wallace to Dr. Adolf Bernhard Meyer, 22 November 1869, partially published by Meyer in "How Was Wallace Led in the Discovery of Natural Selection?," (1895), p. 415. Wallace to Prof. Alfred Newton, 3 December 1887 in F. Darwin, ed., *Charles Darwin* (1908 [1892]), pp. 189–90. Dr. Meyer

unable to do anything else because of a fever, was meditating upon a problem which had long been troubling him. He mentioned this problem in the 1898 account specifically as the "problem of the origin of species;" in the 1903 account as "the possible mode of the origin of new species;" and in the 1908 account as "the possible causes of the change of species." Although Wallace generalized in the 1905 account by saying that "I had nothing to do but to think over any subjects then particularly interesting me," we know already that the species problem was foremost in his thoughts, and it becomes evident that these accounts corroborate each other: the problem occupying Wallace's mind was the species problem.

The second significant point is that in *all accounts* Wallace was considering the species problem *first* in reference to the *human species*. The first account (1898) referred to those checks, observed by Malthus, which kept "all *savage populations* nearly stationary." The second account (1903) stated "somehow my thoughts turned to the 'positive checks' to increase among *savages* and *others*." The third account (1905) mentioned the positive checks "which keep down the population of *savage races* to so much lower an average than that of more civilized peoples." In the last version Wallace stated that the cumulative effect of the chapters on Malthus on "the various causes which keep down the population of *savage* and *barbarous nations* in America, Africa, and Asia" (p. 111), that is the action of the positive checks of "war, plunder and massacres among *men*" (p. 117) provided the final stimulus for him.[2]

In *all four accounts* these facts applicable to human populations were immediately applied to animal species:

----

had also published another account of Wallace's discovery, based on the above cited letter, in his work *Charles Darwin und Alfred Russel Wallace* (1870), pp. xviii & xxiii. I own a microfilm of this very rare book.

Excerpts regarding Wallace's discovery appear in the following works: [Newton?], "Review of *The Life and Letters of Charles Darwin*" (1888), pp. 1–30, ref. p. 24, 2nd fn. Marchant, *WLR*, p. 86.

Therefore, Wallace recounted his story in 1869 [1870 and 1895], 1887 [1892], 1891, 1898, 1903, 1905, and 1908. The various accounts do not agree on every detail. I shall refer to those in 1898, 1903, 1905, and 1908 since they are representative. The full text of these accounts is found in Appendix III. See also Appendix IV for passages from Malthus which influenced Wallace.

2. Italics added by me in all four citations.

It then occurred to me that these checks must *also* act upon *animals,* and keep down their numbers, and as they *increase* so much *faster* than *man* does, . . . it was clear that these checks in their case must be far more powerful. . . . While vaguely thinking how this would affect *any* species, there suddenly flashed upon me the idea of *the survival of the fittest.* (1898, p. 139)[3]

These checks—disease, famine, accidents, war, etc.—are what keep down the population, and it suddenly occurred to me that in the case of wild animals these checks would act with much more severity, and as the *lower animals* all tended to increase more rapidly than *man,* while their population remained on the average constant, there suddenly flashed upon me the idea of the survival of the fittest. (1903, p. 78)

It then occurred to me that these causes [Malthus's positive checks to increase] or their equivalents are *continually acting in the case of animals also;* and as *animals* usually breed much more rapidly than does *mankind,* the destruction every year from these causes must be enormous in order to keep down the numbers of each species. (1905, pp. 361–62)

I then saw that war, plunder and massacres among *men* were represented by the attacks of *carnivora* on *herbivora,* and of the stronger upon the weaker among *animals.* Famine, droughts, floods and winter's storms *would have an even greater effect on animals than on man;* while as the former possessed powers of of increase from twice to a thousand-fold greater than the latter, the ever-present annual destruction must also be many times greater. (1908, p. 117)[4]

During this sudden moment of inspiration, the answers to Wallace's questions flooded him in rapid succession.

The fact that Wallace was led to his great discovery by a considera-tion of the origin *of the human species first* before transferring the emphasis to animal species must immediately focus attention on an interest which Wallace acquired very early in life, his interest in ethnology. As early as 28 December 1845 Wallace discussed this

3. All italics except the last are mine.
4. Italics in these last 3 examples (1903, 1905, 1908) are mine.

interest *in extenso* in a letter to Henry Walter Bates. Wallace's point of view was obviously that of an evolutionist, and he referred specifically to Sir William Lawrence's *Lectures on Comparative Anatomy, Physiology, Zoology, and Natural History of Man* as well as James Cowles Prichard's *Researches into the Physical History of Mankind,* both of which contain many novel and unorthodox thoughts about man.[5]

Wallace's and Darwin's interests in ethnology were expressed in similar ways. Darwin, on his voyage around South America in 1832–35, was profoundly impressed by the Fuegians, who were "without exception the most curious and interesting spectacle I had ever beheld. I could not have believed how wide was the difference between savage and civilized man."[6]

Wallace was equally impressed by his first encounter with man in a state of nature, which he described in the last chapter in his *Travels on the Amazon,* entitled "On the Aborigines of the Amazon":

> I do not remember a single circumstance in my travels so striking and new, or that so well fulfilled all previous expectations, as my first view of the real uncivilized inhabitants of the river Uaupés. Though I had been already three years in the country, and had seen Indians of almost every shade or colour

5. Actually, Wallace's interest in ethnology can be traced back even farther to a long article on "The South-Wales Farmer," dated 1843, in which he discusses their habits, manners, language, character, etc. *My Life,* vol. I, pp. 199, 206–22. Wallace's interest in the origins of mankind, however, apparently began in 1845. See McKinney (1969) for the full text of this letter.

6. *DJR* (1839), p. 228. "Of individual objects, perhaps no one is more certain to create astonishment than the first sight in his native haunt of a real barbarian,— of man in his lowest and most savage state. One's mind hurries back over past centuries, and then asks, could our progenitors have been such as these? Men, whose very signs and expressions are less intelligible to us than those of the domesticated animals; men, who do not possess the instinct of those animals, nor yet appear to boast of human reason, or at least of arts consequent of that reason. I do not believe it is possible to describe or paint the difference between savage and civilized man. It is the difference between a wild and tame animal; and part of the interest in beholding a savage, is the same which would lead everyone to desire to see the lion in his desert, the tiger tearing his prey in the jungle, the rhinoceros on the wide plain, or the hippopotamus wallowing in the mud of some African river." Ibid., p. 605.

and every degree of civilization, I felt that I was as much in the midst of something new and startling, as if I had been instantaneously transported to a distant and unknown country.[7]

Later in life when recalling his explorations in South America, Wallace said there were three particularly impressive features of the Amazon area: the Virgin forest, "the wonderful variety and exquisite beauty of the butterflies and birds," and especially his unforgettable confrontation with primitive man. "The true denizen of the Amazonian forests, like the forest itself, is unique and not to be forgotten."[8] Although Wallace again was greatly handicapped by the loss of his collections, he nevertheless devoted some forty-three pages (in the first edition of his *Travels*) to a separate discussion of the mores and civilization of the Amazonian natives; numerous additional allusions to the natives are interspersed throughout the rest of his book. The first edition of the *Travels* also contained a lengthy appendix (twenty-one pages plus a large chart) describing "Vocabularies of the Amazonian Languages."[9] And once more, the influence of the *Vestiges* may be strongly suspected, for according to Chambers, the modern study of language favors the "supposition that all the great families of men are of one stock," and "the light which is thrown upon the history of mankind [by philological studies] is of a most remarkable nature." He concluded that evidence "which physiology and philology present seems to me decidedly favorable to the idea of one local origin [of man]."[10] One particularly interesting passage in Wallace's chapter on the aborigines suggests that he also suspected a common origin of mankind. He began by pointing out that some of the customs of the Indians of the Amazon valley resemble those of nations far removed. For example, the natives of the Malay Archipelago also use a blowpipe (Borneo), build huge houses like

7. *Travels on the Amazon* (1853), p. 477; (1889), pp. 331–32.

8. *My Life*, vol. I, p. 288.

9. *The Malay Archipelago* likewise has a very lengthy appendix (just over 31 pages in the seventh edition) devoted to the native languages of the Archipelago.

10. *Vestiges* (1845), pp. 197, 205. Lyell also develops this line of argument, and Wallace commended him for his most excellent discussion of this subject. Lyell, "Origin and Development of Languages and Species Compared," (chapter 23) in *The Geological Evidences of the Antiquity of Man . . .* (1863). Letter from Wallace to Lyell, dated 22 April 1863, at the American Philosophical Society.

the Uaupés Indians (Dyaks and Borneo), make similar baskets (Borneo and New Guinea), and shrink heads using the same procedures. Even an isolated Indian tribe in the Amazon, which unlike surrounding tribes used a throwing stick, had its counterpart in the Australian aborigines. He concluded by saying:

It will be necessary to obtain much more information on this subject, before we can venture to decide *whether such similiarities show any remote connection between these nations,* or are mere accidental coincidences, produced by the same wants, acting upon people subject to the same conditions of climate and in equally low state of civilization; and *it offers additional matter for the widespreading speculations of the ethnographer.*[11]

Wallace's desire to compare these customs at first hand may have played some part in prompting him to journey to the Malay Archipelago, for he eventually discussed the natives at every opportunity in his famous book *The Malay Archipelago* as well as in numerous ethnological articles.[12] It is equally significant, however, that Wallace made extensive notes on ethnology in his Species Notebook, which was largely reserved for notes on his proposed book *On the Organic Law of Change,* and in his Journals as well as in his 1854 Notebook. The fact that many of these entries were made between 1 November 1857 and late February 1858—that is *immediately before* he wrote his famous paper "On the Tendency of Varieties to Depart Indefinitely from the Original Type"—furnishes independent evidence corroborating my contention that Wallace was thinking about *human* evolution just before discovering natural selection. As he said, "The human inhabitants of these forests are not less interesting to me than the feathered tribes."[13] Earlier, in January 1857, he had remarked:

11. *Travels on the Amazon* (1853), pp. 517–18. Italics are mine.

12. Chapter XL, "The Races of Man in the Malay Archipelago," *The Malay Archipelago* (1880), pp. 582–98 and frequently throughout the entire book. Henceforth cited as *MA*. The two major articles are: "The Origin of Human Races and the Antiquity of Man Deduced from the Theory of 'Natural Selection' " (1864), pp. clviii–clxx. Discussion of the article continues from pp. clxx–clxxxvii. "On the Varieties of Man in the Malay Archipelago" (1864–65), pp. 196–215. See *WLR,* p. 479 for others.

13. Journal, 1857–58, section 71. He goes on to describe the low state of the existence of the savages, particularly the shockingly bad food supply and consequent misery and vice—in short, a very Malthusian description.

Ethnologists have too often to trust to the information of travellers who, passing rapidly from country to country, have too few opportunities of becoming acquainted with peculiarities of national character, & scarcely ever with those of physical confrontation. Such are exceedingly apt to be deceived in places where two races have long intermixed by looking on intermediate forms & mixed habits as evidences of a natural transition from one race to the other, not an artificial intermingling of the two; & they will be the more readily led into this error if, as is the present case, writers on the subject should be in the habit of classing these races as mere varieties of one stock [who are] as closely related in physical confrontation as from their Geographical proximity one might *a priori* suppose them to be. To me at present the Malay & the Papuan appear to be as widely separated as any two human races can be, the latter possessing the closest affinities, both physical & moral, to the true Negro races. *It is a most interesting question and one to which I shall direct my attention in all the islands of the Archipelago I may be enabled to visit.*

In summarizing his work at Aru, which had been most rewarding, he remarked:

My residence among the natives had given me an intimate acquaintance with the moral features of the Papuan races, not hitherto attained by writers on the subject & has laid the foundation of a knowledge which may perhaps enable me to give a more probable view of their origin than those generally entertained.[14]

He entered extensive notes in his Species Notebook as well. Following a note made about May 1856 apropos of Dr. Samuel Johnson's pronouncement that marriage is not a natural human condition, Wallace recorded Professor Owen's remarks on human color variation:

Prof. [Richard] Owen in his lecture on Orang-utans etc. at [the] B[ritish] As[sociation] says varieties of colour in man have been produced by climate. Instances [are the] Jews of *Syria* who are black, of [the] N[orthern] countries of Europe [where] some [are found] with fair hair, light complexions and blue eyes.

14. Journal, 1856–57, sections 63, 106. Italics are mine.

But there are also Armenian Jews at Singapore [who are] equally fair, and it has little to do with the question as to the Jewish *features often* mentioned [conjectural. The world is illegible], and they, not colours, are the grand characteristics of race. Jews are always pointed to as exhibiting *stability* of physical characters.[15]

As might be expected, Professor Owen—who later became the arch foe of the Darwinian hypothesis—had a quite orthodox point to establish:

nine-tenths, therefore, of the differences . . . as distinguishing the great chimpanzee from the human species, must stand in contravention of the hypothesis of transmutation and progressive development until the supporters of that hypothesis are enabled to adduce the facts and cases which demonstrate the conditions of the modifications of such characters. . . .

Man is the sole species of his genus, the sole representative of his order; he has no nearer physical relations with the brute-kind than those which flow from the characters that link together the primary (unguiculate) division of the placental sub-class of mammalia.[16]

Wallace, of course, would have strongly disagreed with Owen, for he could see man's kinship with other animals, a matter that I shall

15. Ibid., p. 63. Italics are Wallace's. Wallace's reference, no doubt, is to an address "delivered at the request of the Council at the General Anniversary Meeting of the Association." For a summary see Owen, "On the Anthropoid Apes," (1855), pp. 111–13. A paper published in February 1855 (the above address was read in September 1854 in Liverpool) appears to be substantially the same speech, and contains the following: "There are some Jews still lingering in the valleys of the Jordan, having been oppressed by the successive conquerors of Syria for ages,—a low race of people, and described by trustworthy travellers as being as black as any of the Ethiopian races. Others of the Jewish people, participating in European civilization, and dwelling in the northern nations, show instances of the light complexion, blue eyes, and light hair of the Scandinavian families. The condition of the Hebrews, since their dispersion, has not been such as to admit of much admixture by the proselytism of household slaves. We see, then, how to account for the differences in colour, without having to refer them to original or specific distinctions." Owen, "On the Anthropoid Apes, and their Relations to Man," *Notices of the Proceedings . . . of the Royal Institution of Great Britain*, 2 (1854–58), 35–36.

16. Owen (1854–58), pp. 40–41.

examine more closely later in this chapter. The interesting point to observe now is that in his Species Notebook on the page immediately following his notes on Richard Owen's article, Wallace records an observation, to which I shall also return, of a *man with a tail*. On the following page, he continued his examination of the races of the Malay Archipelago by describing the features of the Malay people. He observed that when interbreeding with other races occurs, new and obviously different characters may appear. For example, Hindu, European and especially Arabic features show up among the Rajahs or priests, who have a taller stature, a more yellow skin, a finer and slightly aquiline nose, and a tendency to grow beards.

Wallace pursued his ethnological interests at every opportunity in an effort to discover the origins of the tribes of the Archipelago, and from November 1857 onwards he made an extraordinary number of entries in his Species Notebook[17] and in his Journal, 1857–58. In his Journal, for example, we find the following observation concerning the natives of Amboyna:

> The native Amboynese are a strange mixture, half civilized, half savage, lazy race, who seem [to be] a mixture of at least three nations: Portuguese, Malay, & Papuan or Ceramese with an occasional cross of Chinese & Dutch to give a little variety to the compound.[18]

On 8 January 1858, Wallace arrived at Ternate, one of the small Moluccan Islands, which was to be a headquarters for the years ahead. He stayed only about two weeks before going to Gilolo (now Halmahera) where he stayed until 1 March 1858 when he returned to Ternate.[19] Commenting upon the natives at Gilolo, he wrote:

> The *natives of this large & almost unknown island were examined by me with much interest, as they would help to determine whether* independent of mixed races, *there is any transition from the Malay to the Papuan type.*[20]

17. See Appendix VI.

18. Journal, 1857–58, section 120.

19. Journal, 1857–58, section 125. There is a reference in his Species Notebook, p. 109, dated "Gilolo [Halmahera]. January 20, 1858" which places him there from then until his return on 1 March 1858.

20. Journal, 1857–58, Section 127. Italics are mine.

This discussion continues to the end of the section and the next section begins by describing his return to Ternate, which means that his references to the natives of Gilolo were probably written during late February. Therefore, he was examining the natives of Gilolo "with much interest" to determine their origins *just before he discovered natural selection.* To Wallace the determination of *human* origins was as important as that of the lower animals and this enduring interest is evident in a number of places, for example in his 1854 Notebook, Species Notebook, his great book *The Malay Archipelago,* and his journals. Thus, all these sources furnish independent evidence that Wallace was considering the origin of human races before discovering natural selection.[21]

That Wallace should suddenly switch his attention from the human species to animal species should not at all surprise us. Indeed, William Lawrence in his famous *Lectures on . . . Man,* a book for which Wallace had nothing but praise, had some very interesting words to say on this subject:

> The diversities of physical and moral endowment which characterize the various races of man, must be analogous in their nature, causes, & origin, to those which are observed in the rest of the animal creation, and must therefore be explained on the same principles.
>
> There is no point of difference between the several races of mankind, which has not been found to arise, in at least an equal degree, among other animals, as a mere variety, from the usual causes of degeneration.[22]

In the same letter to Bates in which he praised Lawrence's work, it is obvious that Wallace recognized the close kinship of man and animals; as animals become isolated and vary from the original stock, in like manner are humans isolated and subsequently diverge from their ancestors.[23] If, however, one were to go far enough back in the history of man, some interesting discoveries might be made, so Wallace believed. In his discussion of the habits of the orangutan (see Fig. 6) he wrote:

21. In chapter 8, I shall return to Wallace's story about his discovery of natural selection on Gilolo, not Ternate.

22. Lawrence (1866), p. 183.

23. See Appendix V for "Excerpts Pertaining to Ethnology from Wallace's Letter to Henry Walter Bates of 28 December 1845."

Fig. 6. Orangutan attacked by Dyaks (from Wallace's *The Malay Archipelago*)

It is a remarkable circumstance, that an animal so large, so peculiar, and of such a high type of form as the Orang-Utan, should yet be confined to such a limited district,—to two islands, and those almost at the limits of the range of the higher mammalia; for, eastward of Borneo and Celebes, the Quadrumana and most of the higher mammalia almost disappear. One cannot help speculating on a former condition of this part of the world which should give a wider range to these strange creatures, *which at once resemble and mock the "human form divine,"*—which so closely approach us in structure, and yet differ so widely from us in many points of their external form. And when we consider that almost all other animals have in previous ages been represented by allied, yet distinct forms,—that the bears and tigers, the deer, the horses, and the cattle of the tertiary period were distinct from those which now exist, with what intense interest, with what anxious expectation must we look forward to the time when the progress of civilization in those hitherto wild countries may lay open the monuments of a former world, and and enable us to ascertain approximately the period when the present species of Orangs first made their appearance, and *perhaps prove the former existence of allied species still more gigantic in their dimensions, and more or less human in their form and structure!*[24]

It should also be noted *en passant* that Lamarck and Robert Chambers, among others, thought that man possibly had originated from the orangutan, or a similar creature, and Gerald Henderson has made the interesting suggestion that the following passage from the first edition of the *Vestiges* may have led Wallace to journey to the Malay Archipelago:[25]

According to that theory [of development] we should expect man to have originated where the highest species of the quadrumana

24. Wallace, "On the Habits of the Orang-Utan of Borneo" (1856), p. 31. Italics are mine.

25. Lamarck, *Philosophical Zoology*, p. 171. See Packard's discussion of this point in *Lamarck: the Founder of Evolution*, pp. 357–71, esp. 364 ff. See also Lyell's discussion of "Lamarck's theory of the transmutation of the orangutang into the human species," *Principles* (1857), pp. 575–77. Henderson, (1958), p. 170. Chapter VI in Henderson's dissertation discusses the place of the orangutan in eighteenth- and nineteenth-century thought. See pp. 176–92.

are to be found. Now these are unquestionably found in the Indian Archipelago.

The following year, Chambers qualified this statement somewhat by adding,

> although it now appears, from the investigations of Professor Owen, that the chimpanzee of Western Africa approaches nearer to man than any known species of Indian Simiae.
>
> After all it may be regarded as still an open question whether mankind is of one or more origins.[26]

The following observation from one of Wallace's letters in May 1855 from Sarawak, Borneo appears to confirm Henderson's observation:

> One of the principal reasons which induced me to come here [to Borneo] was that it is the country of those most strange and interesting animals, the orang-utangs, or "mias" of the Dyaks."[27]

If Henderson is correct, however, that Wallace was stimulated by the remark from the *Vestiges,* quoted above, then it would follow that Wallace hoped to find some clue to human evolution; indeed, this is suggested by the conclusion in Wallace's article on the orangutan also quoted above. But according to Henderson,

> in the *Malay Archipelago* and in his scientific papers he *includes no projections* of humanity nor any suggestion that the orang approximates the human status in behavior. The orang appears as a part of the native fauna of Borneo, and Wallace describes him with the same detached interest that he exhibits toward the [so-called] 'flying frog' or remarkable beetles.[28]

Yet both in an article in *Chambers's Journal* for 1856 and in at least one letter home in June 1855, Wallace described a baby orang (which he had for three months) in purely anthropomorphic terms (Fig. 7):

26. *Vestiges* (1844), p. 296; (1845), p. 207.
27. Harrison, "Alfred Russel Wallace and a Century of Evolution in Borneo" (1960), p. 26. See also *MA,* p. 39.
28. Henderson, (1958), pp. 172–73. Italics are mine.

Fig. 7. A young orangutan (from Wallace's *The Malay Archipelago*)

I must now tell you of the addition to my household of an orphan baby, a curious half-nigger baby, which I have nursed now for more than a month. . . . I am afraid you would call it an ugly baby, for it has a dark brown skin and red hair, a very large mouth, but very pretty little hands and feet. . . .

But I must now tell you how I came to take charge of it. Don't be alarmed; I was the cause of its mother's death. It happened as follows:—I was out shooting in the jungle and saw something up in a tree which I thought was a large monkey or orang-utan, so I fired at it and down fell this little baby—in its mother's arms. What she did up in a tree of course I can't imagine, but as she ran about the branches quite easily, I presume she was a wild 'woman of the woods;' so I have preserved her skin and skeleton, and am trying to bring up her only daughter, and hope some day to introduce her to fashionable society at the Zoological Gardens.[29]

29. *My Life,* vol. I, p. 343–44. Wallace, "A New Kind of Baby" (1856), pp. 325–27.

In his equally humorous and deceptive account in *Chambers's Journal,* Wallace cleverly failed to reveal the infant's identity until the last sentence. One may wonder whether it was mere irony or calculation on Wallace's part which led him to submit this particular article to a periodical published by the very man who, according to strong rumors, had written the heretical *Vestiges* which has been quoted above in this very connection. This appears to be the *only* article Wallace ever published in *Chambers's Journal.*

Fortunately, Sir James Brooke's secretary in Sarawak provides us with even stronger evidence showing that Wallace believed the orangs to be very closely related to humans:

> We had at that time [in 1854] in Sarawak the famous naturalist, traveller, and philosopher, Mr. Alfred Wallace, who was then elaborating in his mind the theory which was simultaneously worked out by Darwin—the theory of the origin of species; *and if he could not convince us that our ugly neighbors, the orangoutangs, were our ancestors,* he pleased, delighted and instructed us by his clever and inexhaustible flow of talk—really good talk. The Rajah was pleased to have so clever a man with him, as it excited his mind, and brought out his brilliant ideas.[30]

Two interesting entries in his Species Notebook further illuminate Wallace's views on the subject of man's relationship to animals:

> Mr. Joseph Carter of Ampanam [Lombock] has himself seen in the interior of the Coti River in Borneo a man with a *tail*— about 4 or 5 inches long. He had examined it, but does not know if there is a tribe of the same structure.
>
> July 1856[31]

> Dufour in [his] *History of Prostitution* says that the inhabitants of *ancient Italy* are represented on vases etc. with a tuft

30. St. John, *Life of Sir James Brooke* (1879), p. 274. There were at that time many strange beliefs held even by "eminent men," so we are told; one of these beliefs was that intimacy between orangs and humans sometimes produced incredible results. Brooke, *Ten Years in Sarawak* (1866), vol. I, p. 63–64. Italics are mine.

31. Species Notebook, p. 64. Wallace comments "?gammon." Italics by Wallace.

of hair in place of a *tail.* He says it is evidently a *natural* character!—now lost![32]

These two quotations strongly suggest that Wallace was thinking along the same lines as Charles Darwin when he made the following note in January 1836 in one of his notebooks: "The rudiment of a *tail* shows man was originally quadruped."[33] Darwin discussed this subject of the *os coccyx* at length in the Descent of Man and concluded that man's early progenitors must have had tails, hairy bodies, and pointed, mobile ears, with both sexes having beards.[34] Wallace, of course, would have been familiar with the significance of these observations for the case for evolution since man's vestigial tail had been discussed by Robert Chambers in the *Vestiges:*

> Man, again, has no tail; but the notion of a much-ridiculed philosopher of the last century is not altogether, as it happens, without foundation, for between the fifth and seventh week of the embryo a tail does exist, and in the mature subject the bones of this caudal appendage are found in an underdeveloped state in the *os coccygis* . . . the tail of the human being is shrunk up in the bony mass at the bottom of the back.[35]

Today the evidence of the *os coccyx* forms part of the very substantial case for human evolution.[36]

Once we realize that Wallace considered man to be merely an animal, we can immediately see why it was so easy for him to turn his attention quickly from human to animal species. Indeed, we have already seen this in his 28 December 1845 letter to Bates, quoted in Appendix V; and in his Species Notebook we find him constantly

32. Ibid., p. 91. Italics are Wallace's. Dufour, *Historie de la Prostitution chez tous les peuples du monde* (1851–53). The reference is probably in vol. II.

33. de Beer, ed., *Darwin Notebooks,* vol. 2, no. 5 (1960), p. 169. Italics are Darwin's.

34. (New York, n.d.), second edition, pp. 409 ff., 439 ff., 524. See also the letter from Darwin to Lyell, 11 October [1859]. *LLD,* vol. II, p. 10.

35. *Vestiges* (1845), p. 147. His conclusion regarding man is: "Say it has pleased Providence to arrange that one species should give birth to another, until the second highest gave birth to man, who is the very highest." Ibid., p. 178.

36. Dobzhansky, *Mankind Evolving* (1962), p. 166.

switching his attention from animal and plant species to human species.[37] In fact, on page 116 we find him doing this within the same paragraph:

> Birds nests [are] said to be built by instinct because they don't improve. But they *vary* according to circumstances & does man do more? Any one race of man does not improve in its architecture. The indians of each country have one mode of building their houses which they vary slightly according to circumstances, but do not improve or decidedly change any more than birds. It is only by communication, by the unifying of different races with their different customs, that improvements arise & then, how slowly! A race remaining isolated will ever remain stationary, [culturally] and this is the case with birds. Each species is generally confined to a limited district in which the circumstances are similar and give rise to no diversity of habits.

The various facts adduced above indicate that Wallace had a profound interest in ethnology, and that he felt man had evolved from a lower animal, probably an orangutan or near relative. His query to Darwin in 1857 as to whether he was going to discuss man in his work on species and varieties also shows that Wallace was thinking about man in that connection. During the subsequent year, while considering the problem of how human races come into being—no doubt reflecting upon the various works which he had read on the subject—he happened to recall the work of Malthus, *On the Principle of Population,* and Malthus provided a new perspective and a mathematical demonstration of the interrelationship of population and food supply. A great many of the facts utilized by Wallace were available to the scientific world before 1858, but it was for the prepared mind to appreciate and understand these facts. By February 1858 Wallace's mind was certainly properly prepared to reconsider the work of Malthus.

37 Species Notebook, pp. 36–55, animal (and plant) species; p. 56, ethnology; pp. 57–62, animal and plant species; pp. 63–66, ethnology; pp. 72–90, animal (and plant) species; p. 91, note on ethnology; pp. 92–100, animal and plant species; p. 100, a note on ethnology; pp. 104–06, ethnology; pp. 107–20, animal and plant species.

7 The Influence of Wallace's pre-1858 Work on Sir Charles Lyell and Charles Darwin

The meaning and purpose of Wallace's 1855 Paper are clear: it was the first unequivocal, public indication of his thoughts on the species problem, and considering his cogent arguments and conclusions, it is somewhat surprising that the 1855 Paper evoked no public response. The fact that Edward Forbes, whose "polarity" hypothesis stimulated Wallace to publish in the first place, had died on 18 November 1854— and no one else cared to support his case—probably had an important bearing on the matter; and Wallace, realizing that he might lose an excellent opportunity for a new public hearing of the case for evolution, issued the following last minute challenge as a footnote to his 1855 Paper (p. 192):

> Since the above was written, the author has heard with sincere regret of the death of this eminent naturalist from whom so much important work was expected. His remarks on the present paper,—a subject on which no man was more competent to decide—were looked for with the greatest interest. Who shall supply his place?

Indeed, Forbes would have been the perfect scientist to answer Wallace's excellent arguments. As T. H. Huxley remarked, Edward Forbes and Richard Owen were the two English naturalists preeminent in "learning, originality, and grasp of mind," and in contrasting the two scientists, Huxley observed that Forbes had more claims to the title of philosophical naturalist than any other man in England; He was a scientist of broad interests who was sympathetic, earnest, and blessed with a thoroughly likeable personality which commanded respect and affection. Consequently, his influence on younger naturalists far exceeded that of Owen. And in further contrast to Owen, Forbes was remarkably objective. Huxley commented:

> My notions are diametrically opposed to his in some matters, and he helps me to oppose him. The other night, or rather nights, for it took three, I had a long paper read at the Royal Society which opposed some of his views, and he got up and spoke in the highest terms of it afterwards.[1]

1. Leonard Huxley, ed., *Life and Letters of Thomas Henry Huxley* (1900), vol. I, pp. 94–96

Thus, Forbes's death robbed Wallace of a fair hearing for his case, for Owen apparently was not inclined to enter the lists, nor, for that matter, was anyone else.[2] Even though public response by English scientists was conspicuously absent, the private impact was quite another matter, for it now can be demonstrated that Wallace's 1855 Paper had a profound influence on both Charles Lyell and Charles Darwin.

Wallace's paper appeared in the September 1855 issue of the *Annals and Magazine of Natural History;* shortly thereafter, on 28 November 1855, Sir Charles Lyell opened his own species notebooks, with Wallace's name at the top of the first page of text. Lyell's notes as well as his Index Book reveal that he was arguing specifically and vigorously with Wallace's 1855 Paper. Moreover, it appears that he began his own species notebooks because of the tremendous impact of Wallace's arguments.[3]

It should be especially noted that Lyell's constant inclination was to return to the argument that things are as they are because God has so willed it "by self-imposed laws—by which Man can comprehend the universe." What Wallace thought of as necessary laws were for Lyell merely mysterious events which came to pass to please God, the author of nature. And Lyell did not understand how evolution could have pleased that author since anthropomorphous species, and ultimately man, *must* also be the logical consequence of such a procedure.

That God created everything—male and female, human and animal —was an idea firmly, almost irrevocably, entrenched in Lyell's mind. Consequently, he seized upon one particular point in Wallace's paper as a test case for the entire concept of evolution; ironically, Wallace

2. Owen became a director at the British Museum in 1856 and kept voluminous diaries; Miss Maria Skramovský of the British Museum (Natural History) has kindly informed me in a letter that they have a large collection of Owen's materials. A careful examination of the material may uncover some interesting observations about Wallace's paper. What little notice of his paper did occur is discussed by Wallace in one paragraph of *My Life,* vol. I, p. 355.

3. Entries on Nov. 26 and 27 in his Index Book reveal that Lyell had read Wallace's paper on those days before opening his first notebook on the species question on Nov. 28. See Wilson (1970), p. 65. Entries in the journals themselves will be referred to by *Lyell Journals* to distinguish them from Wilson's own notes and comments.

had already noted in his Species Notebook that this very point "must be proved."[4]

Wallace's central point in his 1855 Paper was that species appear coincident both temporally and spatially with preexisting closely allied species.[5] Although Lyell agreed with this conclusion, he strongly disagreed with the obvious implications of Wallace's paper, and stated that "there are innumerable reasons connected with the past & future as well as with the present which will cause the new species to resemble those wh. exist or wh. lately existed."[6] This belief, of course, was one of long standing with Lyell. As early as 1832 he had published similar views: "It is idle to dispute about the abstract possibility of the conversion of one species into another, when there are known causes so much more active in their nature, which must always intervene and prevent the actual accomplishment of such conversions."[7] And it is these conditions or causes which he adduced to counter Wallace's evolutionary hypothesis.

In the first place, wrote Lyell, "each species must probably be intended to exist for a given term, not an hour or day but for many generations." By the word "intended" he certainly implied a creator; indeed, later he stated that "creation seems to require omnipotence," i.e. an all-powerful God. And yet he examined the case for the introduction of new beings assuming that the creator is not omniscient. The necessary *"conditions"* are: (1) The temperature must be suitable. (2) "All the attributes & instincts of co-existing species must be consid.[d] & their present and future power of increase or diminution—" (3) Past conditions of climate and geography as well as the extinct species must be considered. The new species must also evince adaptations to the total environment—animal, vegetable and mineral. (4) That different organs are required for different environments and a wide range of fluctuating conditions must be considered as well—epidemics, food supply, predators.

Lyell's fifth point is quite interesting for it demonstrates his great perception yet also shows his inability to take the final step. The capacity to produce more offspring or to alter color slightly may protect an organism against contingencies. "Suppose for example an

4. See p. 37, n. 23, above.

6. *Lyell Journals*, I, pp. 2–3.

5. 1855 Paper, p. 186.

7. *Principles* (1832), vol. II, pp. 174–75.

insect destined [by the creator presumably] to live thru the summer into the autumn be of a bright green & concealed by that colour while the leaves are green but not so in autumn—a slight admixture of yellow may cause it to be less readily found & devoured by birds in autumn & so carry it over its period of future danger which might exterminate it 100,000 years hence."[8] We now know that this phenomenon is indeed found in nature, as H. B. D. Kettlewell's excellent work on the industrial melanism of moths has so ably demonstrated.[9] Interestingly enough, Wallace observed in his famous paper of 1858 that "even a change of colour might, by rendering them [species] more or less distinguishable, affect their safety."[10] Lyell was not prepared to say, as would Wallace, that new species might ultimately result.

God rules according to self-imposed laws, and mankind can comprehend the universe by examining and understanding these laws; so wrote Lyell.[11] The laws which regulate species are geological and geographical. Different antecedents necessitate different results; hence, different species arise. Adaptation to an environment was also an important concept to Lyell. He assumed that God had ordered a rational universe, which explained the reasons for gills in fish, lungs in birds, the ability of a species to endure harsh weather conditions and "to fight its way & stand its ground against others, . . ."[12] There were, therefore, sound reasons in Lyell's opinion for rejecting a Lamarckian type of hypothesis concerning the introduction of new species, and Wallace had stimulated Lyell's memory of the evidence which he had already adduced in the *Principles*.[13]

But if Lyell was determined to hold fast to his established ideas, he was also obligated, as an excellent scientist with an omnivorous mind, to weigh all the evidence. And he had to admit that Wallace had presented a very powerful case against established ideas concerning species. He had even quoted Lyell himself as a witness for his own case—that of an evolutionist. The modus operandi of the extinction of species, Wallace wrote "has been well illustrated by Sir C. Lyell in his

8. *Lyell Journals,* I, pp. 1–4.

9. Kettlewell, "Darwin's Missing Evidence" (1959), pp. 48–53.

10. *NS,* p. 34.

11. *Lyell Journals,* I, p. 6.

12. Ibid., pp. 2–6, ref. p. 6.

13. For example as found in *Principles* (1832), vol. II, esp. chap. X.

admirable 'Principles.' Geological changes, however gradual, must occasionally have modified external conditions to such an extent as to have rendered the existence of certain species impossible."[14] Lyell agreed: "Species must die out (see P. of G.) & new ones come in or the Earth would be depopulated."[15] This is the *only* time in his first species notebook that Lyell referred to the P. of G.—the *Principles of Geology,* and it is obviously a direct response to Wallace's remark. There are others. For example, Wallace had observed:

> As generally in geography no species or genus occurs in two very distinct localities without being also found in intermediate places, so in geology the life of a species or genus has not been interrupted. In other words, *no group or species has come into existence twice.*[16]

Lyell in reply again fell back upon his well-established arguments already adduced in the *Principles:*

> The condit.ˢ of existence in climate [and] geogr.ʸ [and of the] plants & animals present, alone, to say nothing of [those present in] the past & future, are innumerable; even the known circum.ˢ, & the unknown probably far greater. *It is scarcely conceivable that they can ever coincide twice in the history of the planet, if it were to endure for millions of millions of years.* Hence that the same species sh.ᵈ reappear may well be regarded as impossible, or that a carbonif.ˢ spec.ˢ could thrive now, or if so that its reappearance sh.ᵈ be consistent with the well-being of all the species wh. are now living, man included.[17]

But Lyell had no effective explanation for the phenomena of rudimentary, i.e. vestigial organs. One series of facts supporting Wallace's evolutionary law was drawn from these phenomena: "the *minute limbs hidden beneath the skin in many of the snake-like lizards,* the anal hooks of the boa constrictor, the complete series of jointed fingerbones in the paddle of the Manatus and whale, are a few of the most familiar instances." He went on to adduce more evidence straight from

14. 1855 Paper, p. 190.
15. *Lyell Journals,* I, p. 6.
16. 1855 Paper, p. 186. Italics are mine. Forbes made the same point (1851–54), p. 429.
17. *Lyell Journals,* I, pp. 7–8. Italics are mine.

Chambers's *Vestiges* as I have shown,[18] and concluded that these facts were the necessary results of natural law. If more fossil forms were available, more "rudimentary" organs would be known. "The great gaps that exist between fishes, reptiles, birds, and mammals would then, no doubt, be softened down by intermediate groups, and the whole organic world would be seen to be an unbroken and harmonious system."[19] To this Lyell's reply was: "Rudimentary organs are a great mystery. They favour the Lamarckian hypothesis tho' the arguments against such variability of species are too powerful to allow us to believe in such a hypothesis—as *that the abortive legs of a snake-like reptile* are the remains of a quadruped altered into a snake."[20] Again the response to Wallace was direct, and Lyell's answer was admittedly unsatisfactory: "It is a mystery like abortion & monstrosities." True, rudimentary organs imply some system or law, and he assumed "that a given term alloted to every species is probably one condition of creation, & the specific century may be another." But this answer is feeble indeed and subject to question—why should an omnipotent creator restrict himself in such a way? To this Lyell said simply first that he does and secondly that "man is enabled thereby to study & understand the mechanism of the org. & inorganic worlds. This may be a very small part of the reasons of fixed laws but one is enough."[21] Lyell thus put himself in the unenviable position of presuming to understand the mind of God.

Wallace had been particularly interested in island flora and fauna. We have noticed this already in his notebook,[22] and the polished version of these specific notes appeared in 1855:

> Such phaenomena as are exhibited by the Galapagos Islands, which contain little groups of plants and animals peculiar to themselves, but most nearly allied to those of South America, have not hitherto received any, even a conjectural explanation. The Galapagos are a volcanic group of high antiquity, and have probably never been more closely connected with the continent than

18. See chapter 4, pp. 50–52.
19. 1855 Paper, pp. 195–96.
20. *Lyell Journals*, I, p. 8. Italics are mine. In his Index Book for this journal he wrote: "Rudimentary organs without any function—limbs hidden beneath the skin in snake-like lizards." Wilson (1970), p. 66.
21. *Lyell Journals*, I, pp. 8–9.
22. See above chapter 3, pp. 36–38.

they are at present. They must have been first peopled, like other newly-formed islands, by the action of winds and currents, and at a period sufficiently remote to have had the original species die out, and the modified prototypes only remain. In the same way we can account for the separate islands having each their peculiar species, either on the supposition that the same original emigration peopled the whole of the islands with the same species from which differently modified prototypes were created, or that the islands were successively peopled from each other, but that new species have been created in each on the plan of the pre-existing ones.[23]

Lyell's implicit comment is terse: "The Galapagos may be sufficiently analog.[s] in many respects to S. America to cause a common type of species tho' diff.[t] in many [respects]."[24] But Wallace also had maintained that the case of the ancient island of St. Helena is similar: it also has a peculiar, although limited flora.[25] To this Lyell replied at greater length, again falling back upon the notion that species are created for a specified length of time. "The St. Helena plants & insects may have lasted for the allotted term. Longevity in species may be as varied as in individuals & there may be some exceptions, but as there is an average in the individuals of a species so there may be a mean durat.[n] in the spec.[s] of a class or Order or Genus for the successive generations." Species are created for specific periods, but accidents sometimes act against the plan: "a volc.[c] island like St. Helena may be destroyed by the ocean or peopled by man & many spec.[s] may be permitted to be prematurely cut off. We cannot affirm this." Perhaps many other islands like St. Helena had species whose preordained terms expired "& the advent of Man was the signal for their extermination."[26]

After wandering back to the general implications of Wallace's paper, Lyell returned to the phenomenon of the uniqueness of island

23. 1855 Paper, p. 188.

24. *Lyell Journals,* I, p. 4. Wilson uses the word "facies" instead of "species" which is probably an error. He also alludes to Darwin's *Journal of Researches.* See Wilson (1970), p. 66.

25. 1855 Paper, p. 188.

26. *Lyell Journals,* I, pp. 9, 10. His remark about "a continent in mid-ocean now submerged" probably refers to the ancient island of Atlantis which Edward Forbes had tried to resurrect in order to explain some anomalies of geographical distribution. See note 34 below.

fauna and reminded himself to examine Darwin's *Journal of Researches* regarding the fauna of St. Helena:

> The Salvages accord.[g] to Woodward & a rock called Cima off
> Baxio, P[ort]° Santo have each a peculiar land shell.
> Maury's charts [of the Atlantic],[27] says W[oodward,] show
> that certain species sh.[d] be common to the Azores & Europe they
> must have gone far round as they could never have crossed the
> Atlantic Abyss.
> St. Helena—see Darwin's voyage for peculiar fauna of.[28]

One of Lyell's greatest difficulties in considering the species problem objectively was that he felt obligated to interject a creator, and in doing so constantly had to rationalize to extricate himself from difficult problems:

> Of innumerable ways in which Omnipotence might fit a new
> species to all the present and future condit.[s] of its existence, there
> may be one which is preferable to all others, and if so, this will
> cause the new species to be in all probability allied to preexisting
> and extinct or with many coexisting species of the same genus.
> *What is called here necessity* may merely mean that it pleases the
> Author of Nature not simply to ordain fitness, but the greatest
> fitness, how far consideration of more beauty in form, of endless
> variety for variety's own sake, may enter into these laws is matter
> for speculation, but independently even of such condit.[s], there
> may be a propriety absolutely exceeding all others, & this may
> always be chosen & may cause many allied species.[29]

27. Samuel Pickworth Woodward (1821–65), a naturalist who concentrated on invertebrate fossils, particularly fossil molluscs. His greatest work was *The Manual of Mollusca, or Rudimentary Treatise of Recent and Fossil Shells* (1851–56), although he published many articles. *Dict. Nat. Biog.*, vol. 21, pp. 897–98. The Salvages are small, rocky islands located about midway between Madeira and the Canary Islands. Porto Santo is near Madeira. Matthew Fontaine Maury (1806–73), an American officer and world-famous oceanographer, in 1847 published an excellent work on winds and currents, *Wind and Current Chart of the North Atlantic. Dict. Amer. Biog.*, vol. 12, pp. 428–31. Wilson (1970), p. 68 says that Woodward referred to Maury's *Physical Geography of the Sea* (1855).

28. *Lyell Journals*, I, pp. 16–17. I have edited the text slightly. I think the "W." refers to Woodward, not Wollaston. See Wilson (1970), p. 68.

29. *Lyell Journals*, I, pp. 11–12. Italics are mine.

Lyell's allusion to "what is called here necessity" is another direct reference to Wallace's conclusion in his 1855 Paper:

> Granted the law [that every species has come into existence coincident in time and space with a preexisting closely allied species], and many of the most important facts in Nature could not have been otherwise, but are almost as *necessary* deductions from it, as are the elliptical orbits of the planets from the law of gravitation.[30]

Although Lyell's religious arguments for divine creation permeate these pages of his first species notebook, he had, as I have already shown, other valid scientific arguments which supported his views. For example, in 1839 William Colchester and Searles Wood discovered some supposed mammalian fossils at Kyson, near Woodbridge in Suffolk. Richard Owen named one *Macacus eocenus*. In 1855, therefore, this evidence tended to refute the idea that man was the last development of the anthropomorphous species. As Lyell said in his notebook: "an Eocene Macacus [is proof] against the theory of anthropomorphous species coming last." In 1862, however, Owen changed his mind and said that the fossil was a pachyderm.[31]

Another argument against evolution was that species could not adapt themselves as fast as species were being exterminated:

> The rate of extermination is now so rapid as compared to the power of species to accommodate themselves to new circums.ˢ that the Lamarckian Hypoth.ˢ seems inadequate.

The problem of ecological adaptation was prominent in Lyell's thoughts. Indeed in his opinion this was a central reason why new species were *introduced,* i.e. created, closely allied to older, already adapted species. In the *Principles* Lyell clearly recognized this relationship of species to environment, and he began this first notebook with these arguments. Obviously, an organism cannot long exist if the climate and geographical conditions are hostile. But Lyell was not consistent. In his notebook he wrote that species frequently die out because their allotted time has expired. True, over the course of time

---

30. 1855 Paper, p. 196. Italics are mine.
31. *Lyell Journals,* I, p. 11. See *Principles* (1857), p. 144. *Principles* (1872), vol. I, p. 162.

the environment may have altered and in some cases precipitate extinction might have occurred, but these are some of the reasons why "creation seems to require omnipotence." As he specifically said only a little farther on, "a given term allotted to every species is probably one condition of creation, & the specific centres may be another." The "term" is of course allotted by an omniscient creator. The idea of specific centers of creation fits very nicely with this point of view, but as Lyell later observed: "It is remarkable how all the hypothesis for the separate and independent Creation [of species] can be turned in favour of the Transmutation theory also." The idea of a specific center of creation for a species is one of those ideas which accommodates the evolutionary hypothesis extremely well.[32]

Wallace had also observed in his 1855 Paper that on islands formed or separated from a continent in a recent geological epoch the species are not peculiar. England was his specific example.[33] Thus it is understandable that Lyell demonstrated an extraordinary interest in the flora and fauna of the British Isles and Europe, a subject treated extensively by Edward Forbes in 1846.[34] An example of this interest is Lyell's observation that "the absence in Irish bogs and peat as well as in the Scotch [ones also] of elephant & rhinoc.[s] [fossils] implies recent emergence."[35] Lyell continued this interesting examination for many pages.

But if Wallace's observation that recently formed islands do not have unique flora and fauna interested Lyell, the following statement by Wallace fascinated him:

> no example is known of an island which can be proved geologically to be of very recent origin (late in the Tertiary, for instance), and yet possesses generic or family groups or even many species peculiar to itself.[36]

In fact, judging from the lengthy notations—over one hundred pages

32. *Lyell Journals*, I, pp. 10–11, 8–9; II, p. 69. But see Darwin's opposition to that concept *LLD*, vol. I, p. 439, and *LLL*, vol. II, p. 216.

33. 1855 Paper, p. 189.

34. Forbes, "On the Connection Between the Distribution of the Existing Fauna and Flora of the British Isles, and the Geological Changes which have Affected their Area, Especially During the Epoch of Northern Drift" (1846), pp. 336–432.

35. *Lyell Journals*, I, p. 19.

36. 1855 Paper, p. 188.

—on the flora and fauna, both fossil and living, of St. Helena, the Galapagos, Madeira, the Azores, Canaries, Porto Santo, and numerous other islands, *Lyell apparently considered this statement of Wallace to be a crucial test of the belief that species have originated by evolution*.[37] The additional inference to be drawn from the statement—and Wallace was fully aware of this—was that if one were to retrace the natural history of an island far enough, to the time when the original inhabitants arrived, one would discover that the fossil remains of those inhabitants would be the same as those of the inhabitants of the closest mainland. As time passed, however, the species of the island and the nearest mainland would begin to diverge and become, eventually, peculiar although similar, as in the case of the Galapagos Islands. And it was precisely to test these points that Lyell collected a mountain of evidence—evidence much too detailed for presentation here. The specific direction of Lyell's thoughts, however, becomes increasingly clear. On 11 April 1856 he had reached some definite conclusions:

> But the land shells of all the 100 British Isles are the same & agree with Germany & France except [for] a few Portuguese, [ones such] as [the] Lyena involuta [of] Ireland. It is only very ancient islands which have their land shells peculiar—Miocene islands as E. Forbes said. Hence a geologist may infer the antiquity of islands by the isolation of their shells.
>
> St. Helena had its own plants & [so also did] the Galapagos [Islands] but each isle of the latter only to a limited extent? Hooker, Linn. Trans. [38]

Two days later, on 13 April 1856, Lyell discussed the migration of plants and shells with Charles Darwin, from whom he learned that

37. *Lyell Journals*, I, pp. 9–131. See also *LLL*, vol. II, pp. 208–13. Lyell remarked in a letter to Professor Oswald Heer on 23 April 1856: "I am extremely pleased with your discussion of the old 'Atlantis,' a subject on which I have been preparing some observations, especially in regard to the fossil and recent shells." *LLL*, vol. II, p. 210. See above footnotes 26 and 34. See also *Lyell Journals*, V, p. 20 and VI, p. 180. Also see Wilson (1970), p. 391.

38. *Lyell Journals*, I, p. 129. According to Wilson (1970), p. 79, the reference is J. D. Hooker, "An Enumeration of the Plants of the Galapagos Islands; with Descriptions of those which Are New," *Trans. Linn. Soc. Lond.*, 20 (1841), 163–233.

In the Galapagos isles the land shells collected were not numerous, but so far as the evidence went, it corroborates the Mad[eir]ᵃ & P[ort]° S[ant]° case[s] in regard to the distinctness of the fauna of each island.

St. Helena has been much changed since the extinct land shells accumulated there.

Darwin also allowed Lyell to read a letter from a Mr. Lowe, dated 12 April 1856, which discussed the flora of Porto Santo, and which said: "There are *very many common* endemic species in Madeira not occurring in P[ort]° S[ant]°."[39] Lyell's intensive examination of island species now abruptly ceases in his notebooks; the important prelude to the Darwin-Lyell conversation three days later appears to have run its course. Before discussing this important meeting, however, a few preliminary words are necessary regarding the relationship of Lyell and Darwin.

It is well known that Darwin, very early in his career, expressed profound admiration for, and was very much influenced by, Lyell's *Principles of Geology,* and that after his return from the *Beagle* voyage, the two formed an enduring friendship. In fact, it was to be Sir Charles Lyell who, along with J. D. Hooker, presented the joint Darwin-Wallace papers to the Linnean Society in 1858. And the Lyell-Hooker letter prefacing that historic presentation sheds some interesting light upon the relationship of Lyell and Darwin. According to that letter the accompanying papers included

> extracts from a MS. work on Species, by Mr. Darwin, which was sketched in 1839, and copied in 1844, when the copy was read by Dr. Hooker, and its contents afterwards communicated to Sir Charles Lyell.

Later, the same letter mentions that "one of us had perused [the memoir] in 1844, and the contents of which we had both of us been privy to for many years."[40]

39. *Lyell Journals,* I, pp. 131, 136. Italics are either Lowe's or Lyell's. Richard Thomas Lowe (1802–74) was a naturalist and Cambridge graduate, who lived in Madeira (1828–54) and made repeated trips back there. He apparently concentrated on the flora and T. V. Wollaston, his friend, concentrated on the fauna of Madeira. *Dict. Nat. Biog.,* vol. XII, pp. 196–97.

40. Loewenberg (1959), pp. 41–42 and pp. 42–43. The reference to 1839 is wrong. The correct year for the sketch is 1842.

Sir Edward Bailey apparently takes this first statement to means that Lyell knew about natural selection in the 1840s, or certainly no later than 1854.[41] The two statements taken together, however, make it clear that *only* Hooker had perused Darwin's manuscript in 1844; the statements "and its contents afterwards communicated to Sir Charles Lyell" and "the contents of which we had both been privy to for many years" are *not* precise statements of time. Although Lyell mentions later that Hooker had known about Darwin's ideas since 1844, he never tells us precisely when *he* learned about natural selection.[42]

On the other hand, it is clear from the letters from Darwin to Lyell, dated 8 October [1845] and from Lyell to C. J. F. Bunbury, dated 13 November 1854, that Sir Charles was aware that Darwin held views on the species question which were directly opposed to the "orthodox faith." However, many others—Thomas Vernon Wollaston, T. H. Huxley, Edward Blyth, Wallace, and W. D. Fox, to name but a few—also knew before June 1858 that Darwin was working on the species question; and some of his other friends were also aware that he entertained heterodox views.[43] To William Darwin.Fox (his cousin, a fellow lover of nature, and an old and very dear college friend) Darwin had mentioned on 19 March [1855] that he was collecting facts and arguments for a book discussing the pros and cons regarding the immutability of species. In a subsequent letter on 27 March 1855 to the same person, he was more specific:

I forgot whether I ever told you what the object of my present work is,—it is to view all facts that I can master . . . in Natural History (as on geographical distribution, palaeontology, classification, hybridism, domestic animals and plants, etc., etc., etc.,) to see how far they favour or are opposed to the notion that wild

41. Bailey, *Charles Lyell* (1963), pp. 158, 186–87.

42. *Principles* (1872), vol. II, pp. 278, 282. Hooker mentioned in 1908 that Lyell knew about Darwin's ideas "some years before the arrival of Mr. Wallace's letter" in 1858, but this statement also is imprecise regarding a specific time. *WLR*, p. 97. See also Lyell, *The Geological Evidences of the Antiquity of Man* (1863), p. 408, and *LLD*, vol. I, p. 384.

43. *LLD*, vol. I, p. 312, and *LLL*, vol. II, pp. 198–99, 212. T.V. Wollaston (1822–1878) studied the coleoptera of Madeira, the Cape de Verdes, and St. Helena. He used the evidence gathered from these sources to support Forbes's belief in a submerged "Atlantis." A Cambridge man, his work *On the Variation of Species* (1856), was dedicated to Charles Darwin. See also *LLD*, vol. I, p. 404. *Dict. Nat. Biog.*, vol. XXI, pp. 780–81.

species are mutable or immutable: I mean with my utmost power to give all arguments and facts on both sides.[44]

A letter of 18 July [1856] to Lyell's friend S.P. Woodward contains a statement that shows clearly that Darwin was not hiding the fact of his dissident views on species:

> I am growing as bad as the worst about species, and have hardly a vestige of belief in the permanence of species left in me; and this confession will make you think very lightly of me, but I cannot help it. Such has become my honest conviction, though the difficulties and arguments against such heresy are certainly most weighty.[45]

As early as 1845, he had remarked to his long-time friend L. Jenyns (the Reverend L. Blomefield):

> The general conclusion at which I have slowly been driven from a directly opposite conviction, is that allied species are co-descendants from common stocks. I know how much I open myself to reproach for such a conclusion, but I have at least honestly and deliberately come to it.[46]

Darwin had also confessed to Huxley on 2 September [1854]: "I am almost as unorthodox about species as the *Vestiges* itself, although I hope not quite so unphilosophical."[47] And this statement was made immediately after Huxley had literally ripped the *Vestiges* to shreds in a scathing review, one which he afterwards regretted "on the ground of needless savagery."

Clearly then, a number of people besides Lyell knew before 1856 that Darwin was working on the species problem and that he entertained heterodox views; however, they did *not* know about Darwin's theory of natural selection, which is quite another matter. For a long time *only* Hooker was privy to Darwin's secret.[48]

44. *LLD*, vol. I, pp. 406, 409.
45. *MLD*, vol. I, pp. 96–97.
46. *LLD*, vol. I, p. 393. See also *MLD*, vol. I, p. 50.
47. *MLD*, vol. I, p. 75. See also pp. 104, 449–50.
48. Darwin requested in 1844 that his wife have his species sketch published in the event of his death. He then suggested Lyell as the best person to edit the sketch, with Forbes, Henslow, Hooker ("would be *very* good"), Strickland, and Owen as other possibilities. However, in August 1854, Darwin wrote the following addendum on the back of the above mentioned request. "Hooker by far best man to edit my species volume." *LLD*, vol. I, pp. 377–79.

When, then, did Lyell first learn from Darwin about natural selection? From 26 November 1855 until 16 April 1856, Darwin's name
is mentioned no less than five times in Lyell's first notebook on the
species question in connection with island flora and fauna, but *not
once* is natural selection ever mentioned. Quite the contrary, we have
seen that Lyell at that time was specifically concerned with Wallace's
1855 Paper and the suggestions of that paper. It was only *after* having
reached certain conclusions that he talked with Darwin about island
species. At this point, it appears that Lyell specifically requested a
meeting with Darwin to discuss his explanation for these phenomena.
Lyell's record of this conversation is also the earliest reference in his
notebooks, or in the published correspondence between the two, to
natural selection:

[Wednesday] April 16, 1856.
With Darwin: On the Formation of Species by Natural Selection—(Origin Q[uer]y?)
Genera differ in the variability of the species, but all extensive
genera have species in them which have a tendency to vary. When
the condit.ˢ alter, those individuals, which vary so as to adapt
them to the new circum.ˢ, flourish & survive while the others are
cut off.

The varieties extirpated are even more persecuted & annihi-
lated by organic than inorganic causes. The struggle for existence
ag.ᵗ other species is more serious than ag.ᵗ changes of climate &
physical geography. The extinction of species has been always
going on. The number of species which migrated into the
Madeiras was not great in proport. to those now there, for a few
types may have been the origination of many allied species.

The young pigeons are more of the normal type than the old
of each variety. Embryology, therefore, leads to the opinion that
you get nearer the type in going nearer to the foetal archetype & in
like manner in Time we may get back nearer to the archetype of
each genus & family & class.

The reason why Mr. Wallace['s] introduction of species, most
allied to those immediately preceding in Time, or that new species was [sic] in each geol.¹ period akin to species of the period
immediately antecedent, seems explained by the Natural Selection
Theory.⁴⁹

49. *Lyell Journals,* I, pp. 137–39.

The reference (at the beginning of this record of their conversation) to "Origin Q[uer]y" also suggests that this meeting was the first time that Lyell had requested a full explanation of Darwin's theory. This record also tells us that Wallace's 1855 Paper was *specifically* mentioned, presumably discussed, and that Lyell (and certainly Darwin) realized Wallace's law could be explained by natural selection. Lyell's note in his Index Book for 27 November 1855 had already observed that Wallace's law went "far towards Lamarck's doctrine." *After this meeting* with Darwin, we have published letters which tell us that Lyell had urged Darwin to publish his theory.[50]

This being the case, the question immediately arises as to *why* Sir Joseph Dalton Hooker learned about natural selection so early—in 1844—whereas Sir Charles Lyell learned about it relatively late—in 1856. A number of explanations are possible. In the first place, very soon after Hooker's return from his Antarctic expedition (on 7 September 1843), Darwin wrote inviting him "to study the botanical collections which he had made in the Galapagos Islands, as well as his Patagonian and Fuegian plants."[51] The obvious intention was to enlist Hooker's aid in his project; but to do so meant confiding in him: Hooker had to know *what* to look for, and this is why in January 1844—that is in the month immediately following his first letter to Hooker—Darwin confessed his heresy and continued after that to divulge more and more to his newly found young friend. Lyell, on the other hand, was an older man, well set in his ways and not amenable to changing his mind quickly. Most important of all, he had not just returned from an extensive and important scientific expedition where he had dealt with the flora of oceanic islands. Therefore, he could not supply the type of scientific help so vital to Darwin's work.

Lyell's subsequent notes on 22 April 1856 are interesting for a number of reasons, not the least of which is that they further corroborate the assertation that Lyell first learned about natural selection on 16 April 1856. Lyell was obviously shaken by Darwin's arguments, in spite of having been prepared by Wallace's 1855 Paper:

Why have we witnessed no new creations since Man existed? Perhaps because the time is too short for what ought to be con-

50. Wilson (1970), p. 66. Wilson agrees that Lyell first learned about natural selection on 16 April 1856. Ibid., pp. xiv. ff.
51. *LLD,* vol. I, p. 381.

sidered a species to be introduced. If most of our species are varieties then genera or sub-genera at any rate are all that originate directly from the hands of the Creator. According to that view it would rarely happen that a new genus came into being.

But perhaps the races of man fill the ecological niches vacated by extinct species. If this were so, then there would be fewer acts of creation. But as Lyell realized, once the door is open, all sorts of concessions must be made: "The objection w.ᵈ be that if we concede the species of a genus so must we [concede] the genera of a family & the families of an Order." Pandora's box would be open. "On the other hand if we revert to the origin of things, how many original generic types do we require?"[52]

In his *Principles of Geology* Lyell had maintained that species would die out quickly in response to extensive alterations of the ecological situation because not enough time would be available for the necessary adaptations.[53] His conversation with Darwin did much to change his opinion. "The immensity of Time even in Pliocene & post-Pliocene periods may greatly facilitate the Lamarckian hypothesis." Moreover, Lyell had already admitted while arguing privately with Wallace's 1855 Paper that the phenomenon of rudimentary organs favors the Lamarckian hypothesis. On 22 April 1856 he again conceded: "Abortive wings, & organs called *rudimentary,* may be indications of a transition from one form or state to another."[54]

Lyell's two greatest stumbling blocks were still the questions of man's origin and how the work of a creator could be reconciled to Darwinian evolution.

But how did Man begin? He was improved out of some anthropomorphous genus & is an *old world* form of that family. To this I object that his progression power causes him to differ wholly from all the Brutes in kind rather than in degree. It is answered that a dog is progressing in a domesticated state, [and] increasing in intelligence. The reply is that he has lost many of his instincts & attributes as a wild dog, possibly as much as he has gained.

52. *Lyell Journals,* I, pp. 139–43.
53. *Principles* (1832), vol. II, p. 173.
54. *Lyell Journals,* I, p. 144. Italics by Lyell.

Terms such as "Creator," "acts of creation," and "creation" occur throughout the notes Lyell entered on that day. As he candidly admitted:

> You require, say my opponents, a perpetual series of miraculous interventions of the supreme [being] or some unknown power to sustain the system of living creatures which Time & the changes of the animate & inanimate world have been always & always now are working.

Furthermore, perpetual creation by natural selection is far easier to understand than creation by unknown fiat:

> You lay yourself open to Whewell['s] objection that creation has ceased, but the Lamarckian machinery supplies a perpetual creation—power of new permanent varieties or species adapted to the new circumstances of climate & geogr.[1] & contempor.[y] botanical & zoological conditions.[55]

Clearly, the armor of Lyell's defenses was weakened as never before. Two days later "after a conversation with [J. S.] Mill, Huxley, Hooker, Carpenter & Busk at Philos[ophical] Club," Lyell observed "that the belief in species as permanent, fixed & invariable, & so comprehending individuals descending from single pairs of protoplasts is growing fainter—no very clear creed to substitute;" that is *these* friends had no clear creed to substitute. They did, however, pose some serious problems which Lyell recorded at length.[56]

55. Ibid., pp. 141–42. (See Lyell's revealing remarks to Darwin just after reading the proofs of the *Origin* in October 1859. *LLD,* vol. II, p. 2.)

56. Ibid., pp. 144–55. William Benjamin Carpenter (1813–85), [son of Dr. Lant Carpenter,] was a naturalist who studied medicine at the Bristol Medical School, University College, London, and Edinburgh where in 1839 he published his greatest work *The Principles of General and Comparative Physiology.* He was well versed in literature and philosophy, no doubt because of the excellent background acquired at his father's famous school at Bristol, and he contributed numerous papers to various scientific journals. In 1854 he published his *Comparative Physiology.* He accepted Darwin's views on evolution in a limited manner, believing that natural selection could not explain the evidence of design in creation. *Dict. Nat. Biog.,* vol. III, pp. 1075–77. George Busk (1807–86) also studied medicine and in 1855 he discontinued his private practice in order to devote full time to science, particularly the microscopal study of the Polyzoa and other lower forms of life. In 1863 and later his interest shifted to ethnology also. He contributed some 70–80 papers to scientific journals and societies after 1841 and was elected F. R. S. (1850),

In a letter to his brother-in-law, C. J. F. Bunbury, on 30 April 1856, Lyell mentioned another assault on the idea of the fixity of species:

> When Huxley, Hooker, and Wollaston were at Darwin's last week, they (all four of them) ran a tilt against species farther I believe than they are deliberately prepared to go. Wollaston least orthodox. I cannot easily see how they can go so far, and not embrace the whole Lamarckian doctrine.[57]

And Lyell's entry of 1 May 1856 in his second notebook on the species question reveals (as Darwin observed shortly thereafter to J. D. Hooker[58]) that he was personally finding it more and more difficult to reject that doctrine:

> The number of generic types, from which reputed species have branched, is much reduced in number if we accept Carpenter's estimate in regard to Orbitolites as a test on Foraminifera & Hooker (N. Zeal.ᵈ Flora) in regard to plants. The more we diminish the number of original types, the rarer will be the birthdays of such stocks; according therefore to the doctrine of successive creation, the fewer will have been the opportunities for man to witness the first starting into being of protoplasts.
>
> On the other hand the concession of a generic type prepares the way for admitting a prototype of an order, & then all we require is the original creation of a certain limited number of vertebrates & invertebrate archetypes, whence the long series of geological assemblages of species were evolved by Lamarckian transmutation.[59]

The inevitable conclusion for Lyell is that once evolution from a few primitive forms is allowed, man's ancestry logically should be explained in similar terms. And the question of man's ancestry was a major stumbling block to Lyell's acceptance of what he labelled the Lamarckian hypothesis. His notebooks made this very clear. They also make clear Lyell's persistent unwillingness to differentiate between Lamarck's evolutionary ideas and those of Wallace and Darwin.

F. L. S. (1846), etc. His most important work was *Report on the Pylozoa Collected by HMS Challenger* (1884–86), 2 vols. See *Dict. Nat. Biog.*, vol. XXII, pp. 357–58.

57. *LLL*, vol. II, p. 212.
58. *MLD*, vol. I, p. 96.
59. *Lyell Journals*, II, pp. 4–5.

Rather than focus on the vast differences between these views, especially the mechanism of natural selection, Lyell preferred to stress their many similarities. In essence, he thought Darwinian evolution was a refurbished, somewhat more scientific, Lamarckianism. His tenacity in maintaining this curious viewpoint greatly annoyed Darwin, who vigorously protested Lyell's lack of perception.

In answer to the question of why more intermediate forms are not found in the geological record, Lyell returned to Wallace's observations:

> Wallace's hint as to the likeness of each succeeding geolog.[1] formation, in reference to its paleontology, is the more deserving of attention when we allow for the multitude of missing documents. We must reply to the question, where are the intermediate types. They are hidden from us, not yet found, many of them destroyed & irrecoverable. This is inevitable. Nature's system is not that of preserving a perfect history of her past creation but only a broken & imperfect one.[60]

Knowing the profound effect which Wallace's paper had on Lyell, we may logically assume that he discussed that paper with his colleagues. Indeed, we know indefinitely that Lyell both recommended Wallace's paper to Darwin and discussed it with him on 16 April 1856 with the observation that if Darwin did not hurry and publish, he would be anticipated—by Wallace who was obviously on the right track. On 3 May [1856] Darwin wrote to Lyell:

> With respect to your suggestion of a sketch of my views, I hardly know what to think, but will reflect on it, but it goes agains my prejudices. To give a fair sketch would be absolutely impossible, for every proposition requires such an array of facts. If I were to do anything, it could only refer to the main agency of change—selection—and perhaps point out a very few of the leading features, which countenance such a view, and some few of the main difficulties. But I do not know what to think; *I rather hate the idea of writing for priority, yet I certainly should be vexed if any one were to publish my doctrines before me.*

60. Ibid., pp. 5–6. This very interesting discussion continues at length and no doubt Wilson will discuss this subject thoroughly in his forthcoming biography of Lyell.

Darwin further revealed his concern, caused by Lyell's exhortations, in a postscript to this letter: "If I did publish a short sketch, where on earth should I publish it?"[61]

After a meeting with Lyell that following week—when Lyell again urged him to publish—Darwin wrote two letters to his good friend J. D. Hooker, one on 9 May [1856] and another two days later, both mentioning Lyell's insistent advice to publish something quickly. Darwin was quite perturbed and in the 11 May letter he wrote: "I begin *most heartily* to wish that Lyell had never put this idea of an Essay into my head."[62] Judging from the somewhat frantic tone of Darwin's letters, Lyell had been *quite* insistent, and had probably reiterated the fact that Wallace might be very close to a solution to the species problem. The culmination of this series of letters is found in Darwin's Journal: "1856. May 14th Began by Lyell's advice writing Species Sketch."[63] Later, Darwin wrote Lyell, as a kind of postscript to the notation in his Journal, "I am delighted that I may say (with absolute truth) that my essay is published at your suggestion." As we know, the Sketch *per se* never materialized, but by beginning work on the Sketch, Darwin had in effect begun work on the *Origin of Species:* "I have found it quite impossible to publish any preliminary essay or sketch; but am doing my work as completely as my present materials allow and without waiting to perfect them. And this much acceleration I owe to you."[64]

In reality, Darwin was prompted by more than Lyell's insistent exhortations, for he had also read and annotated Wallace's paper shortly after it was published in 1855. Furthermore, he took notes on blue paper and pinned them in the back of his copy of the December issue of 1855.[65] Although there are more than thirty-five marks, five

61. *LLD*, vol. I, pp. 426–27. Italics are mine.

62. Ibid., pp. 427–30. Ref. p. 430.

63. de Beer, "Darwin's Journal," vol. 2, no. 1, (1959) p. 14.

64. *LLD*, vol. I, pp. 430, 433.

65. The blue paper may be the same paper he used when taking notes for version three of his *Origin of Species*. Darwin owned *all* the issues of the *AMNH* published in 1855, i.e., Jan. 1855 (vol. 15) to Dec. 1855 (vol. 16). It appears likely that he was a subscriber and received issues regularly. In 1969 these unbound issues were at Down House in Kent, but may have been transferred since then to Cambridge University Library. Many other issues are already at Cambridge. See *Darwin Library. List of Books Received in the University Library Cambridge March–May 1961.*

annotations, and a drawing of a branched scheme in the margin, the additional notes pinned to his December issue suggest that he had curiously failed to understand what Wallace was saying: "Wallace's paper: Laws of Geograph. Distrib. Nothing very new." Considering both the explicit and profound effect on Lyell and Darwin's own marks in the text, his statement is extremely difficult to understand.

In fact, without these and other explicit statements, we might draw the opposite conclusion from his markings beside *seven* of Wallace's ten propositions.[66] Double lines in the left margin beside proposition ten certainly suggests his acceptance of Wallace's law, especially since Darwin added in the margin the word "Nearly" so that the law would read: *Every species has come into existence* nearly *coincident both in space and time with a pre-existing closely allied species.* A very heavy dark mark in the left hand margin beside proposition nine also suggests concurrence, especially since Darwin made similar statements frequently in the *Origin.*[67]

Although Wallace did not claim that his paper was wholly original —and we have seen that parts were taken from Pictet, Chambers, Lyell, and others—Darwin's claim that there was "nothing very new" deserves closer examination, especially since he admitted that Wallace put the facts in a "striking point of view." Moreover, in response to Wallace's statement, "Species of one genus, or genera of one family occurring in the same geological time [i.e. period] are more closely allied than those separated in time," Darwin wrote in the margin "can this be true." Since he had not written on this matter in either his 1842 Sketch or in his 1844 Essay, Wallace's point was clearly novel and interesting to him. So interesting in fact that Darwin later in the *Origin* specifically accepted the statement: "Moreover, if we look to rather wider intervals, namely, to distinct but consecutive stages of the same great formation, we find that the embedded fossils, though almost universally ranked as specifically different, yet are far more closely allied to each other than are the species found in more

66. See Appendix II. Propositions 5, 6 and 7 have no marks beside them in the margins.

67. *On the Origin of Species,* pp. 313, 315–16. "When a species has once disappeared from the face of the earth, we have reason to believe that the same identical form never reappears." "We can clearly understand why a species when once lost should never reappear, . . ." "A group does not reappear after it has once disappeared; or its existence, as long as it lasts, is continuous."

widely separated formations; but," he continued, "to this subject I shall have to return in the following chapter" on geological succession. By 1859 his query had grown not only to certainty but to many pages of discussion under the heading "On the Affinities of extinct species to each other, and to living forms." Perhaps the high point of this discussion is the statement that "fossils from two consecutive formations are far more closely related to each other, than are the fossils of two remote formations." Ironically, Darwin continued by referring to F. J. Pictet—the probable source of Wallace's point! Had Darwin read and understood Pictet before reading Wallace's paper, he would not have asked the specific question he wrote in the margin.[68]

At least six other points were observed by Darwin. As should be expected, he observed the reference to the Galapagos Islands, which probably was inspired by his own *Beagle* voyage, either directly or through Lyell's reference to it. Then there is the matter of the branching lines of affinity which has obvious meaning: "Uses my simile of tree." Moreover, he observed, Wallace argued against the completeness of the geological record, and as for a particularly transparent point in Wallace, rudimentary organs, "Explains Rudimentary organs on same idea."

One last observation is a curious coincidence, for Darwin noticed Wallace's allusion to the necessary deductions from his law "as are the elliptical orbits of the planets from the law of gravitation." Darwin reminded himself to refer to the law of gravitation "for certain, and I quite agree." Since the 1842 Sketch says "our planet has gone circling on according to fixed laws;" the 1844 Essay states "this planet has gone cycling onwards according to the fixed laws of gravity;" and the *Origin* closes "whilst this planet has gone cycling on according to the fixed law of gravity," it is obvious that this metaphor had wide use from Chambers to Darwin.[69]

These facts being clear, one may ask why Darwin nevertheless observed twice "It seems all creation with him," especially since Darwin

---

68. Ibid., pp. 297–98; 329–36, esp. 335. Prof. Camille Limoge's forthcoming edition of Darwin's reading log (Darwin Papers, Cambridge University Library, MS 119) can easily clear up the point of when Darwin read Pictet. Darwin owned copies of both editions.

69. de Beer (1958), pp. 87; 254; *On the Origin of Species,* p. 490. See chapter 4, p. 51 above.

himself was by no means adverse to using the term. Lyell, who firmly believed in creation by God, never placed such an interpretation on Wallace's arguments, nor did anyone else. To observe that "it is all creation" is to close one's eyes to undisputable facts and arguments. Darwin seemed quite determined to flee from the inevitable conclusion that Wallace was an evolutionist and had presented a forceful case for his beliefs. But if Darwin could not bring himself to face these inescapable facts, others did not hesitate to apprise him of the situation.

Probably sometime in February 1856, months after he first read Wallace's paper, Darwin received a letter from his friend and correspondent Edward Blyth, a naturalist who was in Calcutta, India. (Fig. 8). Blyth had both written and mailed his letter on 8 December 1855 in response to a letter from Darwin of 18 October, which he received that morning. The primary focus of his attention was on Wallace: "What think you of Wallace's paper in the *Ann. M. N. H.?* Good! Upon the whole!" Nevertheless, problems immediately popped into his mind. "But what about the *Giraffe,* which has typical representatives" in certain tertiary deposits? "Or the true Elk (=Moose)? Can we suppose *a lost series of relations* connecting these genera with the [word illegible] type, & ramifying off . . . ? Wallace has, I think, put the matter well; and according to his theory, the various domestic races of animals have been fairly developed into *species*." This was of course hitting very closely to home because the first chapter of Darwin's *Origin* discussed variation under domestication, with Darwin using the analogy between human selection and natural selection frequently throughout his book.

In his typically loquacious fashion Blyth continued by citing many instances of variation, particularly of coloring, continually alluding back to Wallace with remarks such as "A triumph of a fact for friend Wallace to have hit upon!" and "capital data for Mr. Wallace. . . . Mr. Wallace could also well support his views by reference" to certain specimens collected in the Philippines and India. He then followed this mass of observations by reiterating his searching question: "What do *you* think of the paper in question? Has it at all unsettled your ideas regarding the persistence of species,—not perhaps so much from novelty of argument as by the lucid collection of facts & phenomena."

Even if Darwin had failed to read Wallace's work before, he cer-

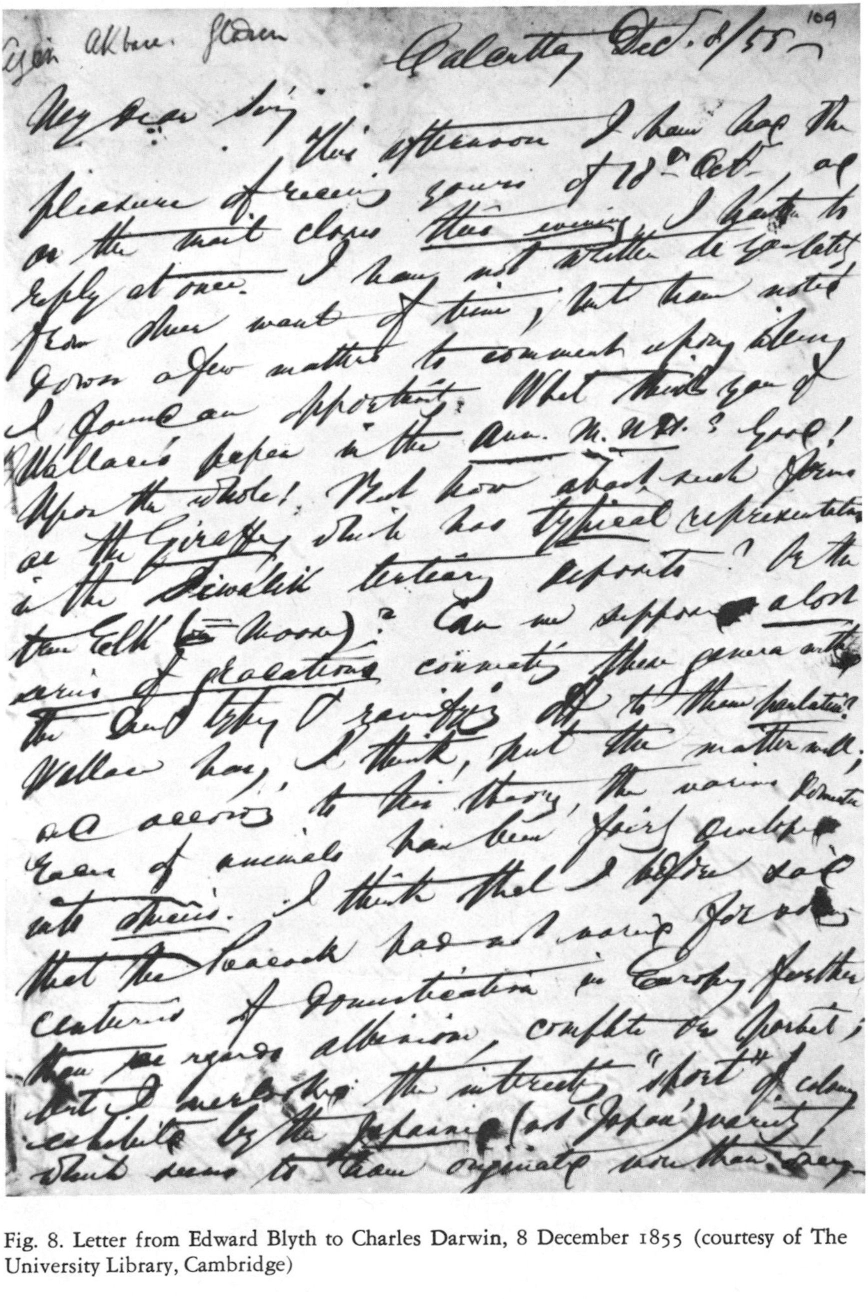

Calcutta Decr. 8/55

My dear Sir,

This afternoon I have had the pleasure of receiving yours of 18th Oct., as on the mail closes this evening, I hasten to reply at once. —

Fig. 8. Letter from Edward Blyth to Charles Darwin, 8 December 1855 (courtesy of The University Library, Cambridge)

tainly would have now and would not have thought that Wallace
was merely talking about "creation." If that viewpoint had been evident, Blyth would have mentioned it since he agreed with Lyell that
providence ordained creation. Quite the contrary, Blyth had a good
grasp of Wallace's points and merely supplied further evidence while
testing some points. In essence his letter was one of warm approbation of Wallace's case, culminated by a question which must have
evoked a fascinating reply. Unfortunately, that reply is lost.[70]

Wallace, who was completely unaware of the reflections stimulated
by his paper, first wrote to Darwin on 10 December 1856, and although Wallace's early letters to Darwin apparently have not survived,[71] except for one fragment at Cambridge, we can deduce from
Darwin's reply of 1 May 1857 that Wallace had discussed his ideas
on species: "By your letter and even still more by your paper in
the *Annals,* a year or more ago, I can plainly see that we have thought
very much alike and to a certain extent have come to similar conclusions." By stating that "This summer will make the twentieth year
(!) since I opened my first notebook on the question [of] how and in
what way do species and varieties differ from each other" and by
agreeing "to the truth of almost every word of your paper," Darwin
had admitted that he was to some extent also an evolutionist. And
his subsequent remark that "I have slowly adopted a distinct and
tangible idea" as to the causes and means of variation in a state of
nature must have greatly aroused Wallace's curiosity.[72]

In fact, Wallace's curiosity may have led him to begin this interesting correspondence. He has told us that he first wrote Darwin
about some ducks which he had sent to England, and a note in his
Species Notebook may have some bearing on that subject:

> The duck of Aru near *Anas Radjah* (Less[on]) is often bred,
> becomes tame & mixes with domestic breeds; the influence of
> its peculiar colours may be constantly seen. The same occurs with
> the Muscovy duck in S. America. The wild cock of Macassar

70. This seven-page letter of 8 Dec. 1855 to Darwin is in the Darwin
Papers, Box 98, Cambridge University Library. Italics by Blyth.

71. Francis Darwin's explanation about the destruction of some of his
father's letters is not completely satisfactory, especially concerning Wallace's
and Lyell's letters. *LLD,* pp. xviii–xix.

72. *WLR,* pp. 107–08.

mixes with the domestic breeds from which it can hardly be distinguished.[73]

This corroborates what we know about Darwin's current interests, for according to his letters of 1855 he was busily engaged in "comparing wild and tame ducks."[74] Wallace, "hearing that Mr. Darwin was interested in travels and collections, and was himself preparing some work on varieties and species," and probably also learning about Darwin's work on ducks, was no doubt eager to discover what another naturalist was thinking about the subject which fascinated him so much. Moreover, in paragraphs three and four of Darwin's first letter to Wallace, he discussed domestic and wild animals, with specific reference to "poultry," "pigeons" and "fowls," which tends to corroborate Wallace's statement.

But in the letter to Mr. Alfred Newton of 3 December 1887 is a statement which needs to be examined: "Through Stevens, my agent, I heard that he [Darwin] wanted curious *varieties* which he was studying." [75] This may very well have been Wallace's source of information about Darwin's interest, but two puzzles remain: (1) Mr. Stevens' name is not mentioned in paragraphs three and four of Darwin's letter which apparently refer to the specific content of Wallace's letter. This may, of course, be a mere oversight; however, (2) a bare, unqualified reference to "the Rajah" *is* found in the important paragraphs three and four. ("The Rajah has sent me some

73. Ibid., p. 86. Species Notebook, p. 91. This undated entry might have been in 1857 in response to Darwin's request for information about "any curious domestic breed" or it could have been made in 1856 as a random entry on a blank page. It is difficult to tell which is the case. My evaluation of these early letters differs from that of Beddall (1968), pp. 291, 314–15. Darwin's letter of 1 May 1857 does not support the contention that Wallace wrote Darwin because he had been reading Darwin's *Journal of Researches.* Nor is there proof that Wallace took a copy of Darwin's book to the Malay Archipelago with him. Quite the contrary, a bibliography of his library holdings, in possession of the Wallace grandsons, indicates he did not own a copy of the book when he was there. Wallace possibly had a copy while in the Amazon—after all the book was quite relevant while he was there—but it would have been lost with all his other possessions when his ship sank in 1852.

74. *LLD,* vol. I, pp. 407–12. *MLD,* vol. I, p. 87.

75. Wallace, "My Relations with Darwin in Reference to the Theory of Natural Selection" (1903), p. 78. *WLR,* p. 108; p. 86.

of his pigeons and fowls and *cat's* skins from Borneo and from Singapore.") The question is why did Darwin not say *which* Rajah, for he certainly could not assume—since this was his first letter to Wallace —that a relative stranger would know whom he was talking about *unless* Wallace had first mentioned the Rajah specifically in his letter to Darwin. It therefore appears that Wallace had indeed first mentioned the Rajah in his letter. The next question is: which Rajah had easy access to specimens from Borneo and Singapore, or to put it another way, was there a Rajah in Borneo or Singapore, or perhaps a Rajah in Borneo who sometimes visited Singapore, who was on friendly terms with Wallace, and evidently Darwin, with perhaps the additional qualification of being a man with some scientific interest? Such a man, uniquely fitting these qualifications, did live in the Malay Archipelago at that time: Sir James Brooke, Rajah of Sarawak on Borneo, was a famous Englishman, a Medalist of the Royal Geographical Society of London and a very good friend of Wallace. During one of his visits to London, he had promised Wallace (in 1852 or 1853) "every assistance" in exploring Borneo, and Wallace wrote that he was "hospitably entertained by Sir James Brooke, and and lived in his house whenever [he] was in the town of Sarawak in the intervals of [his] journeys."[76] The excellent hospitality, conversation, and Sir James Brooke's "admirable" library must have provided Wallace with a pleasant change from the forbidding jungles of the Archipelago, and during these stimulating conversations with his "clever visitor," as Wallace was called, or in a letter sent at a later time, we may assume that Rajah Brooke would refer to any letter he had received from Charles Darwin. Indeed, it would have been most *unlikely* for the Rajah *not* to have mentioned such a letter from another English naturalist who was also interested in the species problem, a problem which Wallace had discussed during his stays in Sarawak.[77]

Thus, we may assume that Wallace wrote Darwin about ducks and that he had heard about Darwin's interest perhaps through his agent Mr. Stevens, or perhaps through Sir James Brooke. We can also deduce from Darwin's responses some of what Wallace said—which probably went something like this: Although you should be certain to keep

76.   *MA*, pp. 34–35. *My Life*, vol. I, p. 341.

77.   St. John, *The Life of Sir James Brooke* (1879), pp. 274, 315–16. Wallace and Sir James definitely corresponded. *MA*, pp. 62–63.

domestic and wild varieties of ducks distinct ("I have acted already in accordance with your advice of keeping domestic varieties, and those appearing in a state of nature distinct." Darwin.), it may very well be that the domesticated and wild varieties have descended from one parent stock [implied by his notes on ducks as quoted from his Species Notebook]. ("I must confess, however, I rather doubt the truth of the now very prevalent doctrine of all our domestic animals having descended from several wild stocks; though I do not doubt that it is so in some cases." Darwin.) In my opinion the differences between the domestic and wild varieties cannot be ascribed merely to the effect of climatic conditions. ("I most entirely agree with you on the little effect of 'climatic conditions' which one sees referred to ad nauseam in all books: I suppose some very little effect must be attributed to such influences, but I fully believe that they are very slight." Darwin.) It also appears that Wallace thought the hybrid animals mentioned above were not sterile as commonly believed. ("I think there is rather better evidence on the sterility of hybrid animals than you seem to admit." Darwin.)[78]

As the words of Darwin must accurately reflect to a large extent what Wallace wrote, so also do Darwin's words perhaps reflect his own subconscious thoughts. We have seen the suggestions by Wallace regarding island flora and fauna which led Sir Charles Lyell to discuss the species question with Darwin on 13 April 1856 and three days later on 16 April 1856. Lyell then insistently exhorted Darwin to publish, and Darwin, quite obviously concerned by these remarks as well as those of Blyth, was quickly moved to action. No doubt he would have liked to discover precisely how far Wallace had progressed since his 1855 Paper. And if this is so, it would account for the closing remark in his first letter to Wallace: "One of the subjects on which I have been experimenting, and which [has] cost me much trouble, is the means of distribution of all organic beings found on oceanic islands, and any facts on this subject would be received most gratefully. Land molluscs are a great perplexity to me.[79]

For some reason—probably because it was his first letter to Darwin and consequently not an appropriate time to reveal heterodox views —Wallace apparently did not refer to his 1855 Paper. Why else

78. These quotations from Darwin's letter to Wallace are found in *WLR*, p. 108.

79. *WLR*, pp. 108–09.

would Darwin be so specific? "By your letter and even still more by your paper in the *Annals, a year or more ago* . . ."[80] By mentioning this paper, however, Darwin had opened the door for additional discussion of the principles set forth therein, and judging from Darwin's lengthy responses, Wallace's letter of 27 September 1857 was long and detailed—once more Wallace had someone like Bates who agreed "to the truth of almost every word" of his views on evolution and was willing to discuss (very cautiously however) the species problem with him. And now it became crystal clear that Wallace was working on a much larger work on precisely the same topic as Darwin himself was: "The mere statement and illustration of that paper is of course but preliminary to an attempt at a detailed proof of it, the plan of which I have arranged, & in fact written. . . ."[81]

On the reverse side of this fragment (Fig. 9) is another interesting response to Darwin who had asked in his 1 May 1857 letters: "Can you tell me positively that black jaguars or leopards are believed generally or always to pair with black?" Wallace replied:

With regard to the black Jaguars always breeding *inter se*, it is of course a point not capable of proof, but the black & the spotted animals are generally confined to separate localities, & among the hundreds & thousands of the skins which are articles of commerce I have never heard of a particoloured one having occurred. I *think* there is a difference of form the black being the more slender & graceful animal.[82]

Other parts of his letter can be inferred from Darwin's prompt reply of 22 December 1857. In addition to his projected plans for a

80. *WLR,* p. 107.   Of course, it had been almost *one year exactly* that Lyell had recommended Wallace's 1855 Paper to Darwin! Italics are mine.

81. Letter fragment, Wallace to Darwin, 27 Sept. 1957; Darwin Papers, Cambridge University Library. See above chapter 3, p. 30.

82. A letter to Darwin from W. B. Tegetmeier of 29 November [1857], located at the New York Botanic Garden Library in the Bronx, alludes to Wallace. "I really now think I shall have material to judge of Poultry of world, for Mr. Wallace is collecting in the Malay Archipelago; but the carriage is costing me a fortune! The Persian Box alone cost £ 4–4s–10d." Dr. Sydney Smith, Cambridge University, kindly supplied me with this transcription. This may mean that Wallace collected some items for him or the "Persian Box" could refer to some items, mentioned earlier in his letter ("I have got skin of common black handsome Persian Cock & Hen, . . . sent me by Hon.[ble] Ch. Murray."). I think the latter is the case.

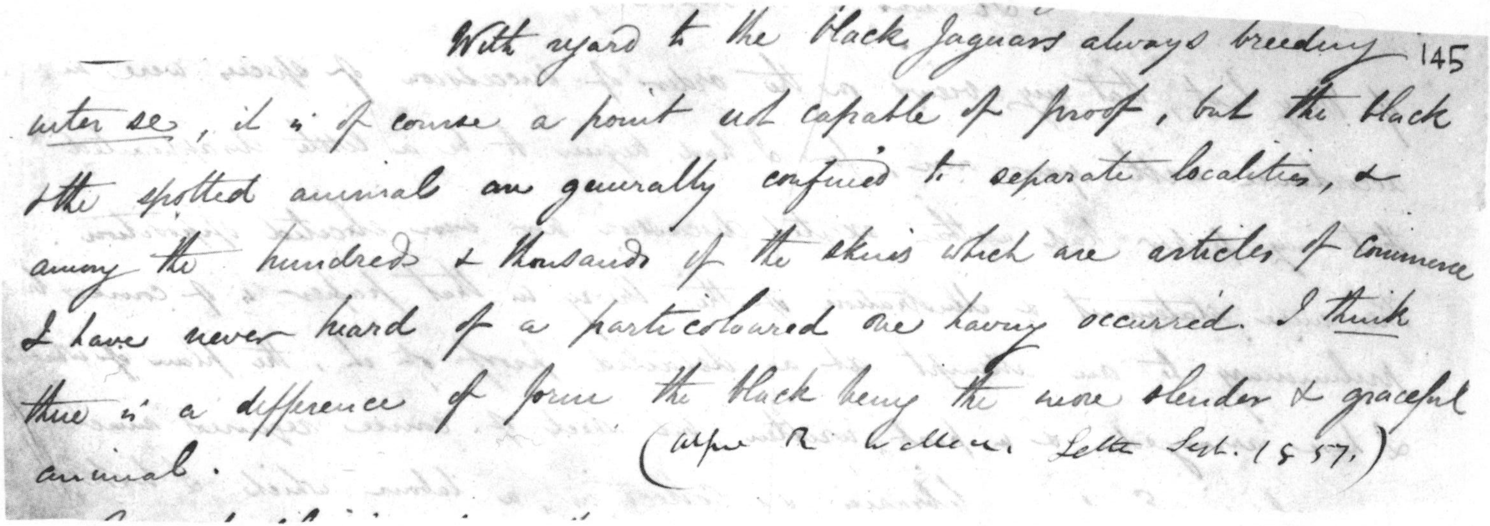

Fig. 9. Fragment of a letter from A. R. Wallace to Charles Darwin, 27 September 1857 (courtesy of The University Library, Cambridge)

lengthy treatment of the species question, Wallace had alluded to the conclusions of his 1855 Paper ("Though agreeing with you on your conclusions in your paper, I believe I go much further than you." Darwin.), and then he had shown how these principles were specifically applicable in the case of the Aru Islands. ("I have not yet seen your paper on [the] distribution of animals in the Aru Islands. I shall read it with the *utmost* interest; for I think that [is] the most interesting quarter of the whole globe in respect to distribution." Darwin.)[83] Wallace's letter had probably described the manner in which he had successfully applied his 1855 law to natural phenomena in the Archipelago, thus explaining why the faunas of New Guinea and Australia, following their separation in the not too distant past, contained many allied species, but few identical ones. His explanation also dispensed with such ideas as "centers of creation." One simple natural law explained the phenomena.[84]

Darwin's reaction to Wallace's ideas on the former connection of islands to continents was strong: "I shall be quite prepared to subscribe to your doctrine of subsidence [regarding the Aru Islands]. . . . But I can see that you are inclined to go *much* further than I am in regard to the former connection of oceanic islands with continents.[85]

Wallace's pointed question regarding land shells on isolated oceanic islands served as another warning signal that Wallace—as Lyell surely

83. *WLR*, p. 109.

84. Wallace, "On the Natural History of the Aru Islands" (1857), pp. 482–83.

85. *WLR*, pp. 109–10. Darwin strongly disagreed with Edward Forbes on the question of subsidence. See *LLD*, Vol. I, pp. 398–99. Wallace received letters from both Darwin (dated 1 May 1857) and Bates (dated 19 November 1856) simultaneously in July 1857 (*WLR*, p. 53) and possibly he wrote to Darwin what he was to reply to Bates a short time afterward: "In this archipelago there are two distinct faunas rigidly circumscribed, which differ as much as do those of Africa and South America, and more than those of Europe and North America; yet there is nothing on the map or on the face of the islands to mark their limits. The boundary line passes between islands closer together than others belonging to the same group. I believe the western part to be a separated portion of continental Asia, while the eastern is a fragmentary prolongation of a former west Pacific continent. In mammalia and birds the distinction is marked by genera, families, and even orders confined to one region; in insects by a number of genera, and little groups of peculiar species, the families of insects having generally a very wide or universal distribution." (*My Life*, vol. I, pp. 358–59.)

had pointed out emphatically—was searching for the right kind of evidence to support the evolutionary hypothesis. ("You ask about land-shells on islands far distant from continents: Madeira has a few identical with those of Europe, and here the evidence is really good, as some of them are sub-fossil." Darwin.[86]) This is precisely the kind of evidence Lyell had carefully examined before talking with Darwin in April 1856. Furthermore, Wallace's question as to whether Darwin was going to discuss man in his work on species and varieties could have only confirmed the conclusion that two of Wallace's letters, a brilliant paper, his own reading of that paper, Blyth's letter, and Lyell's warnings had made inescapable: Wallace was an ardent and intelligent evolutionist quite prepared to "go the whole orang."

Thus, by 22 December 1857 Darwin was fully cognizant of Wallace's progress, for Wallace himself had specifically informed him, and Blyth had also discussed the 1855 Paper at length. Moreover, Lyell had issued repeated warnings, and it is these warnings to which Darwin referred just after receiving Wallace's paper "On the Tendency of Varieties to Depart Indefinitely from the Original Type" in June 1858:

> Some year or so ago [actually more than two years] you recommended me to read a paper by Wallace in the "Annals," which had interested you, and, as I was writing to him [over a year later], I know this would please him much, so I told him. He has to-day sent me the enclosed, and asked me to forward it to you. It seems to me well worth reading. Your words have come true with a vengeance—that I should be forestalled. You said this, when I explained to you here very briefly my views of "Natural Selection" depending upon the struggle for existence.[87]

The sentence "Your words have come true with a vengeance—that I should be forestalled" can now be properly understood. Lyell had pointed out to Darwin that Wallace's law could be explained by natural selection and probably suggested that Wallace, therefore, was a man to watch carefully; he might even anticipate Darwin if something—a sketch perhaps—were not published in order to establish priority. This letter, written in June 1858, also confirms, as does all

86. *WLR*, p. 110.
87. *LLD*, vol. I, 473.

the other evidence, that Darwin first explained to Lyell his views concerning natural selection on 16 April 1856, the date Lyell took notes on his discussion with Darwin on the principle of natural selection, and which he closed by referring specifically to Wallace's 1855 Paper. Considering the numerous explicit storm warnings available, it is incredible that Darwin did not follow Lyell's perspicacious advice sooner.

8 "On the Tendency of Varieties to Depart Indefinitely from the Original Type" February 1858

Everyone has experienced one or more unforgettable moments in his life, moments that never completely fade from memory. Wallace's discovery of natural selection in February 1858 was certainly a moment of genius that never paled in his memory, and his numerous recitations have firmly established his story in the folklore of the history of science. In the following vivid example, he specified even the temperature!

> At that time I was suffering from a rather severe attack of intermittent fever [malaria] at Ternate in the Moluccas, and one day while lying on my bed during the cold fit, wrapped in blankets, though the thermometer was at 88°F., the problem [of how species transformations occur] again presented itself to me, and something led me to think of the "positive checks" described by Malthus in his "Essay on Population," a work I had read several years before [actually about thirteen years] and which had made a deep and permanent impression on my mind.[1]

Additional testimony regarding his specific location during this great moment is provided by his famous paper of 1858 "On the Tendency of Varieties to Depart Indefinitely from the Original Type," which was published with the following words at the bottom of the last page: "Ternate, February, 1858."[2]

Despite this substantial and apparently unimpeachable evidence, Wallace was not on the island of Ternate when he discovered natural selection late in February 1858, and the familiar allusion to Ternate in his story is a fabrication which Wallace's own unguarded words destroy. The truth of the matter is that he was on an island some ten or twenty miles away, the large, but obscure, Dutch island of Gilolo

1. Wallace, *Natural Selection and Tropical Nature* (1891), p. 20.
2. For his other accounts of this discovery see above chapter 6, p. 80, note 1. Wallace customarily stated his location and the date at the end of his articles.

(now more commonly called Halmahera); and he was there during the entire month of February as well as part of the month of January. Part of this chapter will be devoted to the destruction once and for all of another familiar legend in the history of science, a legend consciously manufactured by one of the greatest Victorian naturalists.

TERNATE AND GILOLO: 8 JANUARY TO 1 MARCH 1858.

The story begins in Wallace's personal journal for 1857–58, where he stated that after leaving the island of Amboyna, he arrived at Ternate on the morning of 8 January 1858. "After a fortnight spent on Ternate," he continued, "I determined to visit the island of Gilolo for a month & then return to prepare for a voyage to N. Guinea in one of Mr. Duivenboden's vessels which was expected to leave about the middle of March. We left early in the morning" about 5:00 A.M.[3] Use of the past tense tells us he wrote the words after his departure from Ternate. Since an entry in his important Species Notebook is dated "January 20, 1858, Gilolo"—that is roughly two weeks after 8 January—we may safely assume that he left Ternate according to plan somewhere around that date, possibly January nineteenth or twentieth.[4] The last two manuscript entries I have just cited—the one discussing his decision to leave Ternate and go to Gilolo and the two-page note signed "January 20, 1858, Gilolo"—were no doubt written when he had a few moments to spare, possibly 20 January 1858.

After about two days at Sedingole, Gilolo, Wallace proceeded to Dodinga in the narrow central isthmus of Gilolo where he secured a small hut as living quarters and for which he paid "five gilders for a month's rent"—obviously intending to carry out his plan of staying until March. Judging from a subsequent comment, he did indeed carry out his plan: "On the 1st of March I returned to Ternate to await the return of Mr. Duivenboden's schooner from Macassar in which I had decided to make a voyage to N. Guinea." We also learn that the mail steamer—on which he sent his famous paper "On the Tendency of Varieties to Depart Indefinitely from the Original Type"—stopped at Ternate on 9 March 1858. After leaving Ternate on 25 March 1858, he did not return until 15 August 1858.[5]

3. Journal, 1857–58, section 122, first sentence; section 125.
4. Species Notebook, p. 109.
5. Journal, 1857–58, section 125 (See also *MA*, p. 313); section 128, first sentence; fifth sentence; sections 129 and 149. This is precisely when he could have expected an answer to the letter and paper he sent to Darwin. This journal covers the period from 25 March 1858 to about 29 October 1859.

From the uninterrupted narrative in his journals, it is clear that
Wallace was on Gilolo from about 20 January 1858 until precisely
1 March 1858—certainly the entire month of February. But what does
the published version of his travels in his famous *The Malay Archipelago* tell us about his movements on the island of Gilolo? There we
learn that he "made but few and comparatively shorts visits to this
large and little known island," and the chapter caption refers specifically to *March* and *September* 1858 as the time of his visits.[6] Unknown to the reader, however, his narrative which purportedly described his March 1858 visit, actually described his visit between 20
January and 1 March. Even a cursory comparison of his journal and
his book on the Malay Archipelago will confirm this observation.
Nevertheless, he actually did visit Gilolo on March 28–29 while on his
way to New Guinea, but that brief stay at Gilolo was not his *first*
visit: "My first stay was at Dodinga, situated at the head of a deep bay
opposite Ternate."[7] The chapter caption referring to a March visit
clearly misleads any reader, and Wallace later confused the story even
more by observing in his autobiography published in 1905: "During
my first months of my residence at Ternate I made two visits to the
large island of Gilolo, where my hunters obtained a number of very
fine birds, but owing to the absence of good virgin forest and my own
ill-health, I obtained very few insects."[8] Two points should be observed here. In the first place, contrary to his account in *The Malay
Archipelago*, Wallace made two visits to Gilolo during the early part
of his stay at Ternate. We now know that these visits were from about
20 January to 1 March and 28 March through the afternoon of 29
March. The second significant point is that he was sick during this
period—his precise condition when he discovered natural selection.

6. *MA*, p. 313. Wallace also referred to a later brief stay of a few days
between 5 November 1860 and 3 January 1861 *(MA*, p. 317), but his journal
for that period is completely silent concerning any excursions to Gilolo.

7. Journal, 1858–59, section 129. "On the afternoon of March 25th [I]
left Ternate in schooner "Hester Helena" bound on a trading voyage to the
N. Coast of N. Guinea. . . . Having light air calms we reached Ganeh on the
south end of Gilolo on the 28th & came to an anchor to fill up our water casks
& buy a few provisions. I sent one of my boys to shoot & went myself to look
for insects. The country was forest covered & rugged—very similar to that
about Dodinga and I obtained a few nice insects. . . . in the afternoon of the
29th [we] proceeded on our way to Dorey harbor [New Guinea]."

8. *MA*, p. 313. Journal, 1857–58, section 125. His description of the
Portuguese fort *(MA*, pp. 313–14) comes substantially from Journal, 1857–58,
section 126. *My Life*, vol. I, p. 363.

It is also important that his published narrative in *The Malay Archipelago,* which purports to describe his visit in March 1858, actually corresponds to—and obviously is based on—his journal entries made between 20 January 1858 and 1 March 1858.

These illuminating journal entries are so helpful that we can almost pinpoint the onset of his bout with malaria during February 1858. In his journal he observed with obvious satisfaction: "In my first walk, I obtained a few insects quite new to me and was very pleased with my prospects of making a fine collection."[9] In his published version in *The Malay Archipelago,* this sentence became: "I got some very nice insects here, though, owing to illness most of the time, my collection was a small one."[10] The sentence just quoted from his journal is the last sentence of section 126; the following section—that is section 127—is devoted exclusively to a discussion of the natives of Gilolo, who fascinated him. He observed: "The natives of this large and almost unknown island were examined by me with much interest, as they would help to determine whether, independent of mixed races, there is any transition from the Malay to the Papuan type." His bout with malaria probably followed his description of his first walk on Gilolo but must have preceded his return to Ternate on 1 March 1858. And the only remarks in his journal between that walk and his return to Ternate specifically discuss the native inhabitants of Gilolo. This apparently corroborates my contention earlier in this work that immediately before he formulated the principle of natural selection, Wallace was thinking about the origins of the Malay tribes, specifically from an evolutionist's point of view; "this interest in ethnology led him to recall the work of Malthus, and it was this new perspective which illuminated the species problem for Wallace." Or if I may put it another way, Wallace arrived at this important conclusion about natural selection shortly after section 127 in his journal in which he discussed the natives of Gilolo in a most suggestive manner.

One last example may be adduced which further demonstrates that Wallace altered the narrative in his book *The Malay Archipelago.* In his journal during February 1858 he made the following observation about the natives of Gilolo: "Neither is their hair *frizzly* or *wooly,* but merely *crisp* or *waved,* yet it has a roughness or slight wooliness of

9. Journal, 1857–58, section 126, last sentence.
10. *MA,* p. 314.

appearance produced, I think, by the individual hairs not laying parallel & close together, which is very different from the *smooth & glossy,* though *coarse,* tresses everywhere found in the unmixed Malayan race."[11] In his classic *Malay Archipelago* he observed:: "Neither straight, *smooth* or *glossy,* like all true Malays, nor so *frizzly* and *wooly* as the perfect Papuan type, but always *crisp, waved,* and *rough,* such as often occurs among the true Papuans, but never among Malays."[12] The only basis for this observation in *The Malay Archipelago* for September 1858 is Wallace's journal account for February 1858. The similarities obviously are very pronounced.

Feverish though he may have been, Wallace fully realized where he was during this long-sought moment, and during his subsequent accounts of these events he had ample opportunities to correct any possible misconceptions. He chose not to do this, however, and instead altered the actual story, thus establishing the legend we all know.

TERNATE. 25 JANUARY 1858.

Although this story is already complicated enough, I must refer to an obvious anomaly. In a letter to Henry Walter Bates, his former traveling companion who was still in South America, Wallace added a postscript dated "Ternate. Jan. 25 [, 1858]." In this note he said: "About 10 miles to the E. [of Ternate] is the coast of the large island of *Gilolo* [,] perhaps the most perfect Entomological "terra incognita' now to be found. I am not aware that a single insect has ever been collected there, & can not find it given as the locality of any insect in my catalogues or descriptions. *In about a week I go for a month collecting there,* & then return to prepare for a voyage to N. Guinea."[13] If the note dated "January 20, 1858, Gilolo" in Wallace's *Species Notebook* is correct, then the note to Bates, dated "Ternate. January 25 [, 1858]" is confusing to say the least, since Wallace could *not* move his scientific equipment easily without native helpers and a boat, both of which he almost needed to shanghai! That is, he could not simply jump into any handy boat and quickly return to Ternate on a moment's notice. On a later trip to Gilolo, he spent five days procuring use of a boat and some men, and Wallace described that as an unusually

11. Journal, 1857–58, section 127. Italics are mine.
12. *MA,* p. 316. Italics are mine.
13. *WLR,* p. 55. Italics are mine.

short space of time.[14] Once he arrived on Gilolo, he was essentially stranded there until he returned on March first. However, if the postscript to Bates were dated 15 January, not 25 January, then the postscript would have been written *before* he went to Gilolo and would therefore agree perfectly with the sequence of events which unfolds in the journal and Species Notebook. And the internal evidence of the postscript suggests 15 January rather than 25 January.

You will recall his words just cited, "in about a week I go for a month collecting there, & then return to prepare for a voyage to N. Guinea." Assuming for a moment that 15 January is correct, then approximately one week later—five days to be exact—would be 20 January, which is the entry in his Species Notebook. The big question, of course, is why was the postscript dated 25 January if it should have been dated 15 January? Several answers are possible, but whatever the answer, the date 25 January is apparently erroneous if all the other dates I have cited are correct; but even if it were correct, that date would still have placed him on Gilolo during the month of February. To reiterate for the last time: *"In about a week,* I go for a month collecting there."

What conclusions can we reach from these various facts? In the first place, Wallace's journal and Species Notebook present a straightforward account, complete with dates, and devoid of contradictions. Since they were written contemporary with the events described, they probably are fairly reliable. They describe his arrival on Ternate on 8 January 1858, his trip to Gilolo on about 20 January and his return to Ternate on 1 March. They also relate the important information that the mail steamer arrived at Ternate on 9 March. Wallace's later account in *The Malay Archipelago,* which was first published in 1869, and which was based upon his journals and notebook, contains crucial omissions and errors. Specifically, he failed to mention that he had decided to go to Gilolo after about two weeks at Ternate, that he was in fact on Gilolo on 20 January, and that he returned from there to Ternate on 1 March. Quite the contrary, he conveyed the impression that he was on Gilolo for only a brief time during March, yet described events that occur chronologically in his journal between 20 January and 1 March. Furthermore, he described his trip to Gilolo in September 1858 as his "first attempt at collecting on Gilolo," which is clearly

14. Journal, 1858–59, section 153, last sentence.

an error. His descriptions of the natives, supposedly made in September 1858, actually were made during January or, more likely, February 1858. These alterations in his published account are too numerous and egregious to be mere careless errors, especially when we realize that Wallace normally kept rather careful records. Never openly to admit his presence on Gilolo during February 1858 is clearly a deception.

The pressing question, of course, is *why* did Wallace carry out such a deception? What difference did it really make if he was on Gilolo rather than Ternate? A distance of ten or twenty miles and a mere three to five hours travel time probably had little influence on his actual discovery of natural selection, and catching Wallace in his fib does not alter the fact and importance of his discovery. Nevertheless, Wallace's mendacity does reveal a great deal about his character. While we can never perhaps fully understand his motives, we do know that he was a young man extremely anxious to establish a name for himself. He had pondered upon the question of how species evolve for about thirteen years, and he was acutely aware of the far-reaching significance of his discovery. No doubt he realized that such momentous events tend to be recounted time and again in the pages of history books. It simply would not do to make such a discovery on what he described as the "large and little known island of Gilolo," a veritable "terra incognita."[15] Even half a century after Wallace left there, knowledge of the island was still very incomplete, and it was still politically less important than its small neighbor on the west. Wallace, on the other hand, affectionately described Ternate in quite different terms. It was "one of the most celebrated of the old spice islands" and the sultan of Ternate was once celebrated throughout the East for his power and magnificence. Furthermore, the famous Sir Francis Drake had visited there in 1579; it was a headquarters for the Dutch government in the Moluccas and a relatively civilized place, obviously a place where, to use his own words, he "spent many happy days."[16] The world had heard of marvelous Ternate; after this, the world would never forget her. It was a marriage effected with consummate skill. Moreover, who would know about his deception? He was isolated from civilization, and his letter and paper, which he sent

15. *WLR*, p. 55. *MA*, p. 313.
16. *MA*, pp. 304–12, esp. 306–07.

to Charles Darwin, were actually mailed from Ternate, which was to
be his headquarters for some time and which was, therefore, his mail-
ing address where Darwin would send his eventual reply. That the
deception has been maintained well over one hundred and ten years
clearly demonstrates that Wallace was able to carry it out.

The picture of Wallace that seems to emerge from this curious incident is that of a somewhat romantic scientist, with a definite flair
for a colorful story. Gilolo was an unknown island at the end of the
world, a forbidding and unpleasant wilderness; it lacked the necessary image to accompany a revolutionary scientific discovery. Wallace
evidently preferred to associate his discovery with one of the most
famous and colorful spice islands. Gilolo, the rightful bride, has been
compelled to wait for her moment of glory.

Perhaps this incident also helps us to understand better the later
"aberrations" of Wallace the English naturalist: he was keenly interested in spiritualism, socialism, and the campaign against vaccination;
he supported land nationalization and engaged in other activities
which have done much to vitiate his reputation as a scientist. The
Jekyll side of his character has very deep roots, beginning with his
early naïve acceptance in 1845 of Robert Chambers' heretical theory
of evolution, a theory rejected by most other scientists. His subsequent
alteration of the account of his discovery of natural selection on Gilolo
is simply another illuminating incident in a fascinating career. It is
perhaps the obverse of the story of George Washington and the cherry
tree.

9 MARCH 1858

This examination of Wallace's deception has perhaps uncovered
still another deception. I have mentioned several times that the mail
boat arrived at Ternate on 9 March 1858, when Wallace posted letters
to Frederick and Henry Walter Bates as well as his famous paper to
Darwin.[17] From another unpublished source, written by Wallace
himself, we know that mail normally took about ten weeks to travel

17. Since his letters were written and the mail boat of 9 March 1858 was
the only one he would see for some time, it is safe to assume he mailed these
letters at the same time. Considering the importance he attached to his paper,
he would not have delayed sending it, and in all his versions of the events, he
claimed to have sent the paper on the next mail boat. There is no reason to
believe he would hold on to the letters to the Bates brothers. If he had the
letters would have arrived long after his communication to Darwin.

from Ternate to London. [18] Wallace could therefore anticipate a reply approximately 20 weeks from March 9, or about the first week of August 1858. I have made some allowance for Darwin to compose his reply, but that reply did not arrive until September or October, and it did not bear glad tidings for Wallace; instead, he learned that he was to share the glory of his discovery with Charles Darwin.[19]

What do we know about the fate of Wallace's communication after he mailed it? According to Darwin in a letter to Charles Lyell, he received Wallace's article on the eighteenth; no month or year is provided by him on the letter itself. Darwin's son later inferred that he had received it on 18 June 1858 simply because the letters preceding 1 July seem to have been written in June.[20] No evidence has been previously adduced to establish or question this date of 18 June 1858. But 10 weeks from 9 March, when the communication was mailed, is precisely 18 *May,* one month before Darwin acknowledged receiving it. Knowing the numerous delays in such matters, we should perhaps allow some leeway, although one month appears to be an excessive allowance. Fortunately, an illuminating piece of evidence exists concerning this matter.

Although the article and covering letter to Darwin have been lost, the letters to Frederick and Henry Walter Bates—sent at the same time, with Henry's letter folded and placed inside the letter to Frederick—have survived, and we know from a very clear postmark that the letter to Frederick Bates arrived in London on precisely 3 June 1858 (Fig. 10).[21] It is only reasonable to assume that Wallace's communication to Darwin arrived at the same time and was delivered to Darwin at Down House on 3 June 1858, the same day Bates's letter arrived in Leicester. If this sequence is correct, as it appears to be, we must ask ourselves what Darwin was doing with Wallace's paper during the two weeks between 4 June and 18 June. Without question he was stunned as he had never been before. He had in his hands a manuscript which, so he said, used terms which stood as heads of his

18. Curiously, the end of the first paragraph in his postscript to Bates of 25 {sic} January 1858 is deleted by Marchant. *WLR,* p. 55. And following the word "volcano" are the words: "The Dutch steamer comes here every month & brings letters from England in about 10 weeks." Letter in possession of the Wallace grandsons.

19. Wallace, *My Life,* vol. I, p. 365.

20. *LLD,* vol. I, p. 473.

21. Letter in the possession of the Wallace grandsons.

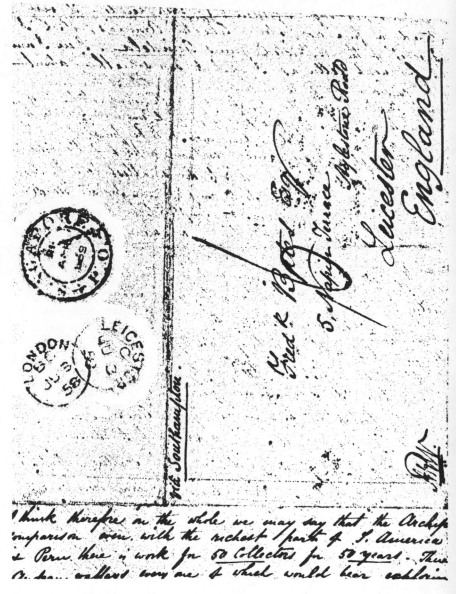

Fig. 10. Envelope stamped June 3, 1858 (in London and in Leicester), to Frederick Bates (courtesy of A. J. R. Wallace and R. R. Wallace; dates unretouched)

chapters. The situation was one of the most remarkable ones in the history of biology. The question was how to respond.

At this point, I must end this discussion with a series of question marks. Assuming Darwin did have Wallace's manuscript for two weeks before telling anyone, what effect did it have on his ideas? According to Darwin's personal Journal, on 14 April he had begun a section on divergence in his long version of the *Origin;* he finished that section on 12 June.[22] Furthermore, the problem of divergence was the one problem which, by his own admission, he had not worked out satisfactorily in his earlier sketch of 1842 and his essay of 1844, although he apparently did discuss the subject briefly in a letter to the American botanist Asa Gray in 1857.[23] Did Wallace's paper provide any special insights for Darwin into this or any other problem? Wallace may simply have reinforced past fleeting ideas or illuminated some obscure point. Before drawing any hasty conclusions about this matter, however, we must now carefully reexamine Darwin's *manuscript* versions of the 1842 Sketch, the 1844 Essay and the long version of the *Origin*.[24] We may ultimately find that all we have is an extended two-week period of extreme trauma on the part of Darwin;

22. de Beer, "Darwin Journal" (1959), p. 14.

23. See de Beer, *Darwin Notebooks, 2*, 2 (1960), 40, who claims Darwin grasped the principle of divergence before 1840; Darwin's statements in his autobiography refer not to the fact of divergence itself, he says, "but to a causal explanation of how it occurs and increases." The letter from Darwin to Gray of Sept. 5 [1857] is at Harvard. See note 27 below. John L. Brooks, Dept. of Biology, Yale University, has hypothesized that "Wallace was the first and the *only* person to conceive of the dynamics of the formation of the observed patterns of organic diversity through the action of inevitable natural process. It is his further contention that Charles Darwin appropriated, without any acknowledgment, the concept of 'divergence' as it appears in the *Origin of Species* from Wallace's 1855 paper and the manuscript that Wallace sent to Darwin from the Dutch East Indies early in 1858." "Report on Grant No. 4595," *Year Book 1968. The American Philosophical Society* (1969), pp. 534–35, ref. p. 534, I have seen none of his evidence, but his argument fails to mention the Asa Gray letter, which seems to bear the correct date and which thereby attenuates the force of Brooks's arguments. Nevertheless, I strongly agree with Prof. Brooks that the subject of divergence bears close examination, especially Darwin's "note on divergence" added to Ch. VI of the long version of the *Origin*.

24. The MS versions are at Cambridge. Professor Robert Stauffer, Univ. of Wisconsin, is publishing the long version of the *Origin*. Although I have examined some of the relevant MSS. at Cambridge, I am not yet prepared to offer final conclusions. The "1842 Sketch" is especially difficult to use because it is

on the other hand, we may find that still another important chapter needs to be written about the Darwin-Wallace relationship.

THE JOINT PAPERS

Whenever Wallace's paper arrived in England, and that point seems clear to me, the history of the subsequent events begins shortly after 18 June when Lyell received Darwin's letter.[25] Although there are still significant gaps in the correspondence between Darwin Hooker, and Lyell, much has nevertheless been written about the flurry of communications preceding 1 July 1858.[26] As a result of adroit handling of the matter by Darwin's "two best and kindest friends," his claim to priority was presented to the Linnean Society of London on that first day of July 1858. Considering the fact that Wallace's paper was the catalyst responsible for the presentation of the papers, and in light of Darwin's cries of self-abnegation in the matter, it is astonishing to find Wallace's brilliant effort at the tail end of the presentation

---

a scrawled jumble of words and ideas, making it difficult to ascertain when some sections were added. After examining many of the relevant manuscripts, Brooks concludes that there is "no evidence that Darwin had a true grasp of 'divergence' before May–June 1858, the period when the Wallace manuscript was in his hands." Brooks, ibid., p. 535. Again, however, the Darwin letter to Gray is conveniently excluded.

25. Letter 58 at the American Philosophical Society. The original is dated "18th [June 1858]," with the June 1858 added either by Lyell or Francis Darwin. Unless the envelope exists or Lyell wrote the date on the letter, the exact date Lyell received it will remain unknown for the moment. The date, the 18th, on the letter by itself, however, proves little. In fact, Darwin could have written the letter June 8th and changed the date later to June 18th. The only concrete, objective evidence is the Bates letter which has the distinct London postmark of June 3, with the additional postmark of June 3 when it arrived in Leicester. It could have been delivered the same day. If Lyell entered a note about the letter in one of his notebooks, we can ascertain precisely when he received the letter.

26. According to Loewenberg (1959), p. 90, note 123, "Documentary evidence for these developments is almost entirely lacking. There are no letters in the published Lyell correspondence relating to these events. Even the replies [in response] to Darwin's letters to Lyell of June 18, 25, and 26 are missing. Hooker's letters to both Lyell and Darwin have disappeared. Wallace's letter and original MS of his essay were never returned to him and have not been found. The published Darwin correspondence does not fill the gaps. Hooker's recollections, recounted in his address to the Linnean Society meeting of July 1, 1908, remain the only source of direct knowledge." See also Beddall (1968), pp. 309–18.

—preceded by a joint statement by Lyell and Hooker, an excerpt from Darwin's 1844 Essay, and an *abstract* of a *copy* of a letter from Darwin to Asa Gray, reputed to have been written in October 1857.[27] These communications, although largely ignored at the time, mark the beginning of the new era in evolutionary biology.

The Wallace-Darwin papers themselves, however, do not discuss the case for evolution per se, but rather, they present arguments and evidence supporting a mechanism—natural selection—which explains why change may occur. The arguments to support the case for evolution itself were not included for good reasons. As far as Wallace was concerned, his 1855 Paper had already set forth numerous reasons for believing that species evolve through natural laws. It was the first part of his hypothesis; the second part was that "there is no difference in nature between the origin of species and varieties"—represented by his paper of 1858.[28]

Darwin, on the other hand, apparently did not think it was necessary to establish priority on the question of evolution as distinguished from its mechanism. After all, many others had argued—at times brilliantly—the case for evolution. The claim to natural selection was the real issue. While remonstrating that "it is miserable in me to care at all about priority," Darwin was clearly very concerned,[29] and he hoped for a favorable resolution of the matter. Had he not, he could easily have insisted that Wallace receive better treatment and could have prevented the situation from developing as it did—which was clearly to Darwin's advantage. One must ask why it was imperative that the joint papers be presented with such celerity if Darwin's priority were not being protected. That Wallace was not consulted on the matter and was presented with a *fait accompli* with no real opportunity to protest—he never saw page proofs nor heard of the resolutions of the matter until his paper was *in print,* nor was his original paper returned—is a black mark on the characters of Darwin, Hooker, and Lyell. Darwin's halfhearted pleas that he would take a back seat to Wallace cannot be taken seriously.

Moreover, Darwin's letter to Lyell, dated 25 June 1858 by Francis

27. The original letter at Harvard University is dated Sept. 5 [1857]. According to Dupree, the copy sent to Gray is in another hand than Darwin's but is corrected by him. "It varies in detail from the version published at the Linnean Society." Dupree, *Asa Gray* (1968), pp. 246–47, 458–59, note 23.
28. *WLR,* p. 54.
29. *LLD,* vol. I, p. 476.

Darwin, contains a significant misconception. Darwin had remarked: "There is nothing in Wallace's sketch which is not written out much fuller in my sketch, copied out in 1844, and read by Hooker some dozen years ago."[30] Since Lyell in all likelihood had not read the 1844 Sketch, he had no way of knowing whether this statement was true or not. In fact, the statement is not true, for the principle of divergence is *not* discussed at all, and for that reason primarily was Darwin's draft of the Asa Gray communication included as part of the Linnean Society presentation. Early in June 1858 Darwin wrote Hooker that the principle of divergence was a keystone of his book along with natural selection.[31] It is curious that he would say this immediately after he had received Wallace's communication, and that he was then writing about divergence. Some questions obviously remain to be answered, but it is clear that Darwin misled Lyell on this point, and that Darwin's case for priority left much to be desired, especially if Wallace had pressed the issue.

Although agreeing on their central tenet of natural selection itself, Wallace and Darwin disagreed or differed on several points. A fundamental difference concerned domesticated animals. In his part of the 1858 papers as well as in the *Origin,* Darwin relied very heavily on the argument that as man selects variations from his stocks of animals, nature—being more powerful—can effect even greater changes on her organisms, given the almost unlimited time at her disposal. After reading Wallace's paper, Darwin observed, "we differ only, [in] that I was led to my views from what artificial selection has done for domestic animals."[32]

Wallace, on the other hand, referred to domesticated species as creatures *protected,* as well as selected, by man. When returned to their primitive state, however, they either reverted to a former, better adapted condition, or perished. Wallace never relied on the analogy between human selection and selection in nature, although some scholars have erroneously claimed that both Darwin and Wallace "took the

30. Ibid., p. 474.

31. Francis Darwin himself observed that the letter to Gray was included because it included "a discussion on divergence, and was thus, probably, the only document, including this subject, which could be appropriately made use of. It shows once more how great was the importance attached by its author to the principle of divergence." See Francis Darwin's comments in de Beer (1958), p. 34. Darwin to Hooker, Down, June 8th [1858], *MLD,* vol. I, p. 109. This letter also establishes that Darwin was at Down early in June 1858.

32. *LLD,* vol. I, p. 474.

variation of domesticated animals and plants as their starting point."[33] While Darwin's argument from analogy was excellent and cogent in 1859, Wallace observed in 1889 that "it has always been considered a weakness in Darwin's work that he based his theory, primarily, on the evidence of variation in domesticated animals and cultivated plants."[34]

Perhaps the greatest impediment for Darwin on the subject of domestic variation was his lack of reliable information on the laws of heredity: "His generalizations, though based on carefully accumulated empirical evidence, never proved entirely trustworthy."[35] The science of genetics, a primary key to understanding the complexities of inheritance under domestication, simply did not exist in 1859. The common man then nevertheless could easily see the gross changes effected by breeders. Wallace was correct that evolution by natural selection could be explained without relying on the analogous argument of domesticated species; nevertheless, from the point of view that his argument was understandable and cogent, Darwin was wise to begin his book as he did and argue persistently from analogy. Modern works have long since abandoned Darwin's approach.

Still another point of difference exists. In his paper Wallace referred to Lamarck and repudiated ideas which he attributed to him.

> The hypothesis of Lamarck—that progressive changes in species have been produced by the attempts of animals to increase the development of their own organs, and thus modify their structure and habits—has been repeatedly and easily refuted by all writers on the subject of varieties and species, . . .[36]

33. Pantin, "Alfred Russel Wallace, F. R. S., and his Essays of 1855 and 1858" (1960), p. 77. He continues his comparison the rest of the page. See also George, *Biologist Philosopher* (1964), p. 68. Both quoted by Camille Limoges, *La sélection naturelle. Étude sur la première constitution d'un concept (1837–1859)* (1970), p. 99.

34. Wallace, *Darwinism*, p. vi.

35. Gienapp, *Animal Hybridization and the Species Question from Aristotle to Darwin* (1970), p. 193. His entire chapter VI, "Darwin, Species, and Hybrids" (pp. 170–94) should be consulted on the subject of Darwin's views on hybridization. See also Müntzing, "Darwin's Views on Variation under Domestication in the Light of Present-Day Knowledge" (1959), pp. 190–220, esp. his summary on 217–19.

36. *NS*, p. 41 or de Beer (1958), p. 277. Wallace's brief summary of Lamarck is inadequate. For Lamarck's evolutionary hypotheses see McKinney (1971), pp. 9–20.

During his long career Wallace never actually yielded to the Lamarckian belief, particularly that characters acquired by use and disuse can be inherited. Like so many of his contemporaries, however, Darwin accepted these ideas when other explanations seemed inadequate—"on purely empirical grounds."[37] Ironically, Lamarck, whose ideas have been derided since he expounded them, could have argued a similar case.

One striking similarity, frequently alluded to, concerns the press of populations on the food supply—"It is the doctrine of Malthus applied in most cases with tenfold force." Several times Darwin explicitly mentioned the name of Malthus as well as his doctrines; Wallace, on the other hand, implicitly referred to Malthus when he said, *"the animal population of a country is generally stationary, being kept down by a periodical deficiency of food, and other checks."*[38] Indeed, the ideas of Malthus also pervade Wallace's essay, and as we have seen, it was the new perspective gained when Wallace recalled Malthus that provided the missing key to his problem.

The important point, however, is that the problem concerning the mechanism for evolution was constantly in his thoughts and the solution barely in the shadows of his mind. The proper stimulus evoked the correct answer, followed by careful consultation of his notebook where he had many excerpts from Lyell, Owen, Blyth, and others. The "bolt from the blue" was in reality the fruition of more than a dozen years of meditation—a vintage crop of ideas constantly guiding his investigations.[39]

37. Ghiselin, *The Triumph of the Darwinian Method* (1969), p. 182. From the first edition of the *Origin* (1859) until the last edition, Darwin accepted this doctrine to some extent. And his provisional doctrine of pangenesis was an attempt to account for the inheritance of acquired characteristics. See Darwin, *The Variation of Animals and Plants Under Domestication* (1868), vol. II, chap. 27, "Provisional Hypothesis of Pangenesis." For the best discussion of Darwin's ideas on this topic see Geison, "Darwin and Heredity: The Evolution of His Hypothesis of Pangenesis" (1969). For Wallace's comments on the influence of the environment on organisms as well as the effects of use and disuse see Wallace, *Darwinism* (1889), ch. 14, esp. pp. 443–44.

38. *NS,* p. 34 or de Beer (1958), p. 273. Italics by Wallace.

39. See also my comments above regarding his paper of 1858. Chapter 5, pp. 56–59 and 75–77.

9 Wallace's Place in Evolutionary Biology
1845–1858

For Alfred Russel Wallace, the path to his discovery of natural selection in 1858 was essentially a direct one. Unlike Edward Blyth, Richard Owen, Sir Charles Lyell, and many others, Wallace was unencumbered by strong religious ties or orthodox scientific dogmas, and was quite receptive to the cogent arguments of the heretical *Vestiges of the Natural History of Creation* by Robert Chambers. Thus, converted as early as 1845 to the idea that species evolve, by a work which Darwin, Huxley, and most of the scientific community at first considered anathema,[1] Wallace examined natural phenomena with a definite predilection. Deciding that, for his purposes, local studies of nature in England were unsatisfactory, he embarked on a long journey to study variation and the geographical distribution of animals in South America in order to solve the species problem.

Unfortunately, most of his efforts were in vain, for while returning to England in 1852, his ship sank, taking with it his natural history collections and many other valuable materials. Confronted with these immense losses, he wisely refrained from openly espousing any evolutionary hypothesis immediately after his return,[2] although his work on zoogeography, published in 1852–53, definitely pointed forward to his first public commitment in 1855 to a natural law, implicitly evolution, as the probable cause of the introduction of new species. Moreover, we know that Wallace himself realized the importance of his work on the geographical distribution of animals because: (1) Before leaving the Amazon jungles in July 1852, he had discussed with Henry Walter Bates what he was to call his species law in 1855. (2) Entries in his 1854 Notebook show the evolutionist trend in his thought. (3) He stated in his 1855 Paper that he had been carefully testing his evolutionary hypothesis at every opportunity *for ten years,*

1. A very long list of Chambers's errors will be found in Gillispie, *Genesis and Geology* (1959), "The Vestiges of Creation," esp. pp. 155–56. See *LLD*, vol. I, p. 399 for one of Darwin's typical references to *Vestiges.*

2. If he expected even the magnanimous Sir Roderick Murchison to help him—as he eventually did—it would have been disastrous to espouse evolution openly at that time.

and then proceeded to adduce cogent zoogeographical evidence, some of which he had personally gathered in South America. That he later utilized this same evidence in his works on the geographical distribution of animals is to be expected.[3]

But if, on the one hand, the loss of his collections was a tragedy, it was at the same time a blessing—so Wallace himself considered it—for as a consequence he resolved to continue his investigations in the Malay Archipelago.[4] And two of his unpublished notebooks—which I have called, respectively, the 1854 Notebook and the Species Notebook—clearly demonstrate that he was continuing his investigations on biological evolution immediately after his arrival in the Archipelago in 1854. Indeed, we find in the Species Notebook the plan and large portions of a book tentatively entitled *On the Organic Law of Change*. These early notes—written before February 1855 as we infer from a letter to Bates—inform us that Wallace's plan was to apply Sir Charles Lyell's uniformitarian geological principles to the organic world: variations now evident in nature, when continued over long geological periods, eventually lead to the introduction of new species and can, if enough time be allowed, account for all organic change. Chambers's *Vestiges* first convinced him of this natural law, and in his Species Notebook, Wallace, while agreeing completely with Lyell's geological uniformitarianism, argued for the defense—Lamarck (per Lyell and Chambers) and Chambers—regarding the species question. I have shown in a number of places that much of Wallace's evidence for evolution came from Lamarck (per Lyell and/or Chambers) or Chambers.

It is particularly interesting that Darwin's interest in the species problem began in a very different manner from Wallace's interest. Darwin, on the one hand, seems to have been led to a careful examination of evolution by the disturbing facts of zoogeography. Wallace, quite the contrary, was first converted to evolution by a widely criticized scientific book—Chambers's *Vestiges*.[5] His search for better facts

---

3. For example, Wallace, *The Geographical Distribution of Animals* (1876), vol. I, pp. 6, 13.

4. Marchant, "A Man of His Time: Dr. Alfred Russel Wallace and his Coming Autobiography" (1903), p. 545.

5. See Darlington (1959), p. 309. But see Richard Owen's pleasant, helpful remarks in a letter addressed to the anonymous author of the *Vestiges*. Owen, *The Life of Richard Owen* (1894), vol. I, pp. 249–52.

to establish evolution as a sound scientific hypothesis led Wallace to examine variation in nature and particularly the geographical distribution of organisms. Darwin had made the *Beagle* voyage before considering evolution seriously; Wallace appears to have journeyed to the tropics *because* he wanted to test his theory in the field. Bates confirmed this by saying that the purpose of their trip to South America (a trip proposed by Wallace) was to assemble a collection of natural history "objects" and gather facts "towards solving the problem of the origin of species, a subject on which we had conversed and corresponded very much." Wallace continued his search in the Malay Archipelago only because he had lost his South American collections and many important notes when his ship sank in 1852 upon his return to England.

A significant similarity between Charles Darwin and Alfred Russel Wallace concerns the work of Malthus, *An Essay on the Principle of Population.* For both men Malthus apparently supplied an important key; however, in neither case did Malthus provide natural selection, an idea contrary to his belief that mankind cannot be improved. What Malthus did provide was a rigorous mathematical demonstration, fortified by numerous cogent examples, that if human or animal populations increased too fast, food supplies would be insufficient. Starvation, death, and possibly extinction could then result. Their own examination of nature as well as Lyell's *Principles* had prepared both Wallace and Darwin to understand this intense struggle for the food supply.[6]

Wallace, although mentally prepared for Malthus in much the same manner as Darwin, recalled the arguments of *On Population* for quite another reason. For many years—from no later than 1845—Wallace had been profoundly interested in ethnology, and from the

6. Ghiselin says that the critical insight provided by Malthus for Darwin has not yet "been adequately explained. De Beer maintains that Darwin overemphasized the significance of Malthus in his discovery. The same conclusion is reached by [Sydney] Smith, who asserts that Darwin had his theory fully in mind from the outset of his work on species, arguing that the idea of natural selection was implicit in Darwin's notebook form 1837 onward, as well as in the writings of Lyell. A number of commentators—there seems almost to be a consensus—support the same general point of view." Ghiselin (1969), p. 49 with refs. on pp. 256–57. See also Vorzimmer, "Darwin, Malthus, and the Theory of Natural Selection" (1969), pp. 527–42; and Herbert, "Darwin, Malthus, and Selection" (1971), pp. 209–17.

evolutionist's point of view. He had sought for clues explaining human variation as well as animal variation, which is not at all surprising since he considered man to have evolved from some simian ancestor—an orangutang or close relative. His very extensive and careful investigations of the inhabitants of the Archipelago led him to conclude they were "all varying forms of one great Oceanic or Polynesian race."[7] It was while considering how and why these variations had arisen, while searching his mind for clues from the works he had read concerning ethnology, that he recalled Malthus. And Wallace's own observations on the natives of Aru had fully prepared him to appreciate the arguments of Malthus regarding the importance of the food supply. Suddenly, the entire problem came into focus and the solution rushed upon him. Realizing that this process was even more applicable in the animal kingdom, he made the logical transfer from human races to animal varieties. The search was ended. While the entire species problem had not been solved, a major breakthrough had been made.

But if there are essential differences between Darwin and Wallace, there are also many similarities as Wallace himself observed: Very early in life both became avid beetle collectors and were thus well acquainted with the variations of those insects; both were infected with "the mere passion for collecting," primarily because of their intense interest in variation in nature; both journeyed to the tropics to examine nature first hand as collectors;[8] but perhaps it is of paramount importance that both read Lyell's *Principles of Geology* and were converted to his uniformitarian principles, which they in turn applied to biology. Lyell, thus, ironically laid the foundations for the overthrow of his own ideas on species. The work of Malthus *by itself,* however, was insufficient reason for even an evolutionist to discover natural selection: Robert Chambers read Malthus and nothing registered on his mind. Perhaps Blyth also read Malthus, but again, no response.[9]

This investigation also furnishes evidence bearing on the question of whether Edward Blyth's papers on varieties were the hidden sources of Darwin's discovery of natural selection. Loren Eiseley has presented a very interesting argument in an attempt to establish this theory—

7. Wallace, "On the Varieties of Man in the Malay Archipelago" (1864–65), p. 212.

8. *WLR*, pp. 95–96.

9. See *Vestiges* (1845), p. 274. See above chapter 5, p. 75, n. 52.

indeed he specifically accuses Darwin of plagiarizing the idea of natural selection from Blyth—but perhaps one strong argument against his view is the fact that Wallace read Blyth's 1835 paper, took notes on it, and saw nothing exceptional in it. It was merely another work which supported his belief that varieties, sometimes radically different, do propagate their own kind. As for the statements regarding the struggle for existence, with extinction being one consequence, Wallace had already observed this in Lyell's *Principles* (and elsewhere). Darwin did in fact read Blyth's papers of 1835 and 1837, but we need not assume that he, any more than Wallace, would find natural selection in them, and not in Lyell's *Principles* which he had read with great care.[10] As for the interesting passages in Darwin's work which Eiseley has adduced as evidence of Darwin's debt to Blyth,[11] the following passage may attenuate the force of that argument:

> I should say the changes [of species] were effects of external causes, of which we are ignorant, as *why millet seed turns a Bullfinch black,* or iodine on glands of throat, or colour of plumage altered during passage of birds (where is this statement?—I remember L. Jenyns talking of it), or how to make Indian cow with hump or pigs foot with cloven hoof.[12]

We find the following statement in Blyth's 1835 paper (p. 44):

> and, as another familiar instance [of the influence of foods on variations], may be cited the fact, equally well known, of bullfinches, and one or two other small birds, becoming wholly black when fed entirely on hempseed.

These two statements taken together perhaps tell us that Leonard Jenyns, afterwards Blomefield—who had published articles in *The Magazine of Natural History*[13]—had discussed Blyth's article with Darwin (and thus probably also recommended it). Nevertheless, remembering the example of Wallace, I see no reason to believe that Darwin would necessarily have attached any especial significance to

10. For an examination of the relationship between the ideas of Blyth and Darwin see McKinney, "Edward Blyth" (1970), pp. 205–07.

11. Eiseley, "Charles Darwin, Edward Blyth, and the Theory of Natural Selection" (1959), pp. 103–04.

12. de Beer, *Darwin Notebooks,* vol. 2, no. 2, (1960), p. 67. Italics are mine.

13. Eiseley (1959), p. 98.

Blyth's statements even if he did read Blyth's paper early in 1837.[14] On the other hand, we must remember that few of Darwin's critics have bothered to utilize the available unpublished manuscript materials at Cambridge and elsewhere to trace the development of his thoughts. Much remains to be done at the manuscript level before we can fully evaluate Darwin's debts to his predecessors.

It has also been possible to show in this work that while we can see several instances where Wallace seized upon passages from Darwin's *Journal of Researches,* particularly on the Galapagos Islands, Darwin had nothing to do with Wallace's discovery of natural selection in 1858. Quite the contrary, Wallace's 1855 Paper can now be seen in proper perspective as a work of profound influence which stimulated Darwin, Lyell, and Edward Blyth. Indeed, Sir Charles Lyell was so impressed by Wallace's paper that he began his own series of species notebooks with direct argumentation against Wallace's ideas, eventually deciding to examine as a test case for evolution the statement that "no example is known of an island which can be proved geologically to be of very recent origin (late in the Tertiary, for instance), and yet possesses generic or family groups or even very many species peculiar to itself." After over one hundred pages of notes had been made in his species notebook, Lyell talked to Darwin on 13 April 1856, and Wallace's statement just quoted was further corroborated by Darwin's evidence as well as by that of the Reverend Richard Lowe. Three days later, apparently at Lyell's request, Darwin first explained his theory of evolution by natural selection to Lyell; Wallace's paper was also discussed. Thereafter followed Lyell's insistent warnings that Darwin publish something quickly or risk being forestalled by Wallace who was obviously giving serious thought to the species problem *from the right point of view.* Darwin's own reading of Wallace's paper as well as Edward Blyth's explicit letter of 8 December 1855 had thoroughly prepared Darwin for Lyell's excellent advice. Furthermore, Wallace's letters to Darwin only confirmed that advice: Wallace knew precisely what he was doing. And his article on the Aru Islands should have caused Darwin to work with even greater fervor. In any event, we know definitely that Wallace's 1855 paper—and Lyell's and Darwin's discussion arising from it—was the immediate reason for Darwin's beginning on 14 May 1856 what he called his Species

14. See also de Beer, *Charles Darwin: Evolution by Natural Selection* (1964), pp. 102–03.

Sketch, which eventually grew to be *On the Origin of Species by Means of Natural Selection* in 1859.

Therefore, Darwin's great shock in June 1858 was not because he was totally unaware of Wallace's work and its implications—Lyell, Blyth, and even Wallace himself had said just about all they possibly could have to forewarn him, and Darwin probably had incorporated in his own work Wallace's point that "species of one genus, or genera of one family occurring in the same geological time [period] are more closely allied than those separated in time" (1855 paper, p. 186). Although Darwin queried this with "can this be so," he went on to accept Wallace's point and to discuss it at length. Wallace's name, however, is not mentioned. Indeed, Darwin always found it difficult to acknowledge his debts to his predecessors on certain points, although his reading and annotations of Wallace's paper as well as the letter of Blyth and Lyell's exhortations to publish focused an inescapable spotlight on Wallace's brilliant essay. Darwin's shock resulted not because he was ignorant of Wallace's work. The shock came from seeing Lyell's prediction about Wallace come true. Clearly, Wallace's paper "On the Tendency of Varieties to Depart Indefinitely from the Original Type" was not a "bolt from the blue," although it was a traumatic shock. Ironically, Darwin could have prevented any possible unpleasantness simply by telling Wallace, as he had Asa Gray, about natural selection.[15] But if he had withheld the story from his good friend Sir Charles Lyell for almost twenty years—a most peculiar but illuminating circumstance—why should we expect Darwin to pour out his soul to a relative stranger like Wallace, especially since he knew Wallace was an evolutionist also and just could have misused what Darwin told him. Quite the opposite, however, appears to have happened, for Darwin received Wallace's paper on natural selection on June third (or, fourth) and held on to it for two weeks before writing Lyell. Since he seems already to have understood the principle of natural selection, we must look elsewhere for any plagiarism—if

15. In the letter from Darwin to Asa Gray, dated 5 September [1857], Darwin says: "You will, perhaps, think it paltry in me, when I ask you not to mention my doctrine; the reason is, if any one, like the author of the 'Vestiges,' were to hear of them he might easily work them in, and then I should have to quote from a work perhaps despised by naturalists, and this would greatly injure any chance of my views being received by those alone whose opinions I value." *LLD,* vol. I, p. 478. Perhaps this has something to do with why Darwin didn't tell Wallace about natural selection.

indeed any took place. Since the principle of divergence was the topic we know he was then working on, it is possible that Wallace illuminated some point for him, but his letter to Gray of 5 September 1857 discussed divergence. The question is what could Darwin have obtained from Wallace's paper while examining it from 3 (or 4) June to 18 June? Perhaps nothing at all, but some doubt must remain until *all* relevant documents are reexamined.

It is clear, nevertheless, that Darwin's desire for priority guided, or at least did not impede, the events in June leading up to the presentation of the joint papers before the Linnean Society on 1 July 1858. But there was danger in such a swift course, for Wallace was not consulted in any way, never saw any page proofs, and did not see the published versions until after the events had passed. For this reason I find it difficult to believe that Darwin destroyed Wallace's— and Lyell's—early letters, for they could have been firm proof that he didn't appropriate natural selection from Wallace.[16] What actually happened to these letters, and *why,* is a matter not easily solved and certainly requires further investigation. Fortunately, Wallace was a perfect gentleman in this matter, thus eliminating many potential problems. We must remember, however, that only Hooker and Lyell were privy to the course of events before July 1 and (with Gray) to *Darwin's evidence for priority.* The 1842 Sketch, and 1844 Essay were not published until 1908. The long version of the *Origin* has still not appeared, although Professor Stauffer has completed his edition for publication.

Since Wallace later acquired his letter of 2 March 1858 to Frederick Bates, which contained within the same envelope a letter to H. W. Bates, he would have known from the postmarks when his paper arrived in England. But any protest would have been beneath his dignity; too much had happened. The matter was a dead issue. Besides he had his own curious deception about Gilolo to remember. It was enough for him that the glory of discovery had been shared with Darwin. His subsequent books and discoveries had elevated him into the ranks of the greatest Victorian naturalists. He was well satisfied.

Finally, the development of Wallace's thoughts on evolution, leading to the discovery of natural selection in 1858, can be traced with

16. Why would Darwin specifically ask Hooker to return Lyell's letters if he were only going to destroy them? In fact he kept Lyell's letters in large numbers. *LLD,* vol. I, p. 439.

considerable precision. His arguments and investigations followed a prescribed plan, and in his 1855 Paper we find a direct application of his theory to well known geological and geographical facts. He also publicly announced his interest in the species problem:

> To discover how the extinct species have from time to time been replaced by new ones down to the very latest geological period, is the most difficult, and at the same time the most interesting problem in the natural history of the earth.[17]

His answer was that they have sprung, temporally and spatially, from previous closely allied species—they have evolved.

From 1855 until 1858 we can trace the elaboration of his ideas. His paper on bird affinity is the direct explanation of the facts of natural phenomena in terms of the complicated branching lines of affinity mentioned in 1855.[18] His work "On the Natural History of the Aru Islands" was a direct test of his belief that the peculiarity of island flora and fauna could reveal much about the nearest mainland and the age of the island itself,[19] a point which Lyell himself tested carefully. From 1855 until 1858, then, was a period of elaboration of his earlier views and a period of the accumulation of facts. And there are many revealing remarks both published and unpublished, which point straight to February 1858. Wallace's discovery was not an example of mere chance or accident, but, quite the contrary, a matter of achieving a long-sought goal. The real wonder in this matter is not that Wallace discovered natural selection in 1858, but that he did not do so much sooner.

17. 1855 Paper, p. 190.
18. Ibid., p. 187.
19. Ibid., p. 188.

Appendix I

Wallace's Request for Aid from the Royal Geographical Society of London

To the President and Council of the Royal Geographical Society of London

Mr. Alfred R. Wallace begs leave to lay before the Council of the Geographical Society an outline of his proposed expedition & to solicit its support and interest.

He proposes leaving England in the Autumn or Winter of the present year, and, making Singapore his headquarters, to visit in succession Borneo, the Philippines, Celebes, Timor, the Moluccas and New Guinea, or such of them as may prove most accessible, remaining one or more years in each as circumstances may determine.

His chief object is the investigation of the Natural History of the Eastern Archipelago in a more complete manner than has hitherto been attempted; but he will also pay much attention to Geography, & hopes to add considerably to our knowledge of such of the islands as he may visit.

It is therefore his earnest desire to provide himself with such Astronomical & Meteorological instruments as are required to determine the position in Latitude, Longitude & Height above the Sea Level, of all his stations.

The expense however of the journey from England is so considerable, that he finds himself unable to make the necessary outlay, and he would therefore wish to know whether the Council of the Royal Geographical Society will feel justified in recommending her Majesty's Government to *grant him a free passage* to any convenient port in the Archipelago, and thereby enable him to supply himself with the necessary instruments.

Through the influence of your Medallist, Sir James Brooke, who has kindly promised him every assistance, he has little doubt of success in exploring the great Island of Borneo. He understands however that the permission of the Governments of Spain & Holland is necessary to visit the interior of any of the Islands where they may have settlements, and he

---

This unpublished manuscript is located at the Royal Geographical Society of London. Italics are Wallace's.

trusts that the Council will give him their support in endeavoring to obtain such permission.

As some guarantee of his capabilities as a traveller he may perhaps be excused for referring to his recent travels for nearly five years, in South America, where alone and unassisted he penetrated several hundred miles beyond any former European traveller, as shown by the map & description of the Rio Negro, which he has had the honour to lay before the Society at its last meeting. [June 13, 1853]

During his travels in South America he relied entirely on his duplicate collections in Natural History to pay his expenses, and he shall follow the same plan in his proposed journey. On his homeward voyage from Pará he suffered the loss of a very extensive and valuable collection together with all his books & instruments by the burning of the Brig *Helen* of Liverpool (in which he was a passenger) on the 6th of August 1852,—a loss which has rendered necessary the present application to the Royal Geographical Society.

Appendix II

Wallace's Summary of the Geological and Geographical Evidence in His 1855 Paper

GEOGRAPHY

1. Large groups, such as classes and orders, are generally spread over the whole earth, while smaller ones, such as families and genera, are frequently confined to one portion, often to a very limited district.

2. In widely distributed families the genera are often limited in range; in widely distributed genera, well-marked groups of species are peculiar to each geographical district.

3. When a group is confined to one district, and is rich in species, it is almost invariably the case that the most closely allied species are found in the same locality or in closely adjoining localities, and that therefore the natural sequence of the species by affinity is also geographical.

4. In countries of a similar climate, but separated by a wide sea or lofty mountains, the families, genera and species of the one are often represented by closely allied families, genera and species peculiar to the other.

GEOLOGY

5. The distribution of the organic world in time is very similar to its present distribution in space.

6. Most of the larger and some small groups extend through several geological periods.

7. In each period, however, there are peculiar groups, found nowhere else, and extending through one or several formations.

8. Species of one genus, or genera of one family occurring in the same geological time are more closely allied than those separated in time.

9. As generally in geography no species or genus occurs in two very distant localities without being also found in intermediate places, so in geology the life of a species or genus has not been interrupted. In other words, no group or species has come into existence twice.

10. The following law may be deduced from these facts:—*Every species has come into existence coincident both in space and time with a pre-existing closely allied species.*

1855 Paper, pp. 185–86. Italics are Wallace's.

Appendix III

Four Accounts Referring to Wallace's Recollection of Malthus's *An Essay on the Principle of Population*

1898

During one of these fits, while again considering the problem of the origin of species, something led me to think of Malthus' Essay on Population (which I had read about ten [actually about thirteen] years before), and the "positive checks"—war, disease, famine, accidents, etc.—which he adduced as keeping all savage populations nearly stationary. It then occurred to me that these checks must also act upon animals, and keep down their numbers; and as they increase so much faster than man does, while their numbers are always very nearly or quite stationary, it was clear that these checks in their case must be far more powerful, since a number equal to the whole increase must be cut off by them every year. While vaguely thinking how this would affect any species, there suddenly flashed upon me the idea of *the survival of the fittest*—that the individuals removed by these checks must be on the whole, *inferior* to those that survived. Then, considering the *variations* continually occurring in every fresh generation of animals or plants, and the changes of climate, of food, of enemies always in progress, the whole method of specific modification became clear to me, and in the two hours of my fit I had thought out the main points of the theory. That same evening I sketched out the draft of a paper; in the two succeeding evenings I wrote it out, and sent it by the next post to Mr. Darwin.[1]

1903

In February, 1858, I was living at Ternate one of the Moluccas Islands, and was suffering from a sharp attack of intermittent fever, which obliged me to lie down every afternoon during the cold and subsequent hot fits which lasted together two or three hours. It was during one of these fits, while I was thinking over the possible mode of the origin of new species, that somehow my thoughts turned to the "positive checks" to increase among savages and others described in much detail in the celebrated *Essay on Population,* by Malthus, a work I had read a dozen [*sic*] years before. These checks—disease, famine, accidents, war, etc.,—are

---

1. Wallace, *The Wonderful Century* (1898), p. 139. Italics are Wallace's.

what keep down the population, and it suddenly occurred to me that in the case of wild animals these checks would act with much severity, and as the lower animals all tended to increase more rapidly than man, while their population remained on the average constant, there suddenly flashed upon me the idea of the survival of the fittest—that those individuals which every year were removed by these causes—termed collectively the "struggle for existence"—must on the average and in the long run be inferior in some one or more ways to those which managed to survive.

By the next post to Darwin

The more I thought of this the more certain it appeared to be; while the only alternative theory—that those who succumbed to enemies of want of food, or to disease, drought, of cold, were in every way and always as well constituted as those that survived—seemed to me impossible and unthinkable. So deeply impressed was I with the importance of this theory, that the very same evening I sketched the outlines, and in the two succeeding evenings, wrote it out in full, and sent it by the next post to Mr. Darwin.[2]

1905

At the time in question I was suffering from a sharp attack of intermittent fever, and every day during the cold and succeeding hot fits had to lie down for several hours, during which time I had nothing to do but to think over any subjects then particularly interesting me. One day something brought to my recollection Malthus's "Principles of Population," which I had read about twelve [sic] years before, I thought of his clear exposition of the "positive checks to increase"—disease, accidents, war and famine—which keep down the population of savage races to so much lower an average than that of more civilized peoples. It then occurred to me that these causes or their equivalents are continually acting in the case of animals also; and as animals usually breed much more rapidly than does mankind, the destruction every year from these causes must be enormous in order to keep down the numbers of each species, since they evidently do not increase regularly from year to year, as otherwise the world would long ago have been densely crowded with those that breed most quickly. Vaguely thinking over the enormous and constant destruction which this implied, it occurred to me to ask the question, Why do some die and some live? And the answer was clearly, that on the whole the best fitted live. From the effects of disease the most healthy escaped; from enemies, the strongest, the swiftest, or the most cunning;

2. Wallace, "My Relations with Darwin in Reference to the Theory of Natural Selection" (1903), p. 78.

from famine, the best hunters or those with the best digestion; and so on. Then it suddenly flashed upon me that this self-acting process would necessarily *improve the race,* because in every generation the inferior would inevitably be killed off and the superior would remain—that is, *the fittest would survive.* Then at once I seemed to see the whole effect of this, that when changes of land and sea, or of climate, or of food-supply, or of enemies occurred—and we know that such changes have always been taking place—and considering the amount of individual variation that my experience as a collector has shown me to exist, then it followed that all the changes necessary for the adaptation of the species to the changing conditions would be brought about; and as great changes in the environment are always slow, there would be ample time for the change to be effected by the survival of the best fitted in every generation. In this way every part of an animal's organization could be modified exactly as required, and in the very process of this modification the un-modified would die out, and thus the *definite* characters and the clear *isolation* of each new species would be explained. The more I thought over it the more I became convinced that I had at length found the long-sought-for law of nature that solved the problem of the origin of species. For the next hour I thought over the deficiencies in the theories of Lamarck and of the author of the "Vestiges," and I saw that my new theory supplemented these views and obviated every important difficulty. I waited anxiously for the termination of my fit so that I might at once make notes for a paper on the subject. The same evening I did this pretty fully, and on the two succeeding evenings wrote it out carefully in order to send it to Darwin by the next post, which would leave in a day or two.[3]

1908

It was the perusal of such statements as these,[4] extending over every part of the world, and very varied in their details, that produced such a deep and permanent impression on my mind, though the individual facts were forgotten. When, ten or twelve [*sic*] years later, while thinking (as I had thought for years) over the possible causes of the change of species, the action of these "positive checks" to increase, as Malthus termed them, suddenly occurred to me. I then saw that war, plunder and massacres among men were represented by the attacks of carnivores on herbivora, and of the stronger upon the weaker among animals. Famine, droughts, floods and winter's storms, would have an even greater effect on animals than on men; while as the former possessed powers of increase from

3. *My Life,* vol. I, pp. 361–63. Italics are Wallace's.
4. See Appendix IV.

twice to a thousand-fold greater than the latter, the ever-present annual destruction must also be many times greater.

Then there flashed upon me, as it had done twenty years before upon Darwin, the *certainty,* that those which, had some little superiority enabling them to escape each special form of death to which the great majority succumbed—that, in the well-known formula, the fittest would survive. Then I at once saw, that the ever present *variability* of all living things would furnish the material from which, by the mere weeding out of those less adapted to the actual conditions, the fittest alone would continue the race. But this would only tend to the persistence of those best adapted to the actual conditions; and on the old idea of the permanence and practical unchangeability of the inorganic world, except for a few local and unimportant catastrophes, there would be no necessary change of species.[5]

5. Linnean Society of London, *The Darwin-Wallace Celebration* (1908), pp. 117–18. Italics are Wallace's.

Appendix IV

Note on the passages of MALTHUS'S ' *Principles of Population* ' *which suggested the idea of Natural Selection to Darwin and myself.*

By ALFRED R. WALLACE.

IN order to refresh my memory I have again looked through Malthus's work, and I feel sure that what influenced me was not any special passage or passages, but the cumulative effect of chapters iii. to xii. of the first volume (and more especially chapters iii. to viii.) occupying about 150 pages. In these chapters are comprised very detailed accounts from all available sources, of the various causes which keep down the population of savage and barbarous nations, in America, Africa, and Asia, notwithstanding that they all possess a power of increase sufficient to produce a dense population for any of the continents in a few centuries.

In order to give an idea, though a very imperfect one, of the nature of the facts adduced by him, I have selected the following passages as being fairly illustrative of the whole. The references are to the sixth edition, London : 1826, vol. i.

CHAPTER IV.

Of the Checks to Population among the American Indians.

Pages 35–37, line 2.

We may next turn our view to the vast continent of America, the greatest part of which was found to be inhabited by small independent tribes of savages, subsisting, nearly like the natives of New Holland, on the productions of unassisted nature. The soil was covered by an almost universal forest, and presented few of those fruits and esculent vegetables which grow in such profusion in the islands of the South Sea. The produce of a most rude and imperfect agriculture, known to some of the tribe of hunters, was so trifling as to be considered only as a feeble aid to the subsistence acquired by the chase. The

---

inhabitants of this new world therefore might be considered as living principally by hunting and fishing * ; and the narrow limits to this mode of subsistence are obvious. The supplies derived from fishing could reach only those who were within a certain distance of the lakes, the rivers, or the sea-shore ; and the ignorance and indolence of the improvident savage would frequently prevent him from extending the benefits of these supplies much beyond the time when they were actually obtained. The great extent of territory required for the support of the hunter has been repeatedly stated and acknowledged †. The number of wild animals within his reach, combined with the facility with which they may be either killed or insnared, must necessarily limit the number of his society. The tribes of hunters, like beasts of prey, whom they resemble in their mode of subsistence, will consequently be thinly scattered over the surface of the earth. Like beasts of prey, they must either drive away or fly from every rival, and be engaged in perpetual contests with each other ‡.

Under such circumstances, that America should be very thinly peopled in proportion to its extent of territory, is merely an exemplification of the obvious truth, that population cannot increase without the food to support it. But the interesting part of the inquiry, that part, to which I would wish particularly to draw the attention of the reader, is, the mode by which the population is kept down to the level of this scanty supply. It cannot escape observation, that an insufficient supply of food to any people does not shew itself merely in the shape of famine, but in other more permanent forms of distress, and in generating certain customs, which operate sometimes with greater force in the prevention of a rising population than in its subsequent destruction.

Page 39, lines 5–21.

In every part of the world, one of the most general characteristics of the savage is to despise and degrade the female sex §. Among most of the tribes in America their

---

* Robertson's History of America, vol. ii. b. iv. p. 127 *et seq.*, octavo edit. 1780.

† Franklin's Miscell. p. 2.   ‡ Robertson, b. iv. p. 129.

§ Robertson, b. iv. p. 103. Lettres Edif. passim. Charlevoix, Hist. Nouv. Fr. tom. iii. p. 287. Voy. de Pérouse. c. ix. p. 492, 4to. London.

condition is so peculiarly grievous, that servitude is a name too mild to describe their wretched state. A wife is no better than a beast of burden. While the man passes his days in idleness or amusement, the woman is condemned to incessant toil. Tasks are imposed upon her without mercy, and services are received without complacence or gratitude *. There are some districts in America where this state of degradation has been so severely felt, that mothers have destroyed their female infants, to deliver them at once from a life in which they were doomed to such a miserable life of slavery †.

CHAPTER VIII.

On the Checks to Population in the different Parts of Africa.

Pages 158–164.

The description, which Bruce gives of some parts of the country which he passed through on his return home, presents a picture more dreadful even than the state of Abyssinia, and shows how little population depends on the birth of children, in comparison of the production of food and those circumstances of natural and political situation which influence this produce.

"At half past six," Bruce says, " we arrived at Garigana, " a village whose inhabitants had all perished with hunger " the year before ; their wretched bones being all unburied "and scattered upon the surface of the ground where the " village formerly stood. We encamped among the bones " of the dead ; no space could be found free from them." ‡

Of another town or village in his route he observes :—

" The strength of Teawa was 25 horse. The rest of the in- "habitants might be 1200 naked miserable and despicable " Arabs, like the rest of those which live in villages .... " Such was the state of Teawa. Its consequence was only " to remain till the Daveina Arabs should resolve to attack "it, when its corn-fields being burnt and destroyed in a night

* Robertson, b. iv. p. 105. Lettres Edif. tom. vi. p. 329. Major Roger's North America, p. 211. Creuxii Hist. Canad. p. 57.

† Robertson, b. iv. p. 106. Raynal, Hist. des Indies, tom. iv. c. vii. p. 110, 8vo., 10 vol., 1795.

‡ Bruce, vol. iv. p. 349.

I

"by a multitude of horsemen, the bones of its inhabitants
" scattered upon the earth would be all its remains, like
" those of the miserable village of Garigana." *

"There is no water between Teawa and Beyla.   Once
"Indedidema and a number of villages were supplied with
" water from wells, and had large crops of Indian corn
" sown about their possessions.   The curse of that country,
" the Daveina Arabs, have destroyed Indedidema and all
" the villages about it; filled up their wells, burnt their
" crops, and exposed all the inhabitants to die by famine." †

Soon after leaving Sennaar, he says: "We began to
" see the effects of rain having failed.   There was little
" corn sown, and that so late as to be scarcely above ground.
" It seems the rain begins later as they pass northward.
" Many people were here employed in gathering grass-seeds
" to make a very bad kind of bread.   These people appear
" perfect skeletons, and no wonder, as they live upon such
" fare.   Nothing increases the danger of travelling and
" prejudice against strangers more, than the scarcity of
" provisions in the country through which you are to
" pass." ‡

" Came to Eltic, a straggling village about half a mile
" from the Nile, in the North of a large bare plain ; all
" pasture, except the banks of the river which are
" covered with wood.   We now no longer saw any corn
" sown.   The people here were at the same miserable
" employment as those we had seen before, that of gathering
" grass-seeds." §

Under such circumstances of climate and political situation,
though a greater degree of foresight, industry and security,
might considerably better their condition and increase their
population, the birth of a greater number of children
without these concomitants would only aggravate their
misery, and leave their population where it was.

The same may be said of the once flourishing and populous
country of Egypt.   Its present depressed state has not been
caused by the weakening of the principle of increase, but
by the weakening of the principle of industry and foresight,
from the insecurity of property consequent on a most
tyrannical and oppressive government.   The principle
of increase in Egypt at present does all that it is possible
for it to do.   It keeps the population fully up to the

---

* Bruce, vol. iv. p. 353.   † *Id.* p. 411.
‡ *Id.* p. 511.   § *Id.* p. 511.

level of the means of subsistence ; and, were its power ten times greater than it really is, it could do no more.

The remains of ancient works, the vast lakes, canals, and large conduits for water destined to keep the Nile under control, serving as reservoirs to supply a dry year, and as drains and outlets to prevent the superabundance of water in wet years, sufficiently indicate to us that the former inhabitants of Egypt by art and industry contrived to fertilize a much greater quantity of land from the over-flowings of their river, than is done at present ; and to prevent, in some measure, the distresses which are now so frequently experienced from a redundant or insufficient inundation *.

It is said of the governor Petronius, that, effecting by art what was denied by nature, he caused abundance to prevail in Egypt under disadvantages of such a deficient inundation, as had always before been accompanied by dearth †. A flood too great is as fatal to the husbandman as one that is deficient; and the ancients had, in consequence, drains and outlets to spread the superfluous waters over the thirsty sands of Lybia, and render even the desert habitable. These works are now all out of repair, and by ill management often produce mischief instead of good. The causes of this neglect, and consequently of the diminished means of subsistence, are obviously to be traced to the extreme ignorance and brutality of the government, and the wretched state of the people. The Mamelukes, in whom the principal power resides, think only of enriching themselves, and employ for this purpose what appears to them to be the simplest method, that of seizing wealth wherever it may be found, of wresting it by violence from the possessor, and of continually imposing new and arbitrary contributions ‡. Their ignorance and brutality, and the constant state of alarm in which they live, prevent them from having any views of enriching the country, the better to prepare it for their plunder. No public works therefore are to be expected from the government, and no individual proprietor dares to undertake any improvement which might imply the possession of capital, as it would probably be the immediate signal of his destruction. Under such circum-stances we cannot be surprised that the ancient works

* Bruce, vol. iii. c. xvii. p. 710.
† Voyage de Volney, tom. i. c. iii. p. 33, 8vo.
‡ Voyage de Volney, tom. i. c. xii. p. 170.

are neglected, that the soil is ill cultivated, and that the means of subsistence, and consequently the population, are greatly reduced. But such is the natural fertility of the Delta from the inundations of the Nile, that even without any capital employed upon the land, without a right of succession, and consequently almost without a right of property, it still maintains a considerable population in proportion to its extent, sufficient, if property were secure, and industry well directed, gradually to improve and extend the cultivation of the country and restore it to its former state of prosperity. It may be safely pronounced of Egypt that it is not the want of population that has checked its industry, but the want of industry that has checked its population.

The immediate causes which keep down the population to the level of the present contracted means of subsistence, are but too obvious. The peasants are allowed for their maintenance only sufficient to keep them alive*. A miserable sort of bread made of doura without leaven or flavour, cold water, and raw onions make up the whole of their diet. Meat and fat, of which they are passionately fond, never appear but on great occasions, and among those who are more at their ease. The habitations are huts made of earth, where a stranger would be suffocated with the heat and smoke ; and where the diseases generated by want of cleanliness, by moisture, and by bad nourishment, often visit them and commit great ravages. To these physical evils are added a constant state of alarm, the fear of the plunder of the Arabs, and the visits of the Mamelukes, the spirit of revenge transmitted in families, and all the evils of a continual civil war †.

In the year 1783 the plague was very fatal, and in 1784 and 1785 a dreadful famine reigned in Egypt, owing to a deficiency in the inundation of the Nile. Volney draws a frightful picture of the misery that was suffered on this occasion. The streets of Cairo, which at first were full of beggars, were soon cleared of all these objects, who either perished or fled. A vast number of unfortunate wretches,

---

* Voyage de Volney, tom. i. c. xii. p. 172.

† Volney, tom. i. c. xii. p. 173. This sketch of the state of the peasantry in Egypt given by Volney seems to be nearly confirmed by all other writers on this subject; and particularly in a valuable paper entitled Considérations générales sur l'Agriculture de l'Egypte, par L. Reynier (Mémoires sur l'Egypte, tom. iv. p. 1).

in order to escape death, spread themselves over all the
neighbouring countries, and the towns of Syria were
inundated with Egyptians. The streets and public places
were crowded by famished and dying skeletons. All the
most revolting modes of satisfying the cravings of hunger
were resorted to ; the most disgusting food was devoured
with eagerness ; and Volney mentions the having seen under
the walls of ancient Alexandria two miserable wretches
seated on the carcase of a camel, and disputing with the
dogs its putrid flesh. The depopulation of the two years
was estimated at one-sixth of all the inhabitants *.

It was the perusal of such statements as these, extending
over every part of the world, and very varied in their
details, that produced such a deep and permanent impression
on my mind, though the individual facts were forgotten.
When, ten or twelve years later, while thinking (as I had
thought for years) over the possible causes of the change
of species, the action of these " positive checks " to increase,
as Malthus termed them, suddenly occurred to me. I then
saw that war, plunder and massacres among men were
represented by the attacks of carnivora on herbivora, and
of the stronger upon the weaker among animals. Famine,
droughts, floods and winter's storms, would have an even
greater effect on animals than on men ; while as the former
possessed powers of increase from twice to a thousand-fold
greater than the latter, the ever-present annual destruction
must also be many times greater.

Then there flashed upon me, as it had done twenty years
before upon Darwin, the *certainty*, that those which, year by
year, survived this terrible destruction must be, on the
whole, those which had some little superiority enabling
them to escape each special form of death to which the
great majority succumbed—that, in the well-known formula,
the fittest would survive. Then I at once saw, that the
ever present *variability* of all living things would furnish
the material from which, by the mere weeding out of those

* Voy. de Volney, tom. i. c. xii. s. ii.

less adapted to the actual conditions, the fittest alone would continue the race. But this would only tend to the persistence of those best adapted to the actual conditions ; and on the old idea of the permanence and practical unchangeability of the inorganic world, except for a few local and unimportant catastrophes, there would be no necessary change of species.

But along with Malthus I had read, and been even more deeply impressed by, Sir Charles Lyell's immortal 'Principles of Geology,' which had taught me that the inorganic world— the whole surface of the earth, its seas and lands, its mountains and valleys, its rivers and lakes, and every detail of its climatic conditions, were and always had been in a continual state of slow modification. Hence it became obvious that the forms of life must have become continually adjusted to these changed conditions in order to survive. The succession of fossil remains throughout the whole geological series of rocks is the record of this change ; and it became easy to see that the extreme slowness of these changes was such as to allow ample opportunity for the continuous automatic adjustment of the organic to the inorganic world, as well as of each organism to every other organism in the same area, by the simple processes of " variation and survival of the fittest." Thus was the fundamental idea of the " origin of species " logically formulated from the consideration of a series of well-ascertained facts.

[Received 28th August, 1908.]

Appendix V

Excerpts Pertaining to Ethnology from Wallace's Letter of 28 December 1845 to Henry Walter Bates

I would observe that many eminent writers give great support to the theory of the progressive development of species in animals & plants. There is a very interesting & philosophical work bearing directly on the subject "Lawrence's Lectures on Man" delivered before the Royal Coll[ege] of Surgeons & which are now published in a cheap form. The great object of these lectures is to illustrate the different races of mankind & the manner in which they probably originated—and he arrives at the conclusion[,] as does also Mr. Pritchard [*sic*] in his work on the Physical history of man, that the varieties of the Human race have not proceeded from any external cause but have been produced by the development of certain distinctive peculiarities in some Individuals which have become propagated through an entire race. Now I sh[ould] say that a permanent peculiarity not produced ["depending" crossed out] in any way by external causes is a distinction of species & not of mere variety & thus if the theory of the "Vestiges" is carried out the "Negro" the red Indian & the European are distinct species of the genus Homo. The Albino which presents as striking a difference as the negro, we have modern & not uncommon instances of the production of but the peculiarity is not propagated so extensively as that of the other varieties. Now it appears to me that the "Albino" and "negro" are very analogous to what are generally considered as "variety" & "species" in the animal world.

McKinney (1969), pp. 372–73.

Appendix VI

Excerpts on Ethnology from Wallace's Species Notebook

Malay races—characteristics
Colour reddish brown of various shades.
Have black straight [hair], on body & beard scanty or none.
Stature low or medium, form robust, breasts very much developed; feet small, thick, short; hands small & rather delicate. Face broad & rather flat; eyes oblique distinctly but slightly. Nose small with no prominent ridge [and] straight; nostrils broad wings inclin[in]g rather downward; cheek bones rather prominent but less so than Chinese; mouth large but lips [are] not thick or prominent.

In many cases principally among Rajahs or priests, a taller stature, yellower skin, finer and slightly aquiline nose with a tendency to beard is observed. [This is] due probably to Arab, Hindoo or European mixture, [the] former principally. Among lower classes, curly or wavy hair, frizzly beard, darker skin & larger nose[s] are often observable; [this is] due probably to Papuan mixture.

Oct. '56. Makassar. ARW

Moral characteristics: reserve, dissimulation, no exhibition of feelings, "Nil admirari," no appreciation of the sublime or beautiful.[1]

[On the following page, Wallace continues his observations]:
Papuan races use bow & arrow. Malays do not.
Query: is this a universal difference?
If so, *good proof of diversity of origin.* [Italics mine]
[The] Dyaks of Borneo [are] totally ignorant of [the] bow.
Malays do not. Javanese used [bows] as a game. by the chiefs etc. ?introduced from India. [The] native[s] of Ke & Aru use bows.

Chinese or Tartar races. ?do they use bows.

Africans—do [they] all use bows?

Alfuros of Minahassa have native names for [the] bow.

Papuans have flat forehead[s], *projecting brows,* large thick nose[s],

1. Species Notebook, p. 65. See also *MA*, pp. 582–97.

[with the] apex *bent down* & wings of [the] nostrils *inclining upwards* from [the] apex, hair on [their] bodies & considerable beard. Papuans have the lips thick, projecting, & *sharply cut.* Malays have rounded foreheads, *flattish brows,* small nose[s], [a] *rounded apex* & nostrils inclin[in]g *downwards* from the apex, scarcely any hair on [their] bodies & no beard[s]. Papuans [are] tall, [and have] rather slender limbs. Malays [are] short, stout [and] thick limbed. Noted at Aru.[2]

[An entry at the bottom of the page containing the following ethnological note is dated Nov. 1857].

Javanese—handsomest of [the] Malay races; nose[s] well formed; mouth[s] often *very small;* chin[s] small; face very oval; [they are] probably an extensive mixture of Hindoo race as many have all the Malay characteristics fully developed. The lower orders of Javanese, however, often approach nearer to the Chinese physio[g]nomy & colour.[3]

The inhabitants of Floris are *Alfuros;* some have frizzly hair; some wavy & some straight [hair] but all *have* dark skins & Papuan features. (Capt. Drysdale)

Inhabitants of Bali have much mixture of Hindoo. In the interior are one or two villages of the indigenes who are Alfuros? *(Mr. King)*

———

Timore people from E. Celebes [who] settled at Batchian almost exactly resemble the *Macassar & Bugis* people; they have all the characteristics of a Malay race.[4]

Lesson says the *Papuans* are a mixed race, Negro & *Malay* inhabiting the N. coast of N. Guinea, Aru, Waigiou, etc. The *Alfuros* & natives of the interior of New Guinea, he says, are *straight haired blacks* and are quite distinct. The Papuans inhabit also New Britain & New Ireland.

———

The bow & arrows [are] unknown over all Australia. Less[on]

———

Alfuros on N[orth] Celebes, Neither of Malay nor Papuan race. Lighter colour than Malays. Hair straight black, rather finer & lanker than that of Malays; beard little; bodies smooth. Features very European; head[s]

2. Species Notebook, p. 66. This probably was written early in January 1857. The "plan to stop further increase of synonyms," occupying the next three pages is dated February 1857. See also Journal, 1856–57, section 63. Wallace's curious interest in whether or not aborigines in the Archipelago use bows and arrows is first mentioned in the 1854 Notebook.

3. Species Notebook, p. 100.

4. Ibid., p. 104.

wide above. Nose straight; apex rather produced, not thickened as a Papuan's. Character mild. ?Philippine or Pacific race.

Lesson's *distribution of the Malay & Polynesian Races*[5]

Hindoo
    Malay—of the Indian Arch[ipela]go & Malacca
    Oceanic—Tahitians, Sandwich Is[lan]ds & New Zealand

Mongolian
    Mongol pelagians of the Philippines, Carolinas & Mulgraves

Black
    Caffre Malegassee including
        Papuans of N. *Guinea coast* & islands
        Tasmanians of Tasmania
    Alfuros including
        Endamene of the interior of N. Guinea & other large islands
        Australians of New Holland

The Malays are Hindoos & Mongol *mixed and isolated* [italics mine]

The true Malays have nothing of *Hindoo;* they are a Mongol race.[6]

5. René Primevère Lesson, "Zoologie," vol. I, first part, in M. L. Duperrey, *Voyage autour du monde, exécuté par ordre du Roi, sur la corvette de la Majesté, La Coquille, pendant les années 1822, 1823 et 1825 (1826),* vol. V, pt. 1, chap. 1, pp. 1–116, esp. p. 36. Wallace read Lesson sometime late in November 1857. See Wallace, "On the Great Bird of Paradise" (1857), p. 415.

6. Species Notebook, pp. 105–06. Except as noted the italics are Wallace's. The last sentence is obviously an afterthought.

Bibliography

MANUSCRIPT MATERIALS

Although many of the following letters, manuscripts, and other materials have not been used in this book, it has nevertheless been my policy to examine, whenever possible, all available materials relating to Alfred Russel Wallace.*

Alfred Russel Wallace Materials

Åbo Academy
    14 letters to Edward Westermarck, 1890–93
Academy of Natural Sciences of Philadelphia
    1 postcard from Wallace to Dr. John W. Harshberger, 1894
The American Museum of Natural History
    31 letters from Wallace to T. D. A. Cockerell, 1890–1913
The American Philosophical Society
    approximately 50 letters from or about Wallace, 1863–1907
Birmingham Public Libraries
    1 letter from Wallace to Sir E. B. Poulton, 1896
British Museum (Bloomsbury)
    approximately 1300 letters to or from Wallace
    book MSS
British Museum (Natural History)
    approximately 20 letters
    2 notebooks: Bird and Insect Register, 1858–62 and Insect, Bird and Mammal Register, 1855–60. The first also contains some later figures for Wallace's bank accounts up to 1865
    drawings of Amazon fish
Brown University
    letters to Lester F. Ward
Cambridge University Libraries
    letters; partial list in *Handlist of the Darwin Papers at the University Library Cambridge* (1960); other letters in the Balfour Library
Cornell University Library
    1 letter from Wallace to H. J. Slack, Oct. 15 [?]
Professor Joseph Ewan, Tulane University
    postcard from Wallace to T. D. A. Cockerell

*A few additional sources are listed in *Archives of British Men of Science* (1972)

Harvard University
  note about a lecture by Wallace in 1886
University of California, Berkeley
  letters from Wallace to Michael Flürscheim, 1892–98
University of California, Los Angeles
  letters; special collections, Norman Douglas Papers
University of Illinois, Champaign
  7 letters to William Allingham, 1877–86
  1 letter (1889) and one postcard (1908) to Mrs. Allingham
Imperial College, London
  7 letters from Wallace to T. H. Huxley, 1863–91;
    listed in W. R. Dawson, *The Huxley Papers: A Descriptive Cata-
    logue* (1946)
University of Kansas
  1 letter to Miss Buckley, June 2 [?]
The Linnean Society of London
  letters; 4 notebooks (Malay Archipelago); 5 journals (one on Ameri-
    can trip); MS of *Palm Trees of the Amazon;* annotated books from
    Wallace's library
The University of Liverpool
  2 letters to the geologist Thomas Mellard Reade, 1879
The London Library
  1 letter which I have not seen
London School of Economics
  2 letters to Frederic Harrison, 1885 and 1892
Royal Botanic Gardens, Kew
  64 letters from Wallace to J. D. Hooker et al., 1848–1913
Royal College of Physicians
  1 letter from Wallace to Mrs. Tebb, 1883
Royal Geographical Society of London
  15 letters from Wallace, 1853–78, as well as some other letters about
    Wallace
The Royal Society
  4 letters, 1868–1908; I have not seen these letters
University of Texas
  letters
Wallace Grandsons' Materials
  letters; part of Wallace's library (partially annotated); lecture notes;
    sketches; miscellaneous materials
Wellcome Historical Medical Library
  8 letters from Wallace, 1863–1910
Yale University
  1. Marsh Collection. 7 letters from Wallace to O. C. Marsh, 1878–87

2. Yale Medical Library. 2 letters in 1904 from Wallace to I. H. L. Jackson, with a 28-page MS. of "A Summary of the Proofs that Vaccination Does Not Prevent Small-pox but Really Increases It."

Henry Walter Bates Materials

Cambridge University Library
Darwin-Bates Correspondence, 1862–79. Robert M. Stecker, M.D., Cleveland Metropolitan Hospital, Cleveland, Ohio, has kindly furnished me a transcript of these letters, which contain a number of interesting remarks about Wallace.

BOOKS

Bailey, Sir Edward. *Charles Lyell.* Garden City, N.Y., 1963.

Bailey, L. H. *Gentes Herbarum.* 8 vols. Ithaca, N.Y., 1920–57.

Bates, Henry Walter. *The Naturalist on the River Amazons.* 2 vols. London, 1863.

———. *The Naturalist on the River Amazons.* London, 1892. A Memoir of the author by Edward Clodd. Reprint of unabridged [1st] ed. [of 1863].

Bell, P. R., ed. *Darwin's Biological Work, Some Aspects Reconsidered.* Cambridge, England, 1959.

Boisduval, Jean Alphonse. *Faune entomologique de l'Océan Pacifique.* Paris, 1832.

———. *Histoire naturelle des insectes:* Vol. I. *Diurnes: papillonides, piérides.* Paris, 1836.

Bonaparte, Charles Lucien J. L. *Conspectus Generum Avium.* Leyden, 1850.

Brooke, Charles. *Ten Years in Sarawak.* 2 vols. London, 1866.

Cambridge University Library, *Darwin Library. List of Books Received in the University Library Cambridge March–May 1961.* Cambridge, England, nd.

———. *Handlist of Darwin Papers at the University Library.* Cambridge, England, 1960.

Chambers, Robert. *Vestiges of the Natural History of Creation.* 1st ed. London, 1844. 3rd ed. New York, 1845. 10th ed. London, 1853.

Cuvier, Georges. *The Animal Kingdom.* 16 vols. London, 1827–39.

Dahlgren, B. E. *Index of American Palms.* Chicago, 1936.

Darlington, C. D. *Darwin's Place in History.* Oxford, 1959.

Darlington, P. J., Jr. *Zoogeography: The Geographical Distribution of Animals.* New York and London, 1957.

Darwin, Charles. *The Descent of Man and Selection in Relation to Man.* 2nd ed. New York, nd. (Modern Library)

———. *Journal of Researches into the Geology and Natural History of the Various Countries Visited by H. M. S. Beagle.* Facsimile Reprint of the 1st ed. of 1839. New York and London, 1952. 2nd ed. London, 1845.

————. *On the Origin of Species by Means of Natural Selection, or The Preservation of Favoured Races in the Struggle for Life.* Facsimile Reprint of the 1st ed. of 1859. Cambridge, Mass., 1964.

Darwin, Francis, ed. *Charles Darwin: His Life Told in an Autobiographical Chapter, and in a Selected Series of His Published Letters.* London, 1908.

————. *The Life and Letters of Charles Darwin.* 2 vols. New York, 1959.

————, and Seward, A. C., eds. *More Letters of Charles Darwin.* 2 vols. New York, 1903.

De Beer, Sir Gavin. *Charles Darwin: Evolution by Natural Selection.* Garden City, N.Y., 1964.

————, ed. *Charles Darwin and A. R. Wallace, Evolution by Natural Selection.* Cambridge, England, 1958.

————, ed. *Darwin Notebooks.* See De Beer, ed., under articles.

Dobzhansky, Theodosius. *Genetics and the Origin of Species.* 1st ed. New York, 1937. 3rd ed. New York and London, 1951.

————. *Mankind Evolving: The Evolution of the Human Species.* New Haven and London, 1962.

Dufour, Pierre [pseud. for Paul Lacroix] *Histoire de la prostitution chez tous les peuples du monde, depuis l'antiquité la plus reculée jusqu'à nos jours.* 6 vols. Paris, 1851–53.

Dupree, A. Hunter. *Asa Gray, 1810–1888.* New York, 1968.

Edwards, William H. *A Voyage Up the River Amazon, Including a Residence at Pará.* New York, 1847.

Eiseley, Loren. *Darwin's Century: Evolution and the Men Who Discovered It.* Garden City, N.Y., 1961.

Elliot, Daniel G. *A Review of the Primates.* 3 vols. New York, 1913.

Forbes, Henry O. *A Handbook to the Primates.* 2 vols. London, 1894.

Gadow, Hans. *The Wanderings of Animals.* Cambridge, England, 1913. Contains a brief history of geographical distribution.

Geikie, Sir Archibald. *The Founders of Geology.* 2nd ed. London, 1905.

George, Wilma. *Biologist Philosopher: A Study of the Life and Writings of Alfred Russel Wallace.* London, 1964.

Ghiselin, Michael T. *The Triumph of the Darwinian Method.* Berkeley and Los Angeles, 1969.

Gienapp, John C. *Animal Hybridization and the Species Question from Aristotle to Darwin.* Doctoral Dissertation, University of Kansas, 1970.

Gillispie, Charles Coulston. *Genesis and Geology.* New York, 1959.

Glass, Bentley et al., eds. *Forerunners of Darwin: 1745–1859.* Baltimore, 1959, 1968.

Gray, J. E. *Catalogue of Monkeys, Lemurs, Fruit-eating Bats in the Collection of the British Museum.* London, 1870.

Greene, John C. *The Death of Adam. Evolution and Its Impact on Western Thought.* Ames, Iowa, 1959.

Henderson, Gerald. *Alfred Russel Wallace: His Role and Influence in Nineteenth Century Evolutionary Thought.* Doctoral Dissertation, University of Pennsylvania, 1958.

Hill, W. C. Osman. *Primates, Comparative Anatomy and Taxonomy.* 5 vols. Edinburgh, 1953–62.

Himmelfarb, Gertrude. *Darwin and the Darwinian Revolution.* Garden City, N.Y., 1959.

Hooykaas, R. *Natural Law and Divine Miracle. The Principle of Uniformity in Geology, Biology and Theology.* Leiden, 1959. 2nd printing with subtitle as title in 1963.

Hubbs, Carl L., ed. *Zoogeography.* Washington, D.C., 1958.

Humboldt, Alexander von, and Bonpland, Aimé. *Personal Narrative of Travels to the Equinoctial Regions of the New Continent, During the Years 1799–1804.* 7 vols. London, 1818–29. Transl. by Helen Maria Williams.

Huxley, Leonard, ed. *Life and Letters of Sir Joseph Dalton Hooker.* 2 vols. London, 1918.

————, ed. *Life and Letters of Thomas Henry Huxley.* 2 vols. London, 1900.

Lamarck, J. B. *Zoological Philosophy: An Exposition with Regard to the Natural History of Animals.* London, 1914. Transl. by Hugh Elliot.

Lawrence, William. *Lectures on Comparative Anatomy, Physiology, Zoology, and the Natural History of Man.* New ed. London, 1866.

Lesson, René Primevère. *Zoologie.* Vol. I, First Part, in M. L. Duperrey. *Voyage autour du monde, exécuté par ordre du Roi, sur la corvette de la Majesté, La Coquille, pendant les années 1822, 1823, et 1825.* Paris, 1826.

Limoges, Camille. *La sélection naturelle. Étude sur la première constitution d'un concept (1837–1859).* Paris, 1970.

Lindley, John. *The Elements of Botany.* 5th ed. London, 1847.

Linnean Society of London. *The Darwin-Wallace Celebration held on Thursday 1st July, 1908, by the Linnean Society of London.* London, 1908.

Loewenberg, Bert James. *Darwin, Wallace and the Theory of Natural Selection Including the Linnean Society Papers.* Cambridge, Mass., 1959.

Loudon, J. C. *An Encyclopedia of Plants.* London, 1836.

Lyell, Sir Charles. *The Geological Evidences of the Antiquity of Man with Remarks on Theories of the Origin of Species by Variation.* 3rd ed. London, 1863.

182   BIBLIOGRAPHY

————. *Principles of Geology.* 1st ed. 3 vols. London, 1830–33; 4th ed.
4 vols. London, 1835; 5th ed. 4 vols. London, 1837; 9th ed. New
York, 1857; 11th ed. 2 vols. London, 1872.
Lyell, Mrs. [Katherine], ed. *Life, Letters, and Journals of Sir Charles
Lyell, Bart.* 2 vols. London, 1881.
Malthus, Thomas Robert. *An Essay on the Principle of Population.* 6th ed.
2 vols. London, 1826.
Marchant, James, ed. *Alfred Russel Wallace: Letters and Reminiscences.*
New York and London, 1916. The English edition in two volumes is
illustrated.
Martius, Karl F. P. von. *Historia Naturalis Palmarum.* 3 vols. Munich,
1823–50.
Mayr, Ernst. *Animal Species and Evolution.* Cambridge, Mass., 1963.
————, ed. *The Species Problem,* Washington, D.C., 1957.
McKinney, H. Lewis, ed. *Lamarck to Darwin: Contributions to Evolu-
tionary Biology, 1809–1859,* Lawrence, Kansas: Coronado Press, 1971.
Meyer, A. B. *Charles Darwin und Alfred Russel Wallace. Ihre ersten
Publicationen über die "Entstehung der Arten" nebst einer Skizze ihres
Lebens und einem Verzeichniss ihrer Schriften.* Erlangen: Eduard
Besold, 1870.
Millhauser, Milton. *Just Before Darwin: Robert Chambers and "Vestiges".*
Middletown, Conn., 1959.
Murray, Hugh, *An Encyclopedia of Geography.* London, 1834.
Newton, Alfred and Gadow, Hans. *A Dictionary of Birds.* London, 1896.
Nordenskiöld, Erik. *The History of Biology.* New York, 1928.
Osborn, H. F. *Impressions of Great Naturalists. Darwin, Wallace, Hux-
ley, Leidy, Cope, Balfour, Roosevelt, and Others.* 2nd ed. New York
and London, 1928.
Owen, Richard. *The Life of Richard Owen.* 2 vols. New York, 1894.
Packard, Alpheus S. *Lamarck: The Founder of Evolution, His Life and
Work, with Translations of his Writings on Organic Evolution.* Lon-
don, 1901.
Peters, James L. *Check-List of Birds of the World.* 7 vols. Cambridge,
Mass., 1931–51.
Pictet, François Jules. *Traité de paléontologie, ou Histoire naturelle des
animaux fossiles considérés dans leurs rapports zoologiques et géolo-
giques.* 4 vols. Paris or Geneva, 1844–46. 2nd ed. 4 vols. Paris,
1853–57.
Prichard, James Cowles. *Researches into the Physical History of Mankind.*
3rd ed. 5 vols. London, 1836–47.
Rádl, Emanuel. *The History of Biological Theories.* London, 1930.
Transl. from German by E. J. Hatfield.
Robinson, Herbert C. *The Birds of the Malay Archipelago.* 4 vols. Lon-

don, 1927.

St. John, Spenser, *The Life of Sir James Brooke, Rajah of Sarawak, from his Personal Papers and Correspondence.* Edinburgh and London, 1879.

Sanderson, Ivan T. *Living Mammals of the World.* Garden City, N.Y., [1955].

———. *The Monkey Kingdom.* London, 1957.

Seemann, Berthold. *Popular History of Palms and their Allies.* London, 1856.

Stephens, J. F. *A Manual of British Coleoptera, or Beetles.* London, 1839.

Swainson, William. *The Natural History and Classification of Fishes, Amphibians, and Reptiles, or Monocardian Animals.* 2 vols. London, 1838–39.

———. *A Treatise on the Geography and Classification of Animals.* London, 1835.

von Buch, Leopold. *Description physique des Iles Canaries.* Paris, 1836. Transl. by C. Boulanger.

Wallace, A. R., ed. *Australasia.* 5th ed. London, 1888.

———. *Contributions to the Theory of Natural Selection.* London, 1870.

———. *Darwinism, an Exposition of the Theory of Natural Selection with Some of its Applications.* London, 1889.

———. *The Geographical Distribution of Animals.* 2 vols. New York, 1876.

———. *Island Life, or The Phenomena and Causes of Insular Faunas and Floras, Including a Revision and Attempted Solution of the Problem of Geological Climates.* London, 1880. 2nd ed. London, 1892.

———. *The Malay Archipelago: The Land of the Orang-Utan and the Bird of Paradise; A Narrative of Travel, with Studies of Man and Nature.* 7th ed. London, 1880. Various editions are similar.

———. *My Life: A Record of Events and Opinions.* 2 vols. London, 1905. The American edition is paginated slightly differently. 2nd ed. London, 1908.

———. *A Narrative of Travels on the Amazon and Rio Negro.* London, 1853. 2nd ed. London, 1889 et seq. Reprinted New York, 1972.

———. *Natural Selection and Tropical Nature.* London, 1891.

———. *Palm Trees of the Amazon and their Uses.* London, 1853. Reprinted Lawrence, Kansas: Coronado Press, 1971.

———. *Social Environment and Moral Progress.* New York and London, 1913.

———. *Studies Scientific and Social.* 2 vols. London, 1900.

———. *The Wonderful Century. Its Successes and Its Failures.* London, 1898.

———. *The World of Life.* London, 1910.

Wallace, George J. *An Introduction to Ornithology.* New York, 1955.

Wichler, Gerhard. *Charles Darwin: The Founder of the Theory of Evolution and Natural Selection.* New York, 1961.

Williams-Ellis, Amabel. *Darwin's Moon. A Biography of Alfred Russel Wallace.* London and Glasgow, 1966.

Wilson, Leonard G., ed. *Sir Charles Lyell's Scientific Journals on the Species Question.* New Haven and London, 1970.

Wollaston, Thomas Vernon. *On the Variation of Species with Especial Reference to the Insecta; Followed by an Inquiry into the Nature of Genera.* London, 1856.

Woodcock, George. *Henry Walter Bates. Naturalist of the Amazons.* London, 1969.

PERIODICAL LITERATURE

Anonymous. "Review of *The Palm Trees of the Amazon and their Uses,* by A. R. Wallace," *Gardener's Chronicle and Agricultural Gazette* (1853), 742.

———. "Review of *Palm Trees of the Amazon,*" *AMNH, 13,* 2 (1854), 56–57.

———. "Review of *A Narrative of Travels on the Amazon and Rio Negro* by A. R. Wallace," *Gardener's Chronicle and Agricultural Gazette* (1853), 838–39.

Barlow, Nora, ed. "Darwin's Ornithological Notes," *Bulletin of the British Museum (Natural History),* Historical Series, *2,* 7 (1963), 201–78.

Bates, H. W. "Contributions to an Insect Fauna of the Amazon Valley," *Transactions of the Entomological Society of London, 5,* 2 (1858–61), 223–28, 335–61.

———. "Contributions to an Insect Fauna of the Amazon Valley. *Lepidoptera: Heliconidae,*" *Transactions of the Linnean Society of London, 23* (1862), 495–566.

Beddall, Barbara. "Wallace, Darwin, and the Theory of Natural Selection," *Journal of the History of Biology, 1* (1968), 261–323.

Blyth, Edward. "An Attempt to Classify the 'Varieties' of Animals, with Observations on the Marked Seasonal and other Changes which Naturally Take Place in Various British Species, and which Do Not Constitute Varieties," *Magazine of Natural History, 8* (1835), 40–53.

Brooks, John L. "Report on Grant No. 4595," *Year Book 1968. The American Philosophical Society* (1969), pp. 534–35.

Darlington, P. J., Jr. "Darwin and Zoogeography," *Proceedings of the American Philosophical Society, 103,* 2 (1959), 307–20.

Dawson, Albert. "A Visit to Dr. Alfred Russel Wallace," *The Christian Commonwealth,* 10 December 1903, 176–78.

De Beer, Sir Gavin, ed. "Darwin's Journal," *Bulletin of the British Museum (Natural History)*, Historical Series, 2, 1 (1959), 1–21.

———. "Darwin's Notebooks on Transmutation of Species," *Bulletin of the British Museum (Natural History)*, Historical Series, 2, 2–5 (1960), 23–73, 75–118, 119–50, 151–83.

——— and Rowlands, M. J., eds. "Darwin's Notebooks on Transmutation of Species. Addenda and Corrigenda," *Bulletin of the British Museum (Natural History)*, Historical Series, 2, 6 (1961), 185–200.

———, Rowlands, M. J., and Skramovsky, B. M., eds. "Darwin's Notebooks on Transmutation of Species. Pages Excised by Darwin," *Bulletin of the British Museum (Natural History)*, Historical Series, 3, 5 (1967), 129–76.

Eiseley, Loren. "Alfred Russel Wallace," *Scientific American*, 200 (1959), 70–83.

———. "Charles Darwin, Edward Blyth, and the Theory of Natural Selection," *Proceedings of the American Philosophical Society, 103* (1959), 94–158.

———. "Darwin, Coleridge, and the Theory of Unconscious Creation," *Daedalus, 94* (1965), 588–602.

Forbes, Edward. "On the Connection Between the Distribution of the Existing Fauna and Flora of the British Isles, and the Geological Changes which Have Affected their Area, Especially During the Epoch of the Northern Drift," *Memoirs of the Geological Survey of Great Britain and of the Museum of Economic Geology in London, 1* (1846), 336–432.

———. "On the Manifestations of Polarity in the Distribution of Organized Beings in Time," *Notices of the Proceedings at the Meetings of the Members of the Royal Institution, 1* (1851–54), 428–33.

Geison, Gerald L. "Darwin and Heredity: The Evolution of His Hypothesis of Pangenesis," *Journal of the History of Medicine and Allied Sciences, 24, 4* (1969), 375–411.

Harrison, Tom. "Alfred Russel Wallace and a Century of Evolution in Borneo," *Proceedings of the Centenary and Bicentenary Congress of Biology in Singapore, December 2–9, 1958,* R. D. Purchon, ed. (1960), 23–38.

Herbert, Sandra. "Darwin, Malthus, and Selection," *Journal of the History of Biology, 4* (1971), 209–17.

Hooker, Sir W. J. "Review of *Palm Trees of the Amazon, and their Uses* by A. R. Wallace," *HJB, 6* (1854), 61–62.

———. "Review of Popular History of Palms and their Allies by Berthold Seeman," *HJB, 8* (1856), 88–92.

Huxley, Julian S. "Alfred Russel Wallace," *Dictionary of National Biography,* Third Supplement (1927), 547–49.

Kettlewell, H. B. D. "Darwin's Missing Evidence," *Scientific American*, 200 (1959), 48–53.

McKinney, H. Lewis. "Alfred Russel Wallace and the Discovery of Natural Selection," *Journal of the History of Medicine and Allied Science*, 201 (1966), 333–57.

―――. "Henry Walter Bates," *Dictionary of Scientific Biography*, 1 (1970), 500–04.

―――. "Edward Blyth," *Dictionary of Scientific Biography*, 2 (1970), 205–07.

―――. "Wallace's Earliest Observations on Evolution; 28 December 1845," *Isis*, 60, 3 (1969), 370–73.

Marchant, James, "A Man of His Time: Dr. Alfred Russel Wallace and his Coming Autobiography," *The Book Monthly* (1903), 544–49.

Mayr, Ernst, "Isolation as an Evolutionary Factor," *Proceedings of the American Philosophical Society*, 103 (1959), 221–30.

Meyer, A. B. "How Was Wallace Led to the Discovery of Natural Selection?," *Nature*, 52 (1895), 415.

Müntzing, Arne. "Darwin's Views on Variation under Domestication in the Light of Present-Day Knowledge," *Proceedings of the American Philosophical Society*, 103, 2 (1959), 190–220.

[Newton, Alfred?]. "Review of *The Life and Letters of Charles Darwin*," *Quarterly Review*, 166 (Jan. 1888), 1–30.

Osborn, Henry Fairfield. "Alfred Russel Wallace," *Popular Science Monthly*, 83 (1913), 523–37.

Owen, Richard. "Description of Certain Fossil Crania, Discovered by A. G. Bain, Esq., in Sandstone Rocks at the South-eastern Extremity of Africa, Referable to Different Species of an Extinct Genus of Reptilia (Dicynodon), and Indicative of a New Tribe or Sub-order of Sauria," [Read 8 January 1845], *Transactions of the Geological Society of London*, 8, 2 (1845–56), 59–84.

―――. "Description of the Skull of a Large Species of *Dicynodon (D. tigriceps, Ow.)*, transmitted from South America by A. G. Bain, Esq.," [Read 16 May 1855], *Transactions of the Geological Society of London*, 7, 2 (1845–56), 233–40.

―――. "On the Anthropoid Apes," *Report of the Twenty-Fourth Meeting of the British Association for the Advancement of Science*, 24 (1855), 111–13.

Pantin, C. F. A. "Alfred Russel Wallace, F. R. S., and his Essays of 1858 and 1855," *Notes and Records of the Royal Society of London*, 14 (1960), 67–84.

―――. "Alfred Russel Wallace: His Pre-Darwinian Essay of 1855," *Proceedings of the Linnean Society of London*, 171 (1959), 139–53.

Poulton, Sir E. B. "Alfred Russel Wallace, 1823–1913," *Proceedings of the Royal Society of London*, 95, B (1924), i–xxxv.

Rockell, Frederick, "The Last of the Great Victorians: A Special Inter-
view with Dr. Alfred Russel Wallace," *The Millgate Monthly*, 7, Pt. 2,
No. 83 (1912), 657–63.

Sanderson, Ivan T. "A Brief Review of the Mammals of Suriname (Dutch
Guiana) Based Upon a Collection Made in 1938," *Proceedings of the
Zoological Society of London*, 119 (1949–50), 760–89.

Sclater, P. L., and Salvin, Osbert. "List of Birds Collected by Mr. Wallace
on the Lower Amazons and Rio Negro," *Proceedings of the Zoological
Society of London* (1867), 566–96.

Smith, Frederick. "Catalogue of the Hymenopterous Insects Collected at
Sarawak, Borneo, Mount Ophir, Malacca, and at Singapore, by A. R.
Wallace," *Journal of the Proceedings of the Linnean Society, Zoology*,
1 (1857), 4–39.

Smith, Sydney. "The Origin of the 'Origin,'" *Impulse*, No. 11 (Nov.
1959), 2–4.

————. "The Origin of the 'Origin,'" *Advancement of Science*, 64
(1960), 391–401.

Stern, Bernhard J. "Letters of Alfred Russel Wallace to Lester F. Ward,"
The Scientific Monthly, 40 (1935), 375–79.

Vorzimmer, Peter. "Darwin, Malthus, and the Theory of Natural Selection," *Journal of the History of Ideas*, 30 (1969), 527–42.

For a more extensive list of Wallace's articles see James Marchant, *Alfred
Russel Wallace: Letters and Reminiscences* (1916), Appendix II.

Wallace, Alfred Russel, "Attempts at a Natural Arrangement of Birds,"
AMNH, 18, 2 (1856), 193–216.

————. "A Disputed Case of Priority in Nomenclature," *The Zoologist*,
16 (1858), 6117–18.

————. "Distribution of Animals," *Encyclopedia Britannica*, Ninth Edition, 7 (1878), 267–86.

————. "The Entomology of Malacca," *The Zoologist*, 13 (1855),
4636–39.

————. "Extracts of a Letter to S. Stevens, Sept. 1849," *AMNH*, 5, 2
(1850), 156–57.

————. "My Relations with Darwin in Reference to the Theory of
Natural Selection," *Black and White*, 17 January 1903, 78–79.

————. "A New Kind of Baby," *Chambers's Journal*, 5, 3 (1856),
325–27.

————. "Notes on the Localities Given in *Longicornia Malayana*, with
an Estimate of the Comparative Value of the Collections Made at
Each of Them," *Transactions of the Entomological Society of London*,
3, 3 (1869), 691–96.

————. "Note on the Theory of Permanent and Geographical Varieties,"
The Zoologist, 16 (1858), 5887–88.

————. "Observations on the Zoology of Borneo," *The Zoologist, 14* (1856), 5113–17.

————. "On the Entomology of the Aru Islands," *The Zoologist, 16* (1858), 5889–94.

————. "On the Great Bird of Paradise, *Paradisea apoda*, Linn.; *'Burong mati' (Dead bird)* of the Malays; *'Fanehan'* of the Natives of Aru," *AMNH, 20,* 2 (1857), 411–16.

————. "On the Habits of the Butterflies of the Amazon Valley," *Transactions of the Entomological Society of London, 2,* 2 (1852–53), 253–64.

————. "On the Habits of the Orang-Utan of Borneo," *AMNH, 18,* 2 (1856), 26–32.

————. "On the Law which Has Regulated the Introduction of New Species," *AMNH, 16,* 2 (1855), 184–96.

————. "On the Monkeys of the Amazon," *Proceedings of the Zoological Society of London,* 20 (1852), 107–10. Also in *AMNH, 14,* 2 (1854), 451–54.

————. "On the Natural History of the Aru Islands," *AMNH, 20,* 2 (1857), 473–85.

————. "On the Orang-Utan or Mias of Borneo," *AMNH, 17,* 2 (1856), 471–76.

————. "On the Ornithology of Malacca," *AMNH, 15,* 2 (1855), 95–99.

————. "On the Phenomena of Variation and Geographical Distribution as Illustrated by the *Papilionidae* of the Malayan Region," *Transactions of the Linnean Society of London, 25* (1865), 1–71, plates I–VIII.

————. "On the Rio Negro," *The Journal of the Royal Geographical Society, 23* (1853), 212–17.

————. "On Some Fishes Allied to Gymnotus," *Proceedings of the Zoological Society of London,* Pt. 20 (1853), 75–76. Also in *AMNH, 14,* 2 (1854), 398–99.

————. "On Some Anomalies in Zoological and Botanical Geography," *The Edinburgh New Philosophical Journal, 19* (1864), 1–15.

————. "On the Tendency of Varieties to Depart Indefinitely from the Original Type," *Journal of the Proceedings of the Linnean Society, Zoology, 3* (1859), 53–62. Reprinted in many places. [Read 1 July 1858 and available in print in August 1858.]

————. "On the Umbrella Bird," *Proceedings of the Zoological Society of London,* Pt. 18 (1850), 206–07.

————. "On the Varieties of Man in the Malay Archipelago," *Transactions of the Ethnological Society of London, 3,* N.S. (1864–65), 195–215.

————. "On the Zoological Geography of the Malay Archipelago," *Journal of the Linnean Society of London, 4* (1860), 172–84.

————. "The Origin of Human Races and the Antiquity of Man Deduced from the Theory of Natural Selection," *Journal of the Anthropological Society of London,* 2 (1864), clvii–clxxxvii.

————. "Proceedings of Natural-History Collectors in Foreign Countries," *The Zoologist, 15* (1856), 5414–16 [21 August 1856]; 5559–60 [27 September 1856]; 5652–57 [1 December 1856]; *16* (1857), 6120–24 [20 December 1857].

————. "Some Account of an Infant 'Orang-Utan,'" *AMNH, 17,* 2 (1856), 386–90.

————. "Some Remarks on the Habits of the Hesperidae," *The Zoologist,* 2 (1853), 3884–85.

———— and Bates, H. W. "Extracts of a Letter to S. Stevens, Oct. 1848," *AMNH, 3,* 2 (1849), 74–75.

Wikman, K. Rob. V. "Letters from Edward B. Tylor and Alfred Russel Wallace to Edward Westermarck," *Acta Academiae Aboensis. Humaniora., 13,* 7 (1940), 3–22.

Index